T0060298

PRAISE FOR

THE
FOUNDLING

"A riveting, intriguing, and inspiring tale . . . For readers who love deep, personal stories of lost and found love and the sometimes strange vagaries of life, this is a book to savor."

—Homer Hickam, author of *Rocket Boys, October Sky,* and *Carrying Albert Home*

"Page-turning . . . will likely appeal to a large swath of readers, from true-crime fans to amateur genealogists."

—*Booklist*

THE
FOUNDLING

THE TRUE STORY OF A KIDNAPPING,
A FAMILY SECRET, AND MY SEARCH
FOR THE REAL ME

PAUL JOSEPH FRONCZAK
and ALEX TRESNIOWSKI

HOWARD BOOKS
New York   London   Toronto   Sydney   New Delhi

An Imprint of Simon & Schuster, Inc.
1230 Avenue of the Americas
New York, NY 10020

Copyright © 2017 by Paul Joseph Fronczak and Alex Tresniowski

All rights reserved, including the right to reproduce this book or portions thereof in any form whatsoever. For information, address Howard Books Subsidiary Rights Department, 1230 Avenue of the Americas, New York, NY 10020.

Some names and identifying characteristics have been changed.

First Howard Books paperback edition August 2018

HOWARD and colophon are trademarks of Simon & Schuster, Inc.

For information about special discounts for bulk purchases, please contact Simon & Schuster Special Sales at 1-866-506-1949 or business@simonandschuster.com.

The Simon & Schuster Speakers Bureau can bring authors to your live event. For more information or to book an event, contact the Simon & Schuster Speakers Bureau at 1-866-248-3049 or visit our website at www.simonspeakers.com.

Interior design by Davina Mock-Maniscalco
All insert photos courtesy of the author.

Manufactured in the United States of America

10   9   8   7   6   5   4

Library of Congress Cataloging-in-Publication Data is available.

ISBN 978-1-5011-4212-3 (hc)
ISBN 978-1-5011-4232-1 (pbk)
ISBN 978-1-5011-4214-7 (ebook)

To Emma Faith, my light and my life. Everything I do is for you.

And to all the foundlings and searchers out there.
My journey is your journey, my dreams are your dreams.
Please know you are worth the fight.

Everything dies baby that's a fact
But maybe everything that dies someday comes back.

—Bruce Springsteen, "Atlantic City"

Contents

Prologue

Southern New Jersey
October 8, 2015

A HALF CENTURY OF SEARCHING, of not knowing, of hoping, led me here. To a nameless dirt road in a trailer park. And all I could think was—shouldn't I bring a gift?

The occasion seemed to call for something. I drove around until I found one of those all-purpose gift stores in a mall, and I walked up and down the aisles, past picture frames and tableware and men's jackets. A young woman asked if I needed help and I politely said no thanks. I didn't know how to explain who the gift was for.

Finally, I came to the artificial flowers. I picked up a small brown pot with a white orchid draped around a green plant stake. Looking at it, you wouldn't know it was fake. I took it up front and paid for it—$12.99. But as soon as I did, I felt uneasy. Not because I didn't like it, but because it was the final diversion.

There was nothing left for me to do now, except what I came to do.

I got back in my rented Nissan and drove down Evergreen Road. The casinos of Atlantic City, the great gray slabs of glass and concrete, were to the east, the ocean right behind them. A trailer park came into view, then another. They had pleasant, resort-style names—something Pines, something Acres. The GPS pushed me one more mile, until I was there—Silver Crest Trailer Park. It was just off a traffic circle, with a liquor store, a Wawa, and Joe's Bar & Grill nearby.

I pulled into the park through a barely marked entrance. Inside, there were two rows of trailers, on either side of the dirt road. The trailers were about twenty feet apart, and there had to be hundreds of them. I drove at ten miles an hour down the road, trying to catch the numbers on them. No. 6. No. 8. No. 10.

No. 18, on the left, was the one I was looking for.

It was double-wide, with brown and tan siding and an aluminum roof. A tall oak tree shaded the trailer and every now and then shot an acorn down on the roof with a clang. A lime-green Ford was parked in front—that likely meant someone was home. The surrounding trailers were in different states of repair, some better kept, some much worse. One had Halloween decorations taped forlornly to the narrow window—a cardboard pumpkin, a witch's hat. Down the dirt road a yellow school bus dropped off a little girl.

I parked on the side of the road across from No. 18. This was it. This was finally it. I took a deep breath and walked up to the gate in the chain-link fence that circled the trailer, and passed through. There were potted plants placed along a stone path that led to the wooden deck that led to the door of the trailer. On the deck, a couple of folding chairs and a flowerpot with an American flag stuck in the soil. It was a warm, cloudless day. I walked up the five stairs about as slowly as I could.

I had never been this close before in my life.

For a moment I didn't know where to knock. The screen? The door behind it? In the dull stillness of the afternoon, all the choices felt like intrusions. I settled on the side of the trailer, and knocked lightly three times.

Nothing happened. Not a sound or movement.

I knocked again, a little more firmly. Still nothing.

I knocked a third time, loud enough for anyone inside to hear. I waited two full minutes after that knock, just standing there. Another acorn clanged on the roof.

Could this be how it ends?

After all the setbacks and false leads, the dead ends and desperate nights, and the miraculous twist of fate that brought me here, to this door—could all of that have amounted only to this? To silence? To nothing?

I'd never lost hope, because for the longest time hope was all I had.

I'd come close to giving up, but never all that close.

I'd stayed strong, but now that strength felt more like delusion.

So I just stood there for a while, outside trailer No. 18. A lost soul with a fake flower in his hand.

—◈—

Probably five minutes went by. I looked around for where to leave the orchid. I decided to knock one last time, because what was the harm? Three hard raps with my knuckles.

"Hello? Is anyone there? This is Paul. Paul Fronczak."

Once again, silence.

But then . . .

Something.

A shadow, visible through the diamond-shaped glass on the door. Movement. Shuffling.

And then, after a few more seconds, the door swung open.

PART ONE
CHICAGO

1

THE FIRST STEP of my long journey was into a dark crawl space.

I was ten years old. I was snooping around for Christmas presents in my family's two-story house in working-class South Side Chicago. I snuck down to the basement one afternoon while my dad was at the factory where he worked and my mom was busy, and I pulled an old gray sofa away from the back wall, and I opened a three-foot by four-foot wooden door that led to the crawl space. It was stuffed with outgrown clothes, forgotten books, and holiday decorations. I got on my hands and knees and went inside, searching for anything that looked new.

And there, toward the back, in a corner behind some framed paintings, I found something that changed my life.

Three shoe boxes and a hatbox.

I shuffled over and lifted the cover off the first shoe box. Inside was a stack of old newspaper clippings. I looked in the second box and saw more yellowed clippings, along with a bunch of letters folded back into their stamped, opened envelopes. The other two boxes held more clippings and more letters. I picked the top clipping off one pile. It was an article from the *Chicago Tribune*, dated April 28, 1964—ten years earlier. The headline, in big bold type, read:

200 SEARCH FOR STOLEN BABY

I looked through more clippings and saw more urgent headlines.

DAD APPEALS FOR BABY'S RETURN
MOTHER ASKS KIDNAPPER TO RETURN BABY
BABY HUNT DRAGS ON IN SAD CITY

I might have put the lids back on the boxes and kept looking for Christmas presents had I not noticed a small, black-and-white photo accompanying one of the articles.

The photo showed a man and a woman in their late twenties or early thirties. They both had dark black hair, and they were both hanging their heads, as if looking up and facing the world was just too painful. The woman wore a simple checkered dress that seemed familiar to me. The man had thick forearms, like those of my father, who worked as a machinist. Below the photo, there was a caption.

> Mr. and Mrs. Chester Fronczak are pictured as they
> prayed for the return of their kidnapped infant son.

Dora and Chester Fronczak were my parents.

I read the caption three or four times, my heart pounding. Then I read the article, squinting through the darkness at the tiny type.

> Police were combing Chicago last night in search for a one-and-a-half-day
> old baby boy who was kidnapped from his mother's arms. The victim of the
> abduction is Paul Joseph Fronczak.

These dozens of newspaper articles, these hundreds of letters from well-wishing strangers—they were all about the same person.

They were all about me.

—∿∿—

The details of the kidnapping were sensational. A woman pretending to be a nurse simply walked into the hospital, took the baby from my mother, and walked out a back door. The hospital went into lockdown, and the FBI and the Chicago PD launched the biggest manhunt in the city's history. Hundreds of homes were searched, hundreds of people questioned. Newspapers ran with the story for weeks.

Later on in the day I found all the articles, I confronted my mother in the kitchen.

"What are these?" I asked, holding out a handful of clippings.

My mother's face went white, then red.

"How dare you snoop around this house!" she scolded. "Those are not your business."

"These are about me, aren't they?" I said. "Paul Joseph Fronczak—that's me, isn't it?"

My mother looked away and fell silent, before turning to face me.

"Yes, those are about you," she said. "You were kidnapped, we found you, we love you, and that is all there is to know."

And that was that. Nothing more. I put the clippings back in their shoe boxes and ate dinner and went to bed. From my mother's tone I knew this wasn't a subject my parents would discuss any further, so I didn't bring it up again, and neither did they. Whatever those yellowing articles meant, whatever truth they hid, stayed buried in the basement.

It stayed buried for the next forty years.

Even before I found the old articles, and for nearly as long as I can remember, I had a strong, persistent feeling about my identity.

I had the feeling I wasn't Paul Fronczak.

Early on, it was more of a sense of not belonging—of being on the outside of things. I didn't physically resemble my parents, or my younger brother Dave—they were all dark-haired, while I had light reddish brown hair. But it was more than just my appearance. I didn't doubt that our parents loved both Dave and me, but they simply didn't show their love for us the same way. Even though Dave was three years younger, for instance, my parents gave him the big bedroom on the second floor with the queen-size bed. I got the much smaller guest room with the little twin bed. I never asked my parents why this was so.

But I never stopped asking myself.

Then I found the clippings in the crawl space, and the rift deepened. Before, all I had was an inexplicable feeling of being on the outside of my own family. But discovering that there had been a kidnapping—that the circumstances of my entrance into the family were out of the ordinary—gave me an actual *reason* to doubt my place in the Fronczak household. Was the story as simple as my mother had put it—I was kidnapped and then I was found—or was it more complicated? I began to dwell incessantly on one question.

Was I really the stolen Baby Fronczak?

The problem was, there was no easy way to answer that question. No test was ever performed to confirm I was the Fronczaks' biological child, and for many years afterward accurate DNA parental testing simply didn't exist. All I had to go on were those few words my mother had uttered after I found the clippings. Those, and my own feelings of doubt and estrangement—of being alone in the world.

Those feelings, and that doubt, came to define my life.

As an adult I was always moving, always searching, never at home. All in all, I probably held a hundred different jobs—musician, cigar salesman, George Clooney's stand-in on the movie *Ocean's Eleven*—and I probably moved forty times. I was married twice, and both relationships fell apart. Something gnawed at me every day of my life—some mysterious longing. I was becoming a failed man and I didn't know why.

After a while, I wasn't even sure I wanted to keep living that way.

Then an amazing thing happened.

A few years ago, my wife, Michelle, and I had a child, Emma Faith. When I held my beautiful daughter in my arms for the first time, I felt something new and surprising and powerful—a connection, a closeness, a gut punch of pure and instant love.

I am sure many first-time fathers feel this intense bond, but for me it was also a kind of answered prayer. All the emotions I'd missed out on and craved as a child—the feeling of belonging to someone, and having them belong to you—were suddenly, miraculously *there*. No disconnect, no sense of being on the outside—no, this was the real thing! This was what being a family meant! I remember kissing Emma's tiny pink forehead and pulling her tight to my chest, and I remember thinking that I never wanted to be anywhere on the planet other than with her.

It was around then that a doctor asked me about my family's medical history. It was a simple question, yet it left me speechless.

I could describe my parents' medical history, but could I be absolutely certain I was also describing my own? I was forty-five years old and I couldn't state with any authority if cancer or heart disease or any other malady had been genetically handed down to me. Unless I could find a way to prove, or disprove, my true identity once and for all, I was doomed to be what I feared I was becoming—a blurry sketch of a man. Somehow I'd found a way to live with that uncertainty for years and years, but the power and sureness of my love for my daughter, Emma, made those doubts feel intolerable. I didn't want to be adrift anymore. I didn't want to have to keep moving from place to place.

I didn't want to ever, ever run away from Emma.

So, after a lifetime of not knowing, I decided to learn the truth about my identity—if not for me, then at least for my daughter. She deserved more than half a father. She deserved someone capable of self-awareness and emotional honesty, someone rooted and solid—a more knowable man. I didn't ever want Emma to feel the estrangement and loneliness I'd felt as a child, but in order to make sure she didn't, I had to resolve, or at least try to, the matter of what caused me to feel so lost.

I had to ask, and hope to answer, the question that had come to shape me:

Was I really Paul Joseph Fronczak?

—⟋⟍—

What do we mean when we talk about identity? Is it just the names and dates and numbers we believe define us? It can't be, because those are so easily taken from us—in this country, someone's identity is stolen every two seconds. Is it our features? Our thoughts? Our memories? No, those are fragile and fleeting, too. So what is it, then? What defines us? What makes us who we are?

When I started my search, I knew I wasn't the only person with these kinds of questions. There are hundreds of thousands of people who were adopted or abandoned or somehow lost who may feel the same longings I felt—people who cling to slim shards of family history, or have no shards at all, as they dig for any clues to their real identities, their true selves.

My journey, I realized, wasn't just mine. Nor was my desire to know where I came from unique to me. The details of my case may have been more dramatic, but what I longed for was universal. It is, I discovered, a longing built into who we are.

A wolf can leave its pack and rejoin it years later, because a wolf always knows its pack, and a pack knows its own. The truth runs through the blood.

What I wanted, what I needed, was the truth.

—m—

Getting to it was the hardest thing I've ever gone through in my life.

I spent many dark, desperate nights staring at a computer screen, hunting for hours without knowing what I was hunting for. There were times it felt like I was being pulled into a black hole, away from everything that was good in my life and toward an endless nothing. Moments when I could feel my mission turning into an obsession—could feel myself becoming withdrawn, isolated, angry. "And when you gaze long into an abyss," Nietzsche famously said, "the abyss also gazes into you." That is what was happening to me—the pitch-black mystery of my uncertain past was swallowing my present.

And so, along the way, there were people who got hurt by my search—people I didn't ever want to hurt. The mother and father who raised me as their own looked at my quest as a betrayal and stopped speaking to me. My brother sided with them and refused to help me in any way. My wife, Michelle, who wanted me to discover my past but didn't want to lose me to it, fought hard to pull me back into the family I already had. Things were said, relationships damaged. There were days when I looked at my pretty, bubbly daughter, Emma, and wondered if I was making a horrible mistake—if I was sacrificing the most precious gift I'd ever been given in a hopeless bid to recover something that was never really mine.

Many, many times I thought of quitting—and many more times, those around me pleaded for me to lay it all down.

But I couldn't. I simply couldn't. I had to keep going. I had to *know*.

And then, when I got to the end of a very long and difficult road, what I found was not what I expected—not at all.

Because sometimes, even in fairy tales, there is a monster lurking.

—⁊⁊—

Still, I realize now that this was a journey I had to take, a journey so many of us must take—the determined voyage to self-discovery.

To knowing why we do what we do, so we can hope to change how we act. To confronting what it means to be a parent or son or daughter. To understanding the dark forces that tear families apart, and the great currents of love that keep them together.

To solving, as best we can, the elemental mystery of identity, the puzzle of all human life:

What is it that makes us *us*?

2

I WAS NOT FINISHED with the boxes in the basement.

A few days after my mother shut down my questioning about them, I waited until my parents were both out of the house and I went back to the crawl space. I was ten, after all, and what ten-year-old wouldn't be fascinated by a good mystery story, much less a mystery in which he's the star? So I dug out the boxes and read all the articles, dozens of them, and I read all the letters, too, and bit by bit the haunting events of ten years earlier came to vivid life.

It was only decades later that I realized what I was doing down in the basement all those afternoons—I was becoming the detective of my own life.

At first, it was sheer fascination that kept me going. The articles were incredibly detailed, and those details became important to me. How much Baby Paul weighed when he was kidnapped. How my parents stayed in the hospital for days after the abduction, my father sleeping in a cot next to my mother's bed. How my mother's brother John showed up to be with her after the freighter he worked on docked in Chicago.

One detail jumped out, because it was something about my parents I hadn't known. The year before the kidnapping, an article explained, my parents "lost a stillborn son in Michael Reese" Hospital. Incredibly, my mother lost her first son before he was even born, then lost another son just hours after his birth, in the same hospital—on the same *floor*, even. "A mother for the second time but still without a child," one article heartlessly declared. Such a fate seemed impossibly cruel to me, even back then, and I felt even sorrier for my mother.

Yet as sad as that was, and as frightening as the abduction was, I can't say the clippings and letters upset me in any real way. In fact, I had a conflicted view of what I was reading. On one hand, believing that I was the Paul at the center of this spectacular story, this brazen crime, was exciting. It was cool. I kind of liked the idea of being this missing kid—the kid everyone was looking for. Part of me couldn't wait to run out and tell my neighborhood friends about my odd celebrity.

Another part of me, though, felt no connection to the child in the articles at all. It was as if I was reading about someone else. The clippings didn't give me nightmares. I didn't develop a fear of being taken again. The gravity of what happened ten years earlier didn't really land on me, perhaps because my parents never talked about it. I was fascinated, to be sure, but that was about it. I didn't feel like some great truth about me was being revealed in the articles. Not yet, anyway.

Still, I kept reading, kept reconstructing the events, kept absorbing the story, until it became a part of me that I would carry everywhere, unsure of its meaning but more and more certain of its importance.

And eventually I realized that this remarkable event—the most notorious Chicago crime in years, which led to the largest manhunt in the city's history, larger even than the search for John Dillinger—would be the founding plank of the mythology of me, whether I was Paul Joseph Fronczak, or I wasn't.

Michael Reese Hospital
Chicago, Illinois
April 27, 1964

Outside, it was sixty degrees and foggy and drizzling. Daylight saving time had started the day before, at 3:00 A.M. The unusually mild winter—the coldest it got that year was two degrees, way off the record of minus twenty-six—had blended into spring.

This was Dora Fronczak's first full day as a mother.

Dora was twenty-eight years old, and she lay in one of the two single beds in Room 418 of Meyer House, the maternity wing of Michael Reese Hospital, a darkly Gothic structure built in 1907 in south Chicago, across from Lake Michigan. In her arms, she held a healthy infant boy with a thatch of dark hair and wrinkly olive skin. This was her son, Paul Joseph. He had been born a day earlier, at 1:20 A.M., and he weighed seven pounds, two ounces. Throughout that day, my mother held him during brief nursing sessions and missed him when he was taken back to the nursery to sleep. The next day, April 27, she got to hold her son for a little bit longer during feedings.

My mother had a roommate in the maternity wing, Joyce Doane, twenty-four, who was expecting her own child soon. But on the morning of April 27, my father Chester Fronczak, thirty-three, wasn't there. He was already back at work. In those days, there was no such thing as paternity leave, so Chester was on the clock as a machinist for the Foote Brothers division of Hewitt-Robins, a factory on South Western Avenue that made conveyor belts, chains and sprockets, transmissions for helicopters, things like that. His plan was to hand out cigars to his co-workers, then rush over to the hospital to see his new son as soon as work was through.

In Room 418, around 9:00 A.M., a nurse brought a swaddled Baby

Paul from the glass-enclosed nursery to my mother's room and handed him to her.

Then, at 9:30 A.M., as Dora happily fed her child, a different nurse walked in.

This nurse was about forty years old, with graying brown hair combed straight back and pressed down by a white hairnet. She wore a typical nurse's uniform—white shoes, white stockings, white smock dress. All that was missing was a white nurse's cap.

The nurse walked to Dora's bed and, without a word, lifted the blue cotton blanket wrapped around Baby Paul. She looked at the boy for a long moment, studying his face. Then she lowered the blanket and—again, without a word—walked out of the room. Nothing seemed too alarming about the nurse, except perhaps for her silence, and maybe her demeanor. "I didn't get the impression that she was a motherly, kindly sort of woman," my mother's roommate, Joyce, would later say.

Just a half hour later, the mysterious nurse walked into Dora's room again. This time, she spoke.

"One of the pediatricians wants to examine your son," she said in a calm, convincing voice. "I need to take him now."

This time, Dora did find it strange that the nurse wanted to take her baby away during a feeding. This was such a precious, sacred time. Still, my mother handed her bundled infant to the nurse.

The nurse took the child and left the room.

She then hurried down the hallway, pushed open the door to a stairwell, descended four flights, and, through a back exit, walked out of Michael Reese Hospital.

A short while later, a Chicago cabdriver, Lee Kelsey, picked up the woman and child on Twenty-ninth Street and Ellis Avenue, just behind the hospital, and drove them several blocks to Thirty-fifth and

Halsted. When the woman stepped out of Kelsey's Checker cab on Halsted Avenue, she might as well have stepped off the earth.

To this day no one has ever reported seeing her again.

—⁓—

Back at Michael Reese Hospital, a young student nurse saw the woman take Baby Paul into the stairwell. She told her supervisor about it, and together they rushed to the nursery. Baby Paul wasn't there. They walked into Dora's room, acting as calm as they could, and saw the infant wasn't there, either. Without alerting Dora, the nursing staff spent the next two hours combing the hospital for any trace of Baby Paul. Their frantic search came up empty.

At 2:55 P.M., hospital officials notified Chicago police. The police issued an all points bulletin and, at 3:00 P.M., began a door-to-door search of the ten-block area surrounding the hospital. Around this time, police also called the foreman at Hewitt-Robins and asked to speak to Chester Fronczak. Earlier, Chester had proudly handed out his cigars. Now he was on the phone with police.

"Your son is missing," my father was told.

In Room 418, Dora still knew nothing. No one asked her to describe the nurse who took her baby—a description that might have helped—because someone deemed it advisable not to tell her anything for several hours. Only after her husband raced to the hospital, knelt beside her bed, and told her what happened did Dora realize she was in a nightmare.

Her son, her angel, was gone.

That day, some two hundred policemen and FBI agents descended on South Side Chicago, searching six hundred homes and interviewing a thousand people by midnight. In the coming days detectives pored over the files of some 2,600 hospital employees. The state director of registration and education had his chief investigator, Jack Hayes, read through the files of hundreds of licensed, registered nurses. Jack Johnson, the warden of the county jail, ordered guards to interview every woman who arrived at the jail after the kidnapping, in case the fugitive nurse had thought to avoid scrutiny by hiding behind bars. Eighteen months' worth of medical records for women with stillborn babies were investigated, along with the histories of thousands of infants whose identities were in any way suspicious. Postmaster General John Gronouski, who like Chester Fronczak was Polish, pledged the support of all 175,000 of his letter carriers.

All told, investigators eventually questioned more than 38,000 people across the country.

At Michael Reese Hospital, police taped single sheets of paper to the walls of the lobby, the exits, and the fourth floor. IMPORTANT NOTICE, the flyers announced in big, black type, before asking any patients, staffers, or visitors for any information they might have about the abductor.

Chicago police questioned my mother, too, and she admitted she never got a good look at the nurse who took her child. Her roommate, Joyce, didn't notice much, either, beyond the observation that "from looking at her, I think she must have hated the world." Even so, interviews with other witnesses, including the cabdriver, helped police sketch artist Otis Rathel create a composite drawing of the kidnapper.

The sketch depicted a white woman somewhere between thirty-five and forty-five years old, somewhere around five feet, three inches tall, weighing between 130 and 145 pounds, with brown eyes and brown hair streaked with gray. Another newspaper sketch showed her in a white cotton dress, white stockings, and white shoes—her nurse outfit. Neither drawing provided anything distinctive about her appearance—

no scar, no lopsided feature, no limp. In the sketches, she looked like any nurse in the world.

Police also released photos of several hospital items, including the type of outfit Baby Paul would have been wearing, the type of blanket he might have been wrapped in, and the small plastic identification bracelet that would have been fastened around his tiny wrist. The bracelet shown in the police photo was a generic bracelet—no name or ID number. The real bracelet, of course—the single item of identification in the absence of handprints or footprints, which weren't yet hospital policy—had vanished along with the child.

Still, hundreds of tips were phoned in to the Chicago Police Department and the temporary office set up for the FBI in the hospital. Reporters were able to conclude that the police and FBI were focusing their search on registered nurses, practical nurses, and nurses' aides who had formerly worked at Michael Reese—and particularly on those who had any record of mental illness, and those who'd had a child die or couldn't have children.

The only certainty about the kidnapper, police admitted, was that she had a thorough knowledge of the hospital layout. She was known to have spent at least four hours in the hospital on the day of the kidnapping. She knew the nursing schedule, and she understood that taking a baby out of the glass-enclosed, segregated nursery would have been far riskier than taking a baby out of a hospital room. The day before the kidnapping, a nurse approached a hospital housekeeper and offered to help her fold linens in the maternity ward—which was odd, the housekeeper later told police, because folding linens wasn't ordinarily something nurses did. But the gesture wasn't strange enough for her to tell anyone about it until after the kidnapping.

Other new mothers at the hospital, too, told police they recalled the nurse coming into their rooms and calmly lifting their babies' blankets so she could see their faces. "I asked her what she was doing," one mother, Leisa Cohen, remembered, "and she turned on her heels and walked out."

The kidnapper, it was clear, was shopping for the perfect baby to take.

—◆◆◆—

For more than two weeks after the abduction, police officers and FBI agents worked twelve- to sixteen-hour days. Many of them simply walked the streets of Chicago, looking for women who resembled the police sketch. They found one woman walking north on the 5500 block of Sheridan Road and stopped her. She wore a babushka head scarf, a green woolen coat, and a white nurse's uniform. "I can't understand why I wasn't picked up before," she told the police. Yet after nearly four hours of questioning, she was released and driven home by police at 4:30 A.M.

Hundreds of other possible suspects came and went. Police looked into a report of a woman in a nurse's outfit who had been kicked out of a different Chicago hospital three months before the kidnapping, after staffers discovered she didn't work there. Nurses remembered her picking up babies from their cribs and commenting on how clean the nursery was compared to the one at Michael Reese. But the woman was never found. As the days went by, FBI agents were less and less forthcoming about what leads they were following. Marlin Johnson, the special agent in charge of the FBI's Chicago office, said, "We defeat our own purpose if we let the kidnapper know what we're doing to find her."

On May 5, eight days after the abduction, doctors at Michael Reese put out an emergency bulletin. "It has just been learned that the family of Paul Joseph Fronczak has a history of multiple allergies," the bulletin read. "Since these allergies may have been inherited by the baby, a change in feeding is necessary."

The family's personal physician went on to describe precisely what the kidnapper ought to do to keep the boy safe.

> Since baby Fronczak may be allergic to cow's milk, the doctor strongly urges that the formula be changed as follows: use Promel powder, a soy-bean milk substitute. Mix one tablespoon of Promel powder with one ounce of water which has been boiled for five minutes. Because Promel powder does not contain vitamins, vitamins C and D should be given separately. The doctor recommends two drops of Drisdol, vitamin D, and 10 drops of Cecon, vitamin C, to be given to the infant each day. The family physician appeals to the kidnapper to follow the above feeding changes to insure the infant's good health. All the ingredients are easily obtained at any drug store.

—◊—

Ten years later, when I read about the doctor's appeal to the kidnapper, I was surprised by how much it assumed about the woman who took Baby Paul. It assumed she had a side to her that was tender and thoughtful and caring, that deep down she had the baby's interests at heart. But how could a woman who so casually stole an infant right from its mother's arms then turn around and be a compassionate mother herself? It didn't make sense to me back then. I saw no grayness in the media descriptions of her—the kidnapper, it seemed to me, was pure evil.

And yet, as I was shocked to learn, my mother, of all people, didn't see it that way.

I came across an article that described my mother's first statement to the media, just three days after the abduction. Remarkably, she told the press she didn't blame anyone for the kidnapping. "It was just something that happened," she said. "All I can say is that this woman must have been desperate for a baby to do such a horrible thing."

Somehow, my mother found it in her to empathize with the kidnapper. I could hardly believe it then, and I still find it hard to believe now. But the more I read, the more I realized my mother wasn't thinking about the kidnapper in the days after the abduction. She wasn't even thinking about herself, or her husband. All of her anguish, her pain, her torment, was secondary. The only thing that mattered to my mother, I learned, was that her child was *okay*.

"Take good care of him and see that he gets enough to eat," she wearily told a reporter who asked if she had anything to say to the kidnapper. "He is everything we built our hopes on for the future. Just so he is taken care of, that's the main thing."

And only then—only after she had expressed the powerful love she held in her mother's heart—did she say anything about herself.

Sitting in a wheelchair in the lobby of the hospital, her eyes red from crying and her face pale and drawn from sleepless, sedative-filled nights—and passing a small crystal rosary nervously through her fingers—she issued a plea to the kidnapper in a voice too soft for most of the huddled reporters to hear.

"Please," my mother whispered, "return the baby to us."

3

EVEN WHEN I first read about the kidnapping, I understood that what my mother went through was hell—a hell beyond my comprehension. Her impossible sadness, the heaviness of it all, was evident in the photos taken of her in the hospital, her pretty face blank from shock, her eyelids drooping, her body limp as my father held her—as if she would crumple to the ground if he let go. In those newspaper photos, my mother is a portrait of utter heartbreak and despair.

But my father? It was easier for me to imagine my mother's pain than it was to picture my father going through the same thing. Maybe it was because I knew my father to be gruff and unemotional, one of those solid, silent types. But then I found an article that gave me a glimpse into what he'd had to endure.

Two days after the kidnapping, someone persuaded my father to make a public statement, just as my mother had. I am sure he did it reluctantly, and probably only because the police convinced him it might help. He met with reporters at the hospital, and sat at a table with a microphone in front of him. There is a photo of him slumped at the table, holding his head up with his left hand, looking dazed.

Did he have a message for the kidnapper? one reporter asked.

"I hope she takes care of the baby," my father answered in a soft voice. "I plead with her to return him."

Someone else asked my father if he had slept at all.

"A few minutes," he replied.

Throughout the brief statement, the articles said, my father fought back tears.

I am sure he did. I would have been surprised to read that my father cried openly in front of reporters. But part of me wished he had, so I could have read about it and known that he was capable of such emotion.

—◊◊◊—

It is seven years before the kidnapping.

My father entered a bank that was two blocks from where he lived in Chicago. There, he saw a pretty, dark-featured woman working as a teller. Her name was Dora, and she'd recently moved to Chicago from Escanaba, Michigan, a small bay town in the state's Upper Peninsula. Dora's father, who worked in a paper mill, and her mother, a housewife, came over from Croatia and raised their children in a primitive home with an outhouse. Dora would forever remember having to brave the brutally cold winter winds just to go to the bathroom in the dark of the night.

As soon as she was old enough, Dora left Escanaba with her sister Bertha and found a place in Chicago. She got a job in a bank and handled a transaction for my father, Chester Fronczak, whose own parents had emigrated from Poland. Chester was darkly handsome, with a broad back and a firm grip. He asked Dora for a date, and she turned him down flat. A few weeks later he asked again, and again she politely said no.

Chester didn't stop asking for the next five years, until finally—worn down, no doubt, by his persistence—Dora agreed to go out with him.

They went to a fancy nightclub for dinner, and they were never apart again.

My parents wed in a Catholic church in Chicago, and two years later, in Michael Reese Hospital, my mother gave birth to a boy she named Paul Joseph.

—⁂—

Besides the crystal rosary beads my mother had with her at all times in the days after the kidnapping, there was something else she kept by her side—a black-and-white photograph of Baby Paul, taken shortly after he was born.

In the photo, which my mother kept in a wooden frame on a table next to her hospital bed, the baby has dark eyes and a pretty good head of black hair. Someone has laid him down on a white sheet, and he's wearing a diaper and a little white shirt. His hands are curled into tiny fists that he holds in front of him, almost like a boxer. The wide plastic ID bracelet is on his left wrist. A card with all his information is placed gently on his stomach. It is numbered 5648, and it includes his name (just Fronczak) and his weight at birth. Lines for the address, city, and doctor are blank. The photographer's name is also listed, though I could never quite make it out.

This is the only known photo of Baby Paul.

I spent a lot of time looking at the photo. I came across it in several articles about the case, and later I got a cleaner copy of the actual photograph. There isn't much to it—even the baby's expression is neutral, neither agitated nor happy—but there was something fascinating about it to me. I think it's that the photo captured a moment of calm, of innocence, that would be so abruptly and tragically lost in only a short while. The photo freezes this moment forever, and in that moment Baby Paul still belongs to my mother, and the nightmare that is to come still doesn't exist, and a future filled with love and happiness is still possible.

But of course time can't be frozen, and so all that remained of the normalcy and joy and innocence of Baby Paul's first few hours on earth was a small, grainy photograph—a photo that was soon pinned up in every police station in Chicago.

—⁓—

My mother clung to the photo, just as she clung to hope. She found hope wherever she could and she held on to it for dear life. She found it in the cards and letters that began to stream in from all over the country, from as far away as Russia and Brazil—the same cards and letters I later found in the basement. *We are praying for you,* most of them said. *Stay strong. Have hope. God will save your child.* She got a letter from a soldier in Germany offering his prayers. She learned that masses were being said in churches everywhere for the return of Baby Paul. She was told that several convents of nuns had joined in prayers for her and her child.

"She reads the cards and keeps them with his picture," Dora's mother-in-law, Ann Fronczak, told reporters. "She still hopes the baby will be returned."

Not long after the abduction, my mother was moved from her double room in the hospital to a single room next door. She chose to stay at the hospital for several days, rather than go home, and I think it was because she believed that if she waited there long enough, the awful nurse would bring her baby back.

But the doctors at Michael Reese wanted her to stay, too, so they could keep an eye on her. They monitored her constantly, and when she couldn't sleep at night they gave her sedatives. Some people worried that keeping my mother in the maternity ward, where newborn babies were everywhere, and other joyous mothers got to take their infants home, might do more harm than good for her mental state. But hospital officials assured the press that it was best for her.

"She is much more emotionally stable now," a spokesman told reporters a week into her stay, "than she was in the first few days after the kidnapping."

I wondered how they could possibly know that was true.

Meanwhile, police officers were stationed outside the door of her room, keeping reporters and other strangers away. Besides investigators, only her doctors, immediate family, and the hospital's Roman Catholic chaplain were allowed to see her. Police also intercepted any phone calls that came in. My father was given time off from the factory and stayed with my mother around the clock. He occasionally left her side, to eat in the cafeteria and talk to the police and FBI agents, but, from what I could tell, my mother never left the room, except for brief strolls with my father to the nearby solarium.

I tried to imagine what these early days were like for my mother. I pictured her struggling to fall asleep, fighting off the terror, and finally swallowing pills and slipping into a haze. I imagined her desperately believing that every visitor to the room, every creak of the door, meant the arrival of good news—and I imagined her shattering disappointment when it was only a nurse or a doctor empty-handed. I am sure there were long stretches of time, hour after silent hour, when my mother's hopes for getting her son back were sorely tested.

There were promising leads and encouraging tips, but investigators decided not to share all of them with my mother, "so that she would not be subject to any more emotional strain than necessary," one article reported. But the police and FBI certainly shared them with the media, and newspapers breathlessly reported each new lead, leaving readers waiting for the next day's paper to learn if it panned out.

As I sat in the basement and read the articles ten years later, I could hardly wait to find out, either.

One of the strongest leads came from a restaurant owner in Freeport, Illinois, a couple of hours west of Chicago.

The owner reported that early one morning, a man and woman came into her café carrying an infant. They asked if they could wash the baby and buy some milk.

"Sure," the owner replied. "How old is he?"

"Three weeks," the woman answered, "I think."

The owner quickly called police, but she didn't stop the couple from getting into their Chevrolet and driving away. Investigators set up surveillance in the area around the restaurant, but the couple and their child were never found.

Then police got a call from Rosetta Alexander, the matron at a railroad station in Dearborn, Michigan, four hours east of Chicago. She reported seeing a woman on the train platform who looked exactly like the woman in the police sketch. Officers picked her up and whisked her to the police station, and word leaked to the press that a suspect was in custody. Believing the kidnapping might be on the verge of being solved, more than sixty reporters rushed to the station and waited outside.

They watched as Lee Kelsey, the cabdriver who'd picked up the kidnapper, was hustled in and out of the interrogation room, followed by a Roman Catholic monk. The longer the reporters waited without word, the more convinced they became that a break was imminent. "That must be the woman who took the baby," they quoted one building staffer as saying, "but where's the baby, then?"

Finally, at 1:17 A.M., Police Captain William Murphy—with "lines of fatigue etched on his round face," one report said—came out of the station to speak to the press. Captain Murphy said that while the woman who was questioned "remarkably resembled" the sketch, she was just a housekeeper who had an alibi and was not the kidnapper. FBI Special Agent Marlin Johnson also addressed the crowd.

"She's not the woman," he said. "We know her whereabouts on the day the baby was kidnapped."

So why, then, had she been wandering around the train station late at night?

"She is just a poor soul who's confused," Johnson said.

Every day, reports of near breakthroughs filled the papers. A woman from the town of Cicero told police she had knowledge of the kidnapping, but her information proved false, and she was ordered to undergo psychiatric evaluation. Another woman brought a baby suffering from malnutrition into the Illinois Masonic hospital, but when police were summoned, they discovered she was in fact the child's mother. Someone reported that the kidnapper had been caught after seeing police rush out of five squad cars and pick up a woman and a baby on Chicago's North Side. It turned out the woman was trying to get her critically ill son to the hospital. Separate tips led police to set up roadblocks in Freeport and stake out ten resort hotels, but neither lead panned out.

Hopes were surely raised when a plaid thirty-by-thirty-six-inch baby blanket, olive and gray on one side and blue and green on the other, was found on 102nd Street and Pulaski Road in Chicago. Police once again brought in Lee Kelsey, who remembered Baby Paul being swaddled in a blanket. But Kelsey couldn't say for sure if this was the same blanket. Not much later, officials at Michael Reese confirmed the blanket wasn't one of theirs.

The one-week mark came and went without news. Finally, on May 5, eight days after the kidnapping, my mother decided it was time to leave the hospital. Sooner or later, she had to face the ordeal of returning to her apartment without her baby. One hospital official asked her if she and my father planned to take some time off and get away somewhere.

"No," my mother replied instantly. "I want to be home in case the woman decides to return the baby."

The morning of May 5, my mother put on a plain red-and-yellow cotton dress and walked out of her room, escorted by my father, in shirtsleeves that showed off his muscled forearms. Her brother John and two Chicago detectives followed behind. They took the elevator to the lobby and were greeted by thirty reporters and photographers. My father held tight to my mother's arm and hustled her through the crowd.

"Do you have any message for the kidnapper?" one reporter yelled out.

"Please return the baby," my mother managed to say.

Outside, reporters kept surrounding her and asking for more comments.

"I just want to get to the car," she told them.

My mother slid into the backseat of an unmarked police car at the curb and bowed her head. My father got in beside her and patted her back.

On her wrist, my mother still wore the hospital bracelet she was given the day Baby Paul was born, identifying her as his mother.

The police car sped away from the hospital, and before long Dora and Chester were back on the tree-lined street where they lived, West Fortieth Place, in the attic apartment of the two-story home owned by my father's parents, Ann and Chester Fronczak, Sr. They'd moved in after getting married two years earlier. Once inside, my mother hunkered down, just as she'd done in her hospital room. A day after she got home she allowed herself to walk less than a block to St. Pancratius Church for mass at 7:30 A.M., again physically propped up by my father. "She barely made it, she's so weak," my grandmother told a reporter.

But other than quick daily trips to morning mass, my mother refused to leave the apartment. "She won't go out," Ann Fronczak said. "She keeps hoping the phone will ring and that will be the call saying he's been found." On their third day home, my father admitted to a reporter, "We will probably have to get her out someday soon for a little fresh air."

Inside the house, two FBI agents—Bernard Carey and Ronald Miniter—set up shop in the small den on the first floor. They lugged in a huge black suitcase, which contained the primitive recording equipment they would use to intercept every phone call. My parents gave the agents a list of the phone numbers of friends and relatives, but all other calls were answered by Carey or Miniter. At first, both agents stayed in the den twenty-four hours a day, one of them sleeping on the sofa, the other on a small cot my parents provided. After a few days, they were allowed to work in separate twenty-four-hour shifts. My mother wheeled in a small black-and-white TV with rabbit ears, and every now and then she took in a plate of cookies, but otherwise the agents carried on their vigil all alone. Years later, I tracked down Bernard Carey in his home in Florida, and I asked him about the days he spent in my parents' home.

"It was a very sad detail," Carey told me. "There was such a sadness in that house. We were waiting every day for anything that seemed like a ransom call, but it never came. We didn't get even one slightly suspicious call. That was the hardest part. Having to go up to your parents every night and say, 'I'm sorry, but there was nothing. No calls, no leads, nothing.'"

Special Agent Miniter stayed for two weeks. Carey lasted one more week after that. Then the FBI ended the detail. When Carey finally packed up the recording equipment and said good-bye to my parents, he had an ominous feeling.

"It's very sad to say," he recalled, "but when I left, I remember thinking that this case would never be solved."

—⁓—

Once my mother was home, my father's parents did everything they could to comfort her, and so did her sister Bertha, who lived nearby. But from the articles, it seemed to me that my mother was inconsolable. Her doctor prescribed a continued regiment of sedatives, and throughout the day she would take them, but eventually the sedatives would wear off and she would "start to cry again," Ann Fronczak told reporters. "But it's better for her to cry the worry out than hold it inside."

For solace, my mother turned to the calendar. Early on, she'd received a letter from a mother whose baby had also been kidnapped. Incredibly, nine days later, the baby was returned. I can imagine my mother counting down to nine days, and feeling dejected when that milestone came and went. Then, she came to believe that Baby Paul would be dropped off at a church on Mother's Day, May 10, nearly two weeks after the abduction. But that day passed without a break, too. A week later, on May 18, my parents would have celebrated their second wedding anniversary, and perhaps my mother believed that would be the day the miracle happened. Instead, all that happened was two neighborhood girls came by the house to drop off a bouquet of flowers.

"No, we have no plans," my father told a reporter who asked how they would spend the day. "There won't be a dinner. Nothing at all."

Eventually, my mother lost track of time altogether. "Someone asked me the other day how long it had been since I left the hospital," she said in one conversation. "I couldn't tell them. Time just goes."

On May 27, Baby Paul had been missing for a month. By then, my mother had been forced to make adjustments—to develop some kind of routine to get through her days. Every morning, she and my father got up at 5:30 and went to 6:15 mass at St. Joseph and Anne Catholic Church on Thirty-eighth Place. Then my father went to work—he finally returned to the factory a month after the abduction—and my mother went home and did what she could to keep busy. "Today, I'm trying to do a little washing," she said in an article. "I try to eat. The doctor says I must."

She also read the twenty or so consoling letters that arrived every day, and took comfort in the tiny shrine to Baby Paul she set up in her bedroom. It consisted of just two things—the framed photo, and a crude crucifix that had been fashioned out of wood by the Poor Clare Sisters, a cloistered order of nuns who lived nearby. What my mother hoped for the hardest, it seemed, was that the kidnapper shared her belief in God's watchful eye. "If she's a woman with any kind of religious beliefs, it's not just the fear of police but fear of her God she must someday meet," my mother told a reporter. "One of the commandments is 'thou shalt not steal,' and what is worse than stealing a human being that belongs to someone else?"

If the kidnapper did indeed have the fear of God in her heart, then she chose not to act on it.

And so my mother continued to suffer, hour after hour. "Sometimes I don't think I'll get through the day," she admitted in an article. My mother also explained that she and my father had stopped going to church together. "It is too hard for us," she said. "He goes early before work and I go a little later, alone."

After more than two months without the return of her child, my mother still refused to go shopping, or visit friends, or otherwise make an attempt to get back to something like normalcy. "I don't even want to go to my sister's for an hour," she said. "I don't want to leave here—I don't want to leave the phone. Someday, there may be just the call we've waited for."

Tips and leads and near breakthroughs continued to happen—an abandoned baby in Georgia, another infant kidnapped in Wisconsin. My mother even received a call from someone demanding ten thousand dollars in a paper bag for the return of her baby. She notified police, who dressed up a female officer to look like my mother and had her drop off a bag filled with newspaper cuttings in the lobby of a building on South St. Louis Avenue, as instructed. When police arrested the young woman who retrieved the bag, there was no baby to be found. It was all an extortion plot.

But the call my mother kept waiting for—the jangle of the phone that would bring her baby back to her—simply didn't come.

It didn't come by the time Baby Paul's first birthday arrived, in April 1965.

It didn't come in time for his second birthday, either.

The tips and leads dwindled, and cops and FBI agents were reassigned. Boxes of evidence were moved to storage. The case of Paul Joseph Fronczak went cold.

Until, in June 1966, more than two years after the kidnapping, the phone call finally came.

4

697 Broad Street
Newark, New Jersey
July 2, 1965

A CHILD HAD BEEN FOUND.

He was found in the middle of a place known as Ladies' Mile. The Mile was a row of several blocks in downtown Newark, New Jersey. Back in the 1960s, Newark was one of the premier shopping destinations in the country, and Broad Street, in particular, was where the most elegant ladies went to shop. The street was home to a number of prestigious department stores—Hahne and Company, Kresge's, Goerke's. One of those stores was on the corner of Broad and Cedar Streets, in a handsome four-story, rectangular brick building, with double-hung windows, a pressed-tin cornice, and a canopy that wrapped around the corner.

A three-story, art moderne sign, visible for blocks, regally announced the store—McCrory's.

The street outside McCrory's was a bustling place. For years, a subway platform poured shoppers right into the store. But even after it closed, the crowds came, for both the shopping and the fine restaurant on the second floor. On weekends, Broad Street was packed; on weekdays, a little less so. But always, the corner of Broad and Cedar was as busy a public space as there was in New Jersey.

Around 3:00 P.M. on Friday, July 2, 1965—a warm, dry day—someone pushed a blond, brown-eyed boy in a stroller up to the entrance of McCrory's.

It was a brand-new stroller, and the boy inside was dressed in clean, bright clothes—a blue suit and a blue cap. To anyone who walked by, the boy looked to be around fourteen months old. There was nothing unusual about the boy or the stroller or the adult who brought him to McCrory's—at least not at first.

But then, whoever it was that brought him let go of the stroller, turned, and walked away. The boy in the blue suit was left behind on the street outside the store.

He sat there in his stroller, alone, for the next two hours.

Finally, at 5:00 P.M., someone called the police and alerted them to an abandoned baby outside McCrory's. The person who called police refused to give a name. When officers arrived, they found the boy just where he'd been left. He had a runny nose and a cold. The officers took him straight to Newark Hospital, where he was weighed—twenty pounds—and measured—thirty inches—and kept overnight.

The next day, Newark Detective Joseph P. Farrell was assigned the task of finding out who the boy was, and who had left him behind. Police also contacted the Newark Bureau of Children's Services, which promptly opened a case file on the child. Since the identity of his parents was unknown, he was given a number and an official designation.

He was designated a "foundling"—an infant abandoned by its parents and left for others to care for.

—〰—

When I was ten and reading the articles about the kidnapping for the first time, I wondered how and when I would reenter the story. Obviously, I'd been found—I was there with my parents, in their house, in their basement. But how did it happen? Was it something dramatic? A ransom payment? A shoot-out?

That's when I had another breathtaking moment of recognition.

I came upon a black-and-white photograph that showed a nurse, this time in a hospital in Newark, New Jersey. She was young and pretty, and her name was Lolita Tana, and she was smiling and holding a young boy against her right hip. I looked at the boy's face, at his sandy hair and his wide eyes, and I knew instantly who he was.

He was me. I was the boy in the blue suit. I was the boy who'd been abandoned.

I was the foundling.

—⚏—

Once Detective Farrell was handed my case, he ran a series of ads in local New Jersey and New York newspapers. They described how I'd been abandoned, and asked anyone with any information to come forward. The ads ran for several days but produced only a single call, which turned out to be a dead end.

Detective Farrell concluded that "someone living outside the Newark area must have abandoned the child," he later told a reporter. "It was obvious that someone wanted him to be found and cared for." Whoever it was that left me behind could have simply dumped me in the woods somewhere. Instead, they dressed me nicely and left me in a busy place trafficked by well-to-do people. This was their final, charitable act on my behalf.

While Detective Farrell investigated my case, I was kept at Newark Hospital for several weeks, because I couldn't shake my cold. Or perhaps it was because there was no better place to take me. Finally, hospital officials transferred my temporary supervision to the state's Bureau of Children's Services. In late July, the bureau placed me in a home in Watchung, about twenty miles southwest of Newark. It was known as an adoption home, a sort of way station for unclaimed kids—the first such home ever established in the state. The owners were Claire and Fred Eckert, who along with their daughter Janet took care of nearly one hundred babies over ten years of operation.

One evening in late July 1965, a Children's Services worker drove me from Newark to the Eckerts' rural home. I was running a temperature and still showing signs of a cold. I wore only a diaper and a half-sleeve shirt, and the official draped a blue blanket over my head as she walked me to the door. Claire, Fred, and Janet Eckert were already there, waiting for me. Claire lifted the blanket slightly so they could all peek under and see my face.

"You smiled," Janet would later remember. "Your eyes were so big."

That night, the Eckerts became my new guardians.

Early on in my time with them, something strange happened. When Claire's teenage son-in-law stopped by for a visit, my reaction was strong and unexpected. As soon as I saw him, I cowered and began to cry. Not small tears, either—I cried "violently" whenever the son-in-law showed up, according to one Children's Services report. The same thing happened when any other young man came near me. It was presumed, the report said, that I'd had "a very bad experience with a young man."

What that experience had been, no one could say.

—◊—

Within a day or two of being dropped off at the Eckerts', I came down with the measles. I was extremely quiet and withdrawn. Eventually I got over the measles and, according to Janet, came out of my shell. I revealed myself to be anything but shy; in fact, I was outgoing and affectionate. When I came to live with them, the Eckerts were caring for several other children, and all the kids slept in separate cribs set up in one room. I took to climbing into the other children's cribs, so I could cuddle with them.

I grew especially close to Claire and Fred. Most days, Claire and Janet watched over me while Fred went off to work as a machinist. Whatever fear I had of younger men did not extend to Fred, who was in his late forties, and I embraced him as if he were my own father. I began to wait at the top of the Eckerts' hilly driveway for him to come home from work, and when I saw him I'd jump up and rush to grab him. Fred would let me carry his lunch box as he held my hand and walked me back to the house. Sometimes he carried me in on his shoulders.

I adapted well to the daily routine the Eckerts set up for the children. Claire would wake me around 7:00 A.M., then give me a breakfast of juice and toast and cereal, or maybe two soft-boiled eggs with butter. I also liked oatmeal, farina, cream of wheat, and Rice Krispies. Sometimes Claire gave me a little dash of her morning coffee in my glass of milk.

By 9:30 A.M., weather allowing, I was outdoors playing, or going for a walk or a ride in my stroller. I'd get a nice chunk of a Parker House bread roll as a midmorning snack. For lunch, Campbell's soup with saltines, and milk and cookies. A short nap at 1:00 P.M., and then more outside time—at first in the small plastic kiddie pool in the Eckerts' backyard (I liked scooping up water in a pail and pouring it over my head) and later in the Eckerts' real pool, where I resisted Claire's efforts to keep a hand on me by saying, "don't want" and "good-bye."

"He has no fear," Claire later wrote. "He climbs to the top of the sliding board, folds his hands in his lap and goes right down."

Around five I'd go in for dinner, which was whatever the Eckerts were having, chopped up. I was given a bath at 7:00 P.M., then put to bed with a bottle of warm milk at 7:30. I'd politely say good night to Claire and Fred when they put me to bed, and I'd chirp "good morning" when they came to get me the next day. I wasn't afraid of the dark, but for some reason I refused to use a blanket or a pillow. I needed to sleep completely uncovered.

The time I spent with the Eckerts was blissfully ordinary. "He gets such a thrill from the simplest things," Claire would write, "from buying new shoes to tasting whatever you may be eating." I had fun helping Claire and Janet do household chores like unpacking groceries and raking up leaves. I could count to six—though often I'd jump past four and five to get there—and I knew the words for my nose, ears, hair, teeth, mouth, fingers and toes, though sometimes I called my knee my toe. I loved to wrestle on the floor with Fred, and I'd follow him around and put up my hands like a little prizefighter and ask, "Want to box?"

I was gentle with the younger babies at the home, and I would stroke their hair and tell them, "Don't cry," and if I tripped and fell and got banged up, I'd tell myself the same thing, over and over, like a mantra—"Don't cry. Don't cry."

"He is one of the most perfect boys I've ever known," Claire would later say. "He has charmed all of us with his dearness and kind little ways. He has such a great love of life, and he has made us aware of so many things. He was my special baby."

The Eckerts did one other remarkable thing for me. A few weeks after I was placed with them, they put me in a special white outfit and took me to St. Joseph's Church in Watchung to have me baptized. It was something they did for all the unclaimed babies in their care. Fred was my godfather, and Janet was my godmother. A priest poured a trickle of water on my forehead, and that afternoon the Eckerts celebrated with a cake, which I ate with my fingers.

In order to be baptized, I had to have a religion and a birth date. So the Eckerts gave me those, too. They made me a Roman Catholic, and they picked a date—April 26—that roughly matched up with my estimated age, and made that my birthday. Most important, the Eckerts gave me a name. Claire came up with it, because she liked the sound of it. Simple, strong, American.

And so the foundling became a boy named Scott McKinley.

—⁓—

Three weeks after I was found in Newark, Detective Farrell played a hunch.

His investigation into who abandoned me was stuck. No one had claimed me, or called in a tip. There were no surveillance cameras at the time, and no eyewitnesses stepped forward. It was as if I'd magically appeared on Broad Street.

Then Farrell remembered a different crime in a different city in a different year. He remembered the Baby Fronczak kidnapping.

It had been a national story, and Farrell recalled that the child had never been found. He dug up a photo of Baby Paul and compared it to the photo he'd taken of me in my blue suit. The age range was roughly right—in July 1965, Baby Paul would have been fourteen months old, which was more or less how old I looked when they found me. Farrell also examined photos of Dora and Chester Fronczak, to see if I bore any resemblance to them. Nothing was conclusive, but Farrell saw enough to take action.

On July 27, 1965, he wrote a letter to Otto Kreuzer, Chicago's chief of detectives, requesting the case file on the Fronczak kidnapping.

—⁓—

In 1965 there was no single blood test that could conclusively prove two people were related. There were roughly fifteen to twenty tests that could determine blood group factors, such as blood type or the presence or absence of proteins on red blood cells. The results of all these tests, taken together, could produce a statistical evaluation that predicted the odds of two people being related. But that's all you could get—a probability, not a certainty.

If, say, a child and a parent both possessed the same rare blood characteristics, then the odds would be even higher that they were related. But a different child could theoretically also have those blood factors. It would be unlikely, but not impossible. The best these tests could do was strongly suggest a relationship. They could not eliminate doubt.

There were other methods of identification police could use in the 1960s. It was becoming a common practice in hospitals to take both fingerprints and footprints of newborn babies, but Baby Paul was stolen before any prints could be taken. Had they existed, they would have been all but definitive proof that someone was or wasn't Baby Paul. In their absence, all police could do was rely on a far less exact method of identification—a comparison of ears.

All of us have ridges, slopes, and bumps on the rims of our ears that are uniquely ours. Theoretically, it was possible to compare the configurations of my left ear to the single existing photo of Baby Paul—which showed the left side of his head—to see if the two ears matched. By itself, this wouldn't have been proof of anything. But coupled with blood tests—and a simple evaluation of whether or not I *looked* like the Fronczaks—it could lead investigators to conclude that it was *likely* that I was the boy who'd been kidnapped, or likely that I wasn't.

Either way, there was only one person on earth who could eliminate all doubt as to whether I was the boy who was taken from Michael Reese Hospital. And that one person—the kidnapper—was nowhere to be found.

—⟋⟍⟋—

In Chicago, Otto Kreuzer got Detective Farrell's request for the Fronczak case file and quickly sent the information along. He also forwarded Farrell's letter to the FBI. It was the best lead the FBI had received in a long while. By the middle of 1965, investigators had medically tested nearly ten thousand children across the country to see if any of them could be Baby Paul. Yet not a single test had led anywhere. Nor were there any leads on the identity of the kidnapper. The Fronczak case had gone cold.

Marlin Johnson, the agent in charge of the FBI's Chicago office, jumped on Farrell's hunch and took control of the new lead. He ordered a series of medical tests—blood, bone, skin, hair, and, yes, ear configurations—to be performed on me while I was under the care of the Eckerts. Shortly after I'd been placed there, in late July, two FBI agents arrived at the Eckerts' home and made a clay mold of the rim of my left ear. That September, Claire took me to a local hospital for a physical examination, and also to have blood samples drawn. She was instructed to bring me to the Trenton office of the Bureau of Children's Services, so staffers there could snap photos of me to forward to the FBI.

The FBI took some of my blood samples and photos and sent them for analysis to Dr. Aaron Josephson, the executive director of

Michael Reese Hospital. In February 1966, FBI agents came to the Eckerts' home, sat me down, and took a fresh round of photos. At that time, the FBI had yet to tell Dora and Chester Fronczak about my existence. They decided not to alert them until, as one government attorney later put it, "all medical possibilities that the child is not theirs had been exhausted."

The FBI continued its investigation of Farrell's hunch for eight long months.

Finally, in March 1966, they were ready to reach a conclusion.

Despite what they called "extensive investigations" and "exhaustive medical studies concerning this child," the FBI could not "absolutely establish that Mr. and Mrs. Chester Fronczak, Jr." were my biological parents.

But, they added, "neither has this fact been excluded."

In other words, out of ten thousand children tested by investigators, I was the only one who could *not* be definitively excluded as being the Fronczaks' lost baby.

That was good enough for the FBI. Toward the end of March 1966, they made the decision to reach out to the Fronczaks.

5

IN MARCH 1966—NEARLY two years after the kidnapping—
the Fronczaks filed a lawsuit against Michael Reese Hospital and
its insurer, Continental Insurance. They accused the hospital of
negligence and carelessness in allowing an unauthorized person in the
maternity ward, and they asked for damages for their "grief, pain, mental anguish and anxiety." The lawsuit sought $1 million—which would
be nearly $8 million today.

When I read about the lawsuit many years later, I wondered if it
was a kind of admission on my parents' part that the chances of getting their son back had all but vanished. If it was a kind of surrender
to the odds. Or maybe they'd just been seduced by a hungry lawyer.
Either way, there was something sad about the lawsuit to me. It was as
if it marked the end of my parents' search for their son.

But just three weeks after they filed the suit, my parents got a letter from the FBI.

"An unknown male child was found abandoned in Newark, New
Jersey," the letter began. "Extensive investigation was conducted by the
Newark Police Department in an effort to determine who abandoned
this child; however, no positive information in this regard was developed."

The letter went on to say that the current estimated age of the
child was twenty-two to twenty-three months—about the same age

the Fronczaks' kidnapped child would have been. Because of the age similarity, the FBI explained, they'd sent the boy's blood samples to doctors at Michael Reese Hospital. The FBI asked the Fronczaks to submit their own blood samples for comparison.

There it was, after nearly two miserable years—*hope*.

—៣—

My parents sent in their samples, which were analyzed at three different hospitals across the United States. This was as close as the Fronczaks had come to a breakthrough yet. The test results could give them the answer they'd been desperately hoping to find.

But they didn't. When the results came back, they were, according to one FBI report, "contradictory."

The New Jersey Bureau of Children's Services, which had legal control over me and worked closely with the FBI, was asked to offer an opinion. Did officials there believe I was the kidnapped child—or even *likely* that child? Or didn't they?

There wasn't much for them to go on. One staffer compared photos of me to photos of the Fronczaks and concluded that I looked "like Mrs. Fronczak from the front and like Mr. Fronczak from the side view." Was that an honest evaluation? Or wishful thinking? Either way, an official at Children's Services told the FBI, "It is our impression that Paul Joseph, who was abducted soon after birth, is in fact the child Scott McKinley."

Based on this, and on their own research, the FBI contacted the Fronczaks once again. It was time for them to come to New Jersey to meet me for themselves.

—៣—

The plan was for the Fronczaks to drive from Chicago to New Jersey and be introduced to me in the district office of the New Jersey State

Adoption Bureau, in the borough of Somerville, about forty miles west of Newark. But first, a vast amount of paperwork had to be generated.

It was understood from early on that if the Fronczaks did indeed claim me as their own, they would have to legally adopt me, since there was no way to prove I was biologically theirs. The New Jersey Children's Services Bureau teamed up with the Illinois Department of Children and Family Services to evaluate the Fronczaks as adoptive parents. This process began weeks before the Fronczaks laid eyes on me.

In early June 1966, both states approved the Fronczaks for adoption. "They are fine, decent people who are interested in the welfare of children," Lloyd McCorkle, New Jersey commissioner of agencies and institutions, told a reporter. "They met all the tests." But since the adoption process would take six months, Chicago officials also applied to give the Fronczaks temporary licenses as child-care providers, allowing them to take me home and care for me, should they choose, before the adoption became legal.

Finally, a date was picked for the Fronczaks to arrive in Somerville—June 9. "The plan is for you to talk things over with the casework supervisor and then be introduced to Scott in the office of the Agency," Ralph Baur, an Illinois Children's Services director, wrote my parents on June 2. By then, the Fronczaks *still* hadn't seen a photo of me. "In any case," Baur assured them, "the caseworker in New Jersey will show you a picture of Scott before you see him face to face."

Baur also sent the Fronczaks a statement they could give to the media, should news of my existence leak to the press. "Mr. and Mrs. Chester Fronczak, Jr., have been studied and approved as adoptive parents . . . for a two-year-old boy found abandoned July 2, 1965, in Newark, New Jersey," the statement read. The Fronczaks "requested they be permitted to adopt the child, establishing legal ties with the child to insure its permanent placement with them. This approval was given."

My fate, it would seem, was sealed before the Fronczaks even met me—before they even saw what I looked like. There was an urgency to the process, an eagerness to connect the child with no parents to the parents with no child. To resolve the unresolved. It was almost as if the other possibility—the possibility that the Fronczaks might take a look at me and decide I *wasn't* their son—had never been contemplated. As if the meeting in Somerville were basically a formality.

—w—

From the beginning, my guardians, the Eckerts, knew about the link between me and the Fronczak kidnapping. They understood that, at any minute, it might be proven the Fronczaks were my real parents. That was the reason I was delivered to the Eckerts' home in the dark of night, with a blanket over my head—in case any reporters had somehow learned about the kidnapping connection.

At the FBI's request, Claire Eckert had taken me in for a number of psychological examinations—all of which found me "to be doing fine in all developmental spheres." Claire also took me in for three separate polio shots. All along, the Eckerts knew I wasn't just another child in their care. I was, potentially, the most famous child they would ever care for.

Early in the summer of 1966, the FBI told the Eckerts about the planned meeting in Somerville. Surely, they understood this meant they would likely be losing me soon. Because I didn't have many clothes—the half-sleeve shirt I wore when I was handed over was the lone item of clothing to my name—Claire saved up a full month's worth of her salary and bought me several new outfits. She chose a bright white jumper suit for me to wear on the day of the meeting.

The FBI allowed the Eckerts to accompany me to Somerville. But they weren't permitted to meet the Fronczaks, or be in the room for the introduction.

The day before the meeting, Claire's son-in-law, Louis—the man who'd made me cry violently, but to whom I had since grown close— gave me a nice, short haircut. He saved some of the hair he'd snipped off, and Claire dropped it in an envelope and put it with all the things she'd prepared for Dora Fronczak. Chief among them, an array of photos of me in the months I'd spent with the Eckerts. Not a single one of those photos featured any of the Eckerts, or any of the other children, with me. The state of New Jersey prohibited the Eckerts from showing themselves with me, for privacy reasons. As a result, in all the photos, I am by myself.

Claire Eckert also typed up a letter addressed to "Scott's Parents."

"For all the sadness you have both known, you are in for so much joy," she assured them, "for you will now see things through Scott's eyes, and he can make them lovely."

Claire added a typical daily schedule for me, which included all the foods I liked. It was titled, "A Complete Diet of Hugs and Kisses." She listed all of my clothing sizes—3 in pants, 6 in socks, 7D in shoes, 4 in pajamas. She fretted that she had packed the heavy navy blue wool jacket she bought me, rather than keep it out in case I got too cold in my shorts the day of the handoff. "Also," she wrote, "Scott skinned his toe when he fell the other day and he tells me about this, so maybe you could take his shoes off while he is riding in the car." I was used to running around barefoot, Claire added, though "he does not like the floor if it is cold on his feet, so I use little slipper socks."

Just before they drove me to Somerville, Claire pinned a small note to one of the undershirts she'd packed in my suitcase. On the note, she'd typed her name, address, and phone number. "We left it in hopes that if the Fronczaks ever wanted to contact us, they could," Claire's daughter Janet, would later explain.

On June 9, the Eckerts and I arrived in Somerville. A caseworker hustled me away, while another staffer moved the Eckerts into an empty room next door to where I was to meet the Fronczaks. Chester and Dora were already there, huddling with a caseworker. Chester wore a dark suit and tie. Dora had on a simple knee-length dress.

Then it was time for the introduction. A caseworker led me into the room by the hand. My short hair was combed neatly across my forehead, and I wore white socks and white shoes to match my jumper. Dora and Chester looked down at me, and I looked up at them.

"My God," my mother nearly yelled, "that is my baby."

—◊—

There was nothing in the newspaper clippings I read years later, or anywhere else I could find, that even hints at any doubts my parents had about my identity.

Vernon Tittle, an attorney who helped them through the adoption process, told a reporter the Fronczaks were convinced I was their child. "The only doubts," he said, "are in the minds of the police." An unnamed source told the *Chicago Tribune* the Fronczaks "believe that this child is the kidnapped one." Even the Eckerts, who heard my mother's exclamation that I was her baby, believed I was being returned to my rightful parents.

"What a wonderful sound that was for us," Claire's daughter Janet later wrote. "We loved you very much, but in our hearts we were happy to see a family that had been apart for so long, reunite again."

But there *was* a dissenting voice.

Many years later, I spoke with a woman named Mary Hendry, whose father, John T. Cartan, was the Chicago Police Department lieutenant who headed the Fronczak kidnapping investigation in 1964. Cartan worked closely with Marlin Johnson, the special agent in charge of the FBI's Chicago bureau. Both the FBI and the Chicago PD signed off on handing me over to the Fronczaks. But that didn't mean they were convinced the case had truly been solved.

In fact, they didn't believe that at all.

"I remember my father standing in the kitchen of our home, shaking his head," Mary told me. "He talked about what good people the Fronczaks were, and how badly he felt for them, and what a good job they would do raising the baby. But he also said that the child they took home was not their baby. He was certain it wasn't the right boy."

Why, then, did the FBI and the Chicago PD allow the adoption to happen?

"My father told us the FBI and the police both agreed the child was not the kidnapped baby," Mary said. "But because the Fronczaks were such good people, they agreed to let it unfold the way it did."

—◊◊◊—

New Jersey officials gave my parents two days to think things over before they officially agreed to adopt me. By the end of the two-day period, my parents had made up their minds. They wanted to take me home with them.

Even so, they had to remain in Somerville for several more days, until more paperwork could be filed. Finally, on a Wednesday, the Fronczaks were allowed to take me, and we traveled back to Chicago. The New Jersey Bureau of Children's Services was still my legal guardian, and they would make several supervisory visits to Chicago to see how I was doing. But, practically speaking, I was suddenly in the sole care and custody of the Fronczaks.

Back in Chicago, a flock of reporters gathered in front of my parents' home, hoping for a glimpse of me and a comment from my folks. They got lucky one morning when Dora carried me out to the family car, with Chester not far behind. It was the first time they'd taken me out of their house since I got there. A reporter from the *Chicago Tribune* asked where we were going.

"We were just leaving to visit some friends," my father said as I sat on my mother's lap in the passenger seat. "I don't feel like talking to anyone about it."

"What's the boy's name?" the reporter persisted.

"Paul Joseph," my father said.

Then the question everyone wanted answered.

"Is this the same baby?" the reporter asked.

"I won't say," my father replied.

That weekend, the attorney Vernon Tittle asked the reporters to respect the Fronczaks' privacy and disband their makeshift camp in front of the house. By the next day—Father's Day—all the reporters were gone. A neighbor would later tell a reporter that for the first time since the kidnapping, laughter could be heard inside the Fronczak house. Dora, one neighbor said, "is really happy."

The next day, my parents dressed me in a small white suit and took me to St. Joseph and Anne Catholic Church—the same church where my mother had prayed every morning for the return of her son.

There, I was baptized into the Catholic faith by Rev. James V. Shannon. Mr. and Mrs. Joseph Majestic—my mother's sister Bertha and her husband—were my godparents. The ceremony took place in a room that was still partially charred by a fire that had gutted the church just two months before.

"Our bombed-out baptistery," Shannon called it.

Three months later, the Fronczaks brought me to Chicago's Civic Center to formally petition to adopt me. Vernon Tittle asked the judge, James Murphy, to hold the hearing in his chambers, away from reporters, and Murphy agreed. Behind a closed door, the Fronczaks were awarded legal custody. Three months after that, on December 12, 1966, the adoption was finalized, and the New Jersey Bureau of Children's Services discharged their guardianship. On January 5, 1967, Tittle forwarded my final adoption decree to my parents.

Chester and Dora Fronczak "are husband and wife, of lawful age and under no legal disability," the decree read. They are "reputable persons of good moral character with sufficient ability and financial means to rear, nurture and educate the said child in a suitable and proper manner." It was therefore "fit and proper" that "Scott McKinley, a minor, shall be to all legal intents and purposes, the child of the petitioners." The decree further stated, "The name of said child shall be changed to Paul Joseph Fronczak."

Nowhere in the three-page petition was the kidnapping mentioned, or my abandonment in Newark, or my parents' identification of me in Somerville. None of those details mattered anymore. In fact, the decree would have been wholly unnecessary if it could have been proven that I was indeed the Fronczaks' natural child. No one can adopt their own son, at least not legally. Thus, Article 4 of the adoption decree was very specific about my connection to the Fronczaks.

"The petitioners," it read, "are *not* related to said child."

Back in New Jersey, in the rural town of Watchung, the Eckerts went on with their lives, raising more children they knew they couldn't keep. They never learned if the Fronczaks found the note they'd pinned inside my T-shirt, and neither did I. All we know is that my parents decided not to reach out to the Eckerts, not even to tell them that I was okay.

"He shall ask for all of us," Claire Eckert predicted in her letter to my parents. "Just try and answer him by telling him that we are gone bye-bye. Before long, he will forget us and stop asking."

And then, one last, heartfelt instruction—or plea—to my parents.

"We kiss him very often and tell him what a good boy he is, and he has thrived on this," Claire wrote. "Let him know you love him, and you are in for the most wonderful experience, because he will return this love over and over and over."

I was not yet three years old, and I was living with my third family.

6

WHEN THE FRONCZAKS adopted me, I didn't just get a new mother and father. I got a new brother, too.

He wasn't yet born when my parents claimed me in New Jersey, in June 1966. But he was on the way. There's a photo of my parents and me taken a month after they brought me back from New Jersey, and in the photo you can plainly see a small bump in my mother's abdomen. You might not notice it if you weren't looking for it, but it's there. My mother was three months pregnant.

She started the year with no children. She would end the year with two.

David was born in December 1966, six months after I came to live with the Fronczaks—and right around the time my adoption was finalized. My mother's first pregnancy had ended in a stillbirth, her second in a kidnapping; now, finally, she got to bring a baby home from the hospital. One of the first people she notified was Ralph Baur, the Illinois official who helped arrange my adoption. She sent him a letter and a photo of me holding my tiny new brother.

"Congratulations on the birth of your brand new baby boy," Baur wrote back. "[In the photo] Paul Joseph seems to have his nose out of joint, which is par for the course when a baby brother arrives."

Looking back, I can't help but think that the timing of my discovery and adoption was unlucky. I wonder if my parents' decision to try to have another child, some fifteen agonizing months after the kidnapping, was a kind of fresh start for them, a chance to let go of the past and begin moving forward. Learning she was pregnant with a new son must have been emotionally fraught for my mother—happiness undercut by guilt, joy ruined by regret. Having another child didn't mean they were giving up on their kidnapped son. But I imagine that, sometimes, it must have felt that way.

And then the past came crashing back, in the form of me.

—⁓—

I can't remember all that much of my first few years with the Fronczaks. Believe me, I've tried—actually sat down for long stretches and tried to reconstruct my early childhood. But very little surfaces. I can remember my mother dressing me in a crazy, multicolored jacket and walking me to the Oak View Elementary School, and me hating the jacket and trying to pull away. I was probably five or six, and that's my earliest memory.

I can also remember Christmas mornings, when my brother Dave would burst into my bedroom and wake me up so we could run down the stairs together and see what Santa had brought.

But that's about it. The rest is just whiteness. I've seen the silent home movies my parents took in the weeks and months after they brought me home, and in those movies I'm the star, the one the camera follows, as I run around the backyard, bouncing all over the place. I'm in the same little white jumper the Eckerts bought for me, and I look happy, excited. In one scene I rush right into my father's arms, and he scoops me up. These images look like anyone's home movies—sweet, precious, ordinary. But I don't feel any connection to them. I know they capture my family, but they might as well be capturing someone else's.

What I remember most about my father is his absence. On work-days, he left for his factory job before dawn, so I never saw him in the mornings. He'd make it home for dinner, in a clean set of clothes after changing at work, and most weekends he'd be home, but even during those times we didn't talk very much. He wasn't mean or imposing, just quiet. He didn't have a lot to say about anything. I can't remember ever sitting down with my father just to talk. I can't remember him ever hugging me or kissing me or telling me he loved me. I can't recall my parents ever fighting or hugging or kissing, not even once. The image I have of my father when I was growing up is of a solid but un-available man.

For that reason, I was much closer with my mother. I do remem-ber hugging and kissing her, and talking to her, though that closeness didn't last very long. It dawned on me pretty quickly that my family was not the type of family to huddle around the dining room table and hash things out. We weren't big on discussions. Things happened, and we moved on. After a while I learned how to work out my problems for myself, and I pretty much stopped sharing anything too personal with my parents.

Not surprisingly, my folks kept an extremely watchful eye on me. They probably would have been strict parents anyway, rooted in their firm Catholic faith, but after the kidnapping they were oppressively careful. Growing up, I wasn't allowed to play in the front yard or on the sidewalk, only out back. I was never allowed to wander off with a friend, or have a sleepover, or anything like that. *We have to see you*— that was the rule. Even as a teenager I had curfews that were hours earlier than any of my friends'. My parents had lost their son once; they weren't about to lose him again.

My mother was also a tireless—some might say obsessive—cleaner, which I think was more fallout from the kidnapping. She needed to be in complete control of her surroundings, and she was constantly vacuuming and mopping and dusting and wiping off surfaces. Two, three, four times a day. Once a room was perfectly clean, my brother and I weren't allowed anywhere near it. The number of places in the house where we could play and frolic and just be kids was very limited. The living room, for instance, was all but off-limits to us. Even our bedrooms had to be spotless. We had to clean and tidy and make our beds every morning, and if we dared leave clothes or a towel on the floor, my mother would scream about it.

Perhaps the most important rule for me growing up—the one my parents hammered into me—was to never, ever tell a stranger my name.

My parents knew full well their last name had a lot of notoriety attached to it, and the last thing they wanted was for anyone to discover who I was. As a result, there was a layer of secrecy built into my childhood. It was as if, from the very beginning, I had to tiptoe around my own life.

Maybe that's why I spent so much of my childhood pretending to be someone else. When I was little, I was always assuming different identities. I was never just Paul—I had to be a werewolf, or a spy, or a talk show host who went around interviewing all his friends. The boys who lived next door, Bud and Eddie, were our best friends growing up, and when they came over to play kickball or build boxcars, I instantly slipped into characters, and got them to play characters, too. I used funny voices and constantly tried out new ones, and it didn't occur to me until later that all this role playing wasn't just a phase.

I assumed different roles because I didn't like the role I'd been given—Paul Joseph Fronczak.

Growing up, I also *loved* aliens. All kinds of aliens—ghosts, ghouls, extraterrestrials, you name it. I believed with all my heart that they existed, and I was drawn to them. The movie *E.T.* really affected me, because it gave a face to the estrangement I felt—the odd, funny face of E.T. himself, stranded a million miles from home. Later on, when *The X-Files* came out, I immersed myself in the show's mythology and creatures (when I was older I got not one but two *X-Files*-themed tattoos). I read everything I could about Area 51 and the Roswell UFO incident. I had a deep-rooted fascination with aliens—so deep that I began to think of myself as an alien, too.

—m—

One of the hardest things about my childhood was the lack of connection I felt to my brother Dave.

We were only about three years apart in age, yet we seemed to have nothing in common. Not one thing. Whatever I liked, he didn't, and vice versa. Other than the memory of Dave rushing into my bedroom on Christmas mornings and yelling, "Santa was here! Let's go!" I have a hard time recalling one moment of fun and sweetness and lightness between us. Mainly, what I remember is distance.

I also began to notice that my brother was much closer to my parents than I was. It wasn't just me feeling like Dave was the favorite son—a lot of kids feel that. It was me sensing that Dave was connected to our parents in a way I could never hope to be. He had an easy familiarity with them that I simply couldn't summon. I could feel it in how they spoke to him, how my mother held him, how he ran to my father when he came home from work.

Not long after bringing me home from New Jersey, my parents moved out of my grandparents' house and into their own three-bedroom, split-level home in Chicago's Oak Lawn neighborhood. My parents had the biggest bedroom upstairs, but the second biggest room wasn't mine—it was Dave's. I had the smallest bedroom, which was separate from the other two and had the smallest bed, too. Early on that didn't bother me, but as I grew up I began to wonder why, as the older brother, I didn't have the better bedroom.

Looking back, I can see that the dynamic of my family often felt like three against one. In the playground, on family trips, even at the dinner table, there was always an imbalance. My brother noticed it, too, because as we got older he began to condescend to me—to treat me as the problem son, the outcast, the one who didn't fit. The emotional connectivity of a family—that fierce magnetic pull toward each other—was there for my parents and my brother. But it was missing for me.

The tension between Dave and me finally exploded on a family vacation to Florida, when we were both in our teens.

We were staying at a hotel, and Dave and I began to argue about something. I can't remember what it was, though I remember the song "Jack and Diane" was playing on the radio. All of a sudden, Dave and I were rolling around on the carpet, fighting and punching. It was a nasty battle. I think my father broke it up, but before he did I grabbed a fistful of Dave's hair and pulled it straight out of his head. I stood there, holding the clump of hair like a trophy.

Dave and I never had another physical fight after that, because, essentially, that fight marked the end of our relationship. If we were distant before the fight, afterward we were basically strangers.

—m—

When I was in the fourth grade at St. Catherine's School, a red-haired girl named LeAnn sat a few desks over from me. One afternoon, I got up and dropped a pencil by her desk. That gave me an excuse to be near her and talk to her.

I think that was the moment I discovered girls.

My first kiss happened in the eighth grade, thanks to a dark-haired seventh grader named Gena. She let it be known that she wanted to kiss me, so one day after school my friends and I got together with her and her friends in the park across the street. I didn't make a move because I didn't know what a move was. So Gena leaned in and kissed me. I remember thinking, *This is cool.*

One of my first serious girlfriends was Cheryl, whom I met at the community pool. She was in a leopard-print bikini, and we chatted for a while. The next day I looked out my front window and saw Cheryl circling on her ten-speed bicycle, motioning for me to come out and join her. I didn't need much encouragement, and soon we were an item.

That was the start of my dating life, which only increased the friction between my parents and me. My mother, in particular, did what she could to undermine my dating adventures. As a God-fearing Catholic, she staunchly disapproved of premarital sex, or even premarital fooling around, and she was suspicious of all my girlfriends. When I brought them to the house to meet her, she was cold and unfriendly. It got to where I stopped introducing my girlfriends, and just snuck them into the house when my parents were busy or working.

With Cheryl, I had a perfect system. I'd pick her up after school on my bike, bring her home, and make out with her in the living room while my folks were away. From there I could see the driveway, so I always knew when my father was home from work. At the first glimpse of his Buick LeSabre turning up the drive, I'd hustle Cheryl out through the backyard. I never got caught, though my father did once notice Cheryl's gloves, which she'd forgotten on the sofa. He didn't say anything about them.

Eventually my father allowed me to use the LeSabre—with its powder-blue paint job and powder-blue crushed-velour seats—to go on dates. I still had to be home at an absurdly early hour, but at least I got to pick up my girlfriends in a car, not on a bike. One night, after taking my girlfriend Brenda out to dinner, I drove us to my home and parked out front. I lived on a quiet street, so I knew we could sit in the car and fool around there.

But just a few minutes later, the car door swung open and Brenda and I were hit with a stream of ice-cold water. It was my mother, dousing us with the hose.

"Get in the house right now!" she yelled.

I'm pretty sure I never brought another girl home after that.

But I didn't stop dating or partying. I'd wait for my parents to go away to a wedding or on a business trip, then throw a wild keg party in the house. Dave, who hated it when I snuck girls in, *really* hated it when I had parties there. He was already disapproving of most of what I did, and these infractions only made it easier for him to shake his head at me. He was the good, obedient, studious son, and I was the reckless troublemaker. He never ratted me out, but he made it clear that he was disgusted by me.

But I didn't care. Sneaking around to party and be with girls was *fun*. It was a way to break through the confinements of my childhood. I became a rebel—or rather, I took to the role of a rebel really nicely. It felt good to do what I wanted to do and be who I wanted to be. I was developing an identity that had nothing to do with my parents or my brother, and I liked it.

Without even realizing it, I was correcting my family's three-against-one imbalance by jumping off the seesaw altogether.

There was another odd rupture in my family, however, that I could never fix. It had to do with music.

For as long as I can remember, I loved music. I mean *really* loved it. When I was just two years old and living with the Eckerts in New Jersey, I'd jump around their house pretending to play a plastic toy guitar.

"His love of music," Claire Eckert wrote to my parents, "runs from rock-n-roll to Mantovani."

When I was twelve, the band Rush released an album titled *2112*, and the moment I heard a song from it on the radio, my life changed. I had a paper route then, and I saved up enough to buy the album. I brought it home and loaded it on my parents' big stereo console, and—when no one was home—I played the entire record at top volume. I remember the furniture in the living room vibrating.

Then I ditched my paper route and got a job as a stock boy at the local Sears for $3.35 an hour. When I'd saved $100, I ran out and bought my first bass guitar—a heavy Fender rip-off called a Hondo—and I taught myself to play. I started a band called Arias, covered songs by Rush, AC/DC, and the Scorpions, and played at a lot of weekend parties. I grew my hair long, down to my shoulders, and I began to think of myself as a musician. It was the most comfortable role I'd ever assumed.

Yet my passion for music wasn't something I could share with my family. None of them cared much for it or had any musical talent they felt compelled to explore. Even back then, I found this strange. How could I have such an inherent love of music while my closest relatives didn't seem moved by it at all? It was yet another thing that set me apart from my parents and Dave—the most serious thing yet. The deeper I got into music, the further I pulled away from my family.

Even growing my hair long—while my father and Dave wore theirs short—wound up intensifying the disparities in our appearance. In photos from those days, my father and Dave look exactly alike—wide, roundish faces, slightly droopy eyes. And there I am, with my angular face and jutting jaw and long hair and perpetual scowl. I look like I've been Photoshopped into the pictures.

My dating girls and playing in a band led to a lot more fighting with my parents. Some of it was typical teenage stuff, but some of it wasn't. Some of it sprang straight from the kidnapping. My mother's resistance to my girlfriends, for instance, probably derived from her belief that each new girlfriend represented another chance for me to talk about the kidnapping with someone new. And this was my parents' great fear—that the story they'd tried so hard to bury and forget would somehow slip out, and be retold, and circulate among the neighbors, and embarrass and torment them all over again.

That people would point at their house and say, "That's where the kidnapped boy lives."

For me, all these differences and fractures and arguments ran together into a single, powerful sense of not belonging. The closeness most families feel, the comforting familiarity, the friendships that deepen over time—those things just didn't exist for me. Instead of being bound to and grounded by each other, it was as if we were all victims of an opposite effect—a repulsion, like you see with warring magnets, always squirming to flee each other. For a long time, this reality about my family made me angry and frustrated and confused. It may have even made me desperate to be loved and accepted. But after a while, all I wanted was to escape it.

One afternoon, my mother and I got into a heated argument in my bedroom. She may have been mad about all the rock-and-roll posters I had on the walls, I can't remember. But I do remember screaming at her, and I remember her slapping me in the face with her open hand. Her wedding ring cracked one of my teeth.

"I wish they'd never found you," she said.

—⁓—

I don't want to blame my parents for anything that happened during my childhood. They are good, strong, caring people, and I know they loved me in their way. They were also understandably traumatized by the kidnapping, and determined not to let any harm or misfortune befall me. They were trying to protect me, but instead they held me back. It was not a mistake born of meanness or neglect. They did what they did because they were afraid.

But the effect was the same. A bonsai tree never grows because its pot deliberately hems in its roots. It is not meant to stretch and lengthen. It's meant to stay the same. But we are not. We are meant to reach and wander and grow.

Not long after graduating high school, I moved out of my family's house and struck out on my own.

7

I WAS NINETEEN AND HAVING DINNER with my girlfriend, Anne, in a diner in Chicago when I overheard two guys talking in the booth behind us.

"All we need is a bass player," one of them said.

I spun around and joined the conversation.

"I'm a bass player," I said.

"Oh yeah? What do you play?"

"Mostly Rush."

The two guys sized me up.

"Can you audition tomorrow?" one of them asked.

I told them I could.

The next day I showed up at someone's house with my new Rickenbacker bass guitar, which I'd saved up nine hundred dollars to buy. The two guys—brothers named Tony and Eddie—asked if I knew Rush's "New World Man," and I did. The three of us ripped through the song.

As soon as we stopped playing, Eddie asked, "Can you move to Arizona?"

"Hell yeah," I said.

And that, pretty much, was that.

It took me a few days to work up the nerve to let my parents know I was leaving. I dreaded having to tell them, but I was determined to go. I knew they had plans for me—enroll at the University of Illinois and study business. They'd been supportive of my first band, Arias, and even let us practice in the basement. But I'm sure they thought it was just a hobby. They never saw this coming.

One night, right after we finished dinner, I blurted it out.

"Mom, Dad, I'm moving to Arizona."

They didn't take it well. When my parents were unhappy with something I did, or if I didn't do something the way they wanted me to do it, they always let me know. And this time, they were *really* unhappy.

"You're blowing your whole future," my mother pleaded.

"You need to go to school and get a job," my father said.

They were probably right. I had no money, no job, no prospects. All I had was a high school degree, a love of music, and a deep desire to leave. The strictness of my upbringing—the constant surveillance and the long list of rules—had created a wanderlust in me. I yearned to break out and run free. And this was my chance. My parents were devastated, but in the end they couldn't stop me from going. So I went.

I broke up with Anne, bought a plane ticket with the little money I'd saved from my stock boy job at Sears, packed some clothes in a duffel bag, and took off. I honestly can't remember saying good-bye to my parents, or to Dave. I'm sure I did, but I can't remember it. It must not have been a very warm moment.

As I look back now, what stands out is how easy it was for me to close one chapter in my life and move on to the next. There was no soul-searching, no agonizing. I didn't even feel bad about disappointing my parents. I simply slipped out of one set of roles—son, brother, boyfriend—and slipped into another—band member, single guy, Arizonan. It wasn't any trickier than going from a pretend werewolf to a pretend spaceman, like I did when I was young.

Whatever forces had shaped me—the unknown trauma of my first two years, the deep-rooted feelings of not belonging anywhere—had given me the ability to morph seamlessly from one persona to another. Maybe this was a defense mechanism, my way of adapting to what I perceived as unwelcome surroundings. For sure it was a handy skill, though maybe not a healthy one.

I landed in Tucson, and my new bandmates picked me up in a beat-up blue Caprice. I stayed with them in their mother's home (their father was out of the picture), and we started up the band. We called ourselves Montreal, because our favorite group, Rush, was from Canada. Actually, they were from Toronto, but that name was already taken.

The band lasted five good years. We wrote our own songs, built a local following, and played a lot of clubs and frat parties. We still needed day jobs to get by, so we worked as handymen at an apartment complex Eddie's mother's boyfriend managed. Our goal was to land a record deal, but it never happened.

Then Eddie started dating a girl who was below the legal drinking age and couldn't come into the clubs to watch us play. He got it in his head that his girlfriend was cheating on him during our gigs, and he couldn't handle it. Eddie quit the band and moved to India to follow a guru. Tony and I filled his slot, but it didn't work out. Montreal was finished, and so was my time in Arizona.

At twenty-four, I moved back to Chicago, and back in with my parents.

—∭—

I didn't really want to go back, but I didn't have many options. I was broke and I needed a job, and at least in Chicago I could save on rent. My parents were happy to have me back, long hair and all. At the time my buddy Jim worked in a warehouse stacking industrial lightbulbs, and he got me a job there.

One afternoon, I helped the vice president of the lighting company carry some boxes to his car. We talked for about ten minutes. He slammed his trunk, looked me in the eye, and offered me the job of managing his new lighting outlet store in Wrigleyville, two blocks from where the Cubs play.

"Cut your hair and the job is yours," he said.

That's how I became a store manager. No application, no interview, no grand plan. I didn't realize it then, but that would be the template for the next twenty years of my life. I basically walked in and out of jobs with uncanny ease. I was a good talker, polite and respectful, and people seemed to like me. I never worried about my next job, because I knew there'd always be one waiting for me somewhere.

This fluid approach to employment suited me well. I got bored easily, and I was always looking for the next challenge, the next role. I rarely stayed in any job for more than two or three years. The same was true of relationships. I dated lots of women, but never seriously. It was as if I could never convince myself that I belonged where I was, or with the woman I was with. Everything felt good, but nothing felt right. So I just kept moving.

Just two years after coming back home, I was ready to leave again. This time, I decided to join the Army.

—w—

Once again, there wasn't any grand plan. I drove to a recruitment office in Oak Lawn and saw an Air Force officer and an Army officer both standing there. The Army guy rushed over and grabbed me first, so that's where I wound up.

I went to boot camp at Fort Sill in Oklahoma as a private first class. A sergeant took a liking to me and taught me how to fold and crease my private's cap in a way that made me look more like a veteran soldier when I wore it. My cap, plus the fact that I was a couple of years older than most of the other soldiers, allowed me to avoid the usual hazing and misery that befalls lowly privates in boot camp.

I also did well on tests and was sent to work in communications, specifically central switching/trunking repair. I can't say I loved my time in the Army, but unsurprisingly I adapted nicely and did fine. At the end of my stint, which lasted about a year, I could have re-upped and gotten a free education. But by then I was bored again, so I took an honorable discharge and went looking for whatever came next.

What came next, to my own surprise, was marriage.

Her name was Dannette, and I had met her before I joined the Army, in a sports bar in Chicago. She had jet-black hair and shining green eyes. She sat at the bar and had men draped all over her. For some reason, she brushed them aside and came over to me.

"You're not from here, are you?" she asked, looking at my long, shaggy hair. "No one here looks like you. What's your story?"

That night, she let other men in the bar buy her cocktails and slid them over to me to drink. I immediately liked her a lot. She'd grown up on Chicago's North Side, the good side, and she worked as an executive assistant for some lawyers. She was funny and smart, and we talked for hours without an awkward silence. Just a few weeks later, we moved in together in a small, one-bedroom apartment with wooden floors just off Lake Michigan. We started having serious talks about getting married.

But the thought of marriage scared me. I was used to slipping in and out of relationships, and I hadn't been serious about anyone until Dannette. And even with her, it wasn't as if I felt hopelessly, head-over-heels in love. It wasn't as if I was absolutely certain of our future together. At best, I was hopeful. I worried about how easy it was for me leave a girlfriend, and I wondered if I even had it in me to put down roots and be a husband. But I did love Dannette, and I wanted to give it a try.

We put our plans on hold when I joined the Army, but toward the end of my stint we arranged to get married on a weekend when I was on leave. I drove from my Army base in Georgia to Chicago in a red Sunbird I'd recently bought. The ceremony was in a small chapel, and my folks and brother were there. It was all very low-key. A modest reception, no honeymoon. But it was a happy time for me, at least at first.

Dannette and I moved to Las Vegas, where her parents lived. We found an apartment in central Vegas, and I got a job at a Mazda dealership. My interview, typically, was short.

"You're from Chicago?" the dealership owner said. "*I'm* from Chicago!"

Then he asked when I could start.

I was good at selling cars, good at interacting with customers, but I was restless within a few months. My next job was repairing amplifiers and line extenders for a cable company. Then, two billionaire brothers who were friends with the lawyers Dannette worked with decided to get into the cigar business, and hired both of us to set up events and parties for them. Before long, I was the general manager of their cigar operation, overseeing the sale of Cohibas and Macanudos at twelve Las Vegas casinos. When the billionaire brothers opened a premium cigar store in Grand Central Terminal in New York City, Dannette and I moved there to run it.

Then the bottom fell out of the cigar industry. For years, demand had outpaced production, but when production finally caught up, the quality of cigars had lowered, and demand disappeared. Dannette and I moved back to Las Vegas, sold the home we'd bought five years earlier, and moved into a town house.

It was a strange time for us both. I had no job, and we had no savings. We'd talked about having kids, but we never did. The cracks in our relationship had long since started to show, especially during the cigar boom, when we both worked seventy hours a week and rarely saw each other. When we got back to Las Vegas, it was hard to find a reason to stay together. We'd grown apart, and we weren't at all sure we were right for each other. After ten years of marriage, we reached the end of our run.

What stands out in my memory once again is how easy it was for us to leave each other's lives. There were some fights along the way, but no major blowouts. In the end, we simply sat down and had a calm discussion about our future. We agreed it was best for us both to go our separate ways, and so we did. We did the paperwork for the divorce ourselves, for $120. Dannette kept the town house and Magnum, our German shepherd. I moved out with some clothes and a couple of boxes of things.

In retrospect, I see something sad, maybe even tragic, about how my marriage ended. I should not have been able to leave the marriage as easily as I would leave a job, but I was, and I did. I just packed up and moved on. It didn't seem strange to me at the time; it seemed normal. That's how I'd always ended relationships, cleanly and unemotionally, at least on my end of things. I can't even say I felt bad about leaving Dannette, and for sure I wasn't heartbroken.

But shouldn't I have been? Hadn't our ten years together amounted to something worth fighting for—or at least commemorating in some way? Or was this who I was—a leaver? A vagabond who never stayed anywhere for long, and slipped easily and silently out any open door?

Had I even been a real husband to Dannette? Or had I just been pretending?

—⁓—

I turned forty divorced, jobless, and broke. By then I'd had more than thirty different jobs and at least as many relationships. Yet nothing was sticking. Nothing was taking hold. I didn't feel like I had any meaningful ties to anything or anyone. I was wandering through my own life, going wherever the current took me.

That's when, after years of easing in and out of roles, I finally found the most obvious job for me—actor.

I'd done some print modeling in my twenties, but hadn't taken it seriously. Now, I got new head shots and an agent and hit the audition circuit. I dropped my last name, and called myself Paul Joseph. That choice was liberating in a way I hadn't expected it to be. Symbolically, it was me excising my family from my life.

My career as an actor and model took off quickly. I landed some lucrative national commercials, including one for a protein-bar dog bone. I was in print ads for banks, casinos, restaurants. I filmed two instructional videos for the people who ran McCarran International Airport, in which I played a passenger going through security. More people recognized me from those videos than from any other job I ever had. In fact, the videos are still playing on monitors throughout the airport. Every time I fly anywhere, I look up and see my younger self incorrectly packing a travel bag.

My steadiest gig was playing several characters in a live Las Vegas show called Star Trek: The Experience. It was a huge production funded by Sony and run out of a big soundstage. We did several shows a night for hundreds of people, and we'd shuttle through different sets as the action unfolded around them. I played someone called Commander Marcus, and I wore a Star Trek costume and wielded a phaser rifle. My job was to shepherd the guests to safety after a team of Borgs invaded the Starship.

"The station is under attack!" I'd yell. "We sustained tremendous damage, but we have a plan to get you out of here. You'll be safe as long as you follow me."

Then I'd break down a door and shoot a few Borgs with my phaser, before dying a heroic death.

Later on, I took the role of Commander Ross, and had a giant Borg arm come down from the rafters and lift me thirty feet in the air to my death. It wasn't until I got to play a character named Major Elkins that I made it through the whole show alive. I remember missing my dramatic death scenes.

I also got hired to be the stand-in for George Clooney—the actor who stands in his spot on the set so technicians can light him—on the Las Vegas heist film *Ocean's Eleven*. He and I had roughly the same measurements—five eleven, 175 pounds—and the same jawline. I only had a few talks with him, but he was a lovely, friendly guy. Mostly I hung around the set trying not to stare at Brad Pitt, Matt Damon, and all the other big stars.

The irony and significance of being someone's stand-in didn't occur to me at the time. Only now, when I look back on it, can I see how that job pretty much defined who I was back then. Not to get too metaphoric about it, but in a way I'd spent years and years being my *own* stand-in, inhabiting my place in the world temporarily, until it was time for the real person to show up. Except in my life, the real person never showed up.

I made a pretty good living as an actor and model, and I didn't get bored because the parts were always different. If I had any kind of identity back then, it was as an actor. I wasn't the Fronczak baby any-more. I was Paul Joseph, actor. It wasn't a very stable career, or a stable lifestyle, and the chances of me becoming any kind of major actor were slim, but that was okay with me. I still didn't have any grand plan for my life. Drifting and pretending suited me just fine.

That changed when I decided to run a personal ad on the dating site Match.com. I had a free three-day trial, so I threw up a photo and a profile out of curiosity. I still cringe when I think of the tagline I chose: "Cool guy looking for cool girl."

My first day on the site, I got a message from a woman named Mi-chelle. I liked her picture; she was gorgeous and holding a martini glass. I answered her note, and we chatted online for a while. She said she was planning on going to a party in San Diego that week, and asked if I wanted to come. We made arrangements for me to pick her up at a friend's apartment and go to the party together. When I got there, Michelle came out from a back bedroom in jeans and a white T-shirt. She had just showered, and her long dark hair was still wet. She came over and gave me a hug and said, "I'll be ready in a few min-utes." I was smitten.

We saw each other a few times after that night. Michelle was fun and friendly and sweet, and I liked being with her, but as with all of my relationships, I never looked too far into the future. At the time, Michelle had a home in Las Vegas and I was temporarily living in Los Angeles for a job. I accepted that we were dating, but I didn't yet see it as anything serious. As usual, I was too busy drifting to be able to take stock of what I had in front of me.

One afternoon, when I was in Las Vegas for a day to film a com-mercial, my car was T-boned by another car making an illegal left turn. The crash broke my collarbone and my sternum. I called Michelle to tell her about it, and she let me stay with her for the next two weeks to recover. Michelle was a teacher, and she was very nurturing, and in those two weeks she took wonderful care of me. It began to feel to me like she was not only nursing me back to health but also saving my life. *She is good for me*, I kept thinking. *She grounds me.* And then I thought the unthinkable.

This is it. This is her. I can finally put down roots.

I'd told myself I wasn't interested in getting married again, or settling down, or even being in a real relationship. I was happy dating women I met on movie sets and living the bachelor life. Nothing about my past suggested I'd ever be a good husband, or a good father. Nothing inside me burned to have my own family.

And yet there had to be *something* there, burrowed down deep, that moved me in the direction of committing to Michelle. She was, by nature, organized and in control, while I was wild and scattered, and those opposing personalities shouldn't have worked together, but somehow they did. Michelle was the one who could finally make me stop drifting. She was the one who could pin me to a spot. I hadn't thought this was something I wanted, and yet it was happening all around me. It was already *under way.* More than that, it was actually pleasing to think about. It dawned on me that this was my chance to be a normal person. A regular guy with a regular wife and a regular family. This was my chance at actual happiness.

This, I thought, *is how it's supposed to be.*

I asked Michelle to marry me on a bridge over the Chicago River. It was snowing, and a horse-drawn carriage was going by. I got down on one knee, and she said yes. We were married on a sunny day in Las Vegas, at the Wildhorse Golf Club. My parents flew out to be there, and so did Dave. I wore a black tuxedo, and Michelle wore a stunning white dress. We looked like a golden couple.

It wasn't much later that Michelle took a pregnancy test and called me with the result. She was pregnant, and I was ecstatic. Genuinely, authentically joyful. I was surprised by how happy I was, because I'd never imagined that this was something that could make me happy. But when it happened—when I found myself on the verge of having my own family, of finally having a place where I belonged—I felt my heart swell with emotions I'd never felt before.

I began to dream about having a baby daughter. I guess I didn't want my child to experience the hardships I'd gone through as a boy, and having a girl felt like a kind of fresh start. When Michelle and I went in for an ultrasound, I was so nervous my knees felt like they might buckle. The technician passed the wand over Michelle's belly and casually told us we were having a girl. I jumped up in the air and literally cried out with excitement. We picked a name for our daughter—Emma Faith—because we liked how those two names sounded together.

For the first time ever, I had reason to be hopeful about my future.

Then I was asked a question that forever changed the course of my life.

8

IT WAS A SIMPLE QUESTION from a doctor. A question she'd probably asked a thousand expectant fathers.

"What is your medical history?"

This was during a routine visit to Michelle's ob-gyn. Michelle had no problem discussing her family's history, but when it was my turn, I just didn't know what to say. I was about to recite what I knew about Chester and Dora Fronczak, but before I did I stopped myself, and instead said nothing. I remember the doctor looking at me as if something was wrong.

The truth was, I didn't *know* my family's medical history. Or at least I couldn't be certain I did. After more than thirty years of burying the questions I had about my true identity, suddenly all those doubts came rushing back. It occurred to me that the whole nagging mystery was no longer just about me. Now, it was about my *daughter*, too. It was about her life, her health, her well-being, not just mine. This hidden part of my past—that I had been returned to the Fronczaks after a horrible kidnapping and an equally horrible abandonment—was no longer just my secret. It now belonged to Emma as well.

Since finding the newspaper articles about the abduction in the crawl space, I hadn't had one substantive conversation about those events with anyone. Not one. I had the brief talk with my mother, when she assured me I was her son, but I never got a similar assurance from my father. Beyond telling me never to mention the kidnapping to anyone, my parents simply never brought it up. My mother's angry statement that she wished I'd never been found was about as close as we ever got to confronting the matter of the kidnapping with any real emotion. Otherwise, it was a buried secret.

But the doubts that entered my mind after reading those clippings—and living with people who seemed so different from me— never went away. I didn't summon them to the surface too often, but they were always there. When I did think about it, it seemed all but impossible to me that I could be the Fronczak boy. What were the chances that a child abandoned in one state could be the same child who was kidnapped in another? Out of all the orphans and foundlings in the country, what was the likelihood that I was the one who was taken from the Fronczaks? Wasn't that too long a shot to be believed?

And it seemed to me that the driving force behind my delivery to the Fronczaks was not the righting of a terrible wrong, but rather the papering-over of a crime everyone wanted to forget. If I wasn't the Fronczaks' real son, well, then, at the very worst I was a homeless child being given to a childless family.

Which would make me a kind of consolation prize.

In all the articles I read about the kidnapped boy, and later about myself, there were only two tiny pieces of information about my medical history. The New Jersey Bureau of Children's Services sent them along to the Fronczaks when they took me back to Chicago. My parents were told that I'd had the measles, and that my blood type was O negative. And that was it. Nothing else. There was no way to guess at any genetic irregularities, or disease tendencies, or anything. It was simply unknowable. I was indeed like an alien who'd been dropped out of a spaceship and rescued by some baffled family. Medically, I was a blank slate.

So what was I supposed to tell Michelle's doctor?

When I met Michelle, I didn't know how to tell her about the kidnapping, so I turned it into small talk. "Hey, you want to hear a cool story about me?" I asked, before dropping the details of how I came to be Paul Fronczak. It wasn't the first time I'd told my story to a girl I was trying to impress. I'd noticed that it made them feel protective of me, and maybe even want to hug me. In a way, I used my buried secret as a pickup line.

From time to time, Michelle and I would joke about the kidnapping. "You *can't* be the same kid," she'd say. "You're nothing like your family." Or we'd laugh about which famous people my real parents could actually be. Sometimes we'd even joke about swiping some of my parents' hair when they slept over at our house, so we could finally get to the truth of who I was.

But after Michelle got pregnant, the kidnapping wasn't small talk anymore. If I was ever going to delve into my murky past, this was the time to do it. Not for me, but for Michelle and Emma. They deserved to know the truth. No—they *needed* to know. I was forty-five years old, a soon-to-be-father, and what had long been just an annoyance now became an obligation.

It was my duty, once and for all, to find out who I was.

—⟶⟵—

And still, I was hesitant. I knew that unearthing the kidnapping details would be extremely messy and painful, and it wasn't anything I wanted to do. My relationship with my parents was in good shape. We weren't really close but we got along fine, and they were extremely excited about Emma's arrival. Did I really want to rip open the wound they'd worked so hard to close? Maybe it could wait. Maybe I didn't have to do it at all.

About seven weeks before Michelle's due date, we drove to see her ob-gyn for a routine ultrasound, on the way to a nice restaurant for dinner. But when her doctor looked at the scan, her face tightened into a frown.

"Your fluid is low," she told Michelle. "You have to have this baby *right now*."

Neither of us panicked. We went back home so Michelle could gather up her things, then drove to St. Rose Hospital. We were set up in a large suite, and the next day, Michelle was taken to the delivery room. I was there with her. I was holding on to her, and probably squeezing too tight, when Emma began to appear. Michelle was pushing and pushing and a nurse was holding Emma's head, which was covered in a shock of dark hair. I stood there in utter amazement.

Then, quickly, Emma was here. The nurse cradled her and held her up in front of Michelle's face, just inches away, and I watched as my wife and my daughter looked at each other for the first time, their eyes locking together.

That was the single most beautiful moment I'd ever witnessed.

That is our child, I said to myself. *This is my family*.

The nurses quickly bundled Emma up and handed her to Michelle. Just a few minutes later, I got to hold her for the first time. The effect was immediate and profound. I was overwhelmed by a kind of love I hadn't experienced before. It was brand-new but also ancient. It was real, and inescapable, and inevitable. It was something that I was on the inside of, not outside, looking in. It was exactly the kind of bone-deep, primal connection I'd been missing all my life. It was the answer to the question I didn't even know was tearing me apart.

What is it like to have a real family?

I held Emma's tiny body and stared into her squinty eyes. She was impossibly beautiful in every way. I gently kissed her forehead, and in that instant I felt a father's instinct—*nothing bad will ever happen to this child. I will see to that.*

And in that instant, too, I decided that I wouldn't let Emma out of my sight at the hospital. Not for one second. Wherever she was, I'd be there, too.

We wound up staying in the hospital for a little over two days, and in that time I never left the delivery suite. If other people hadn't brought food in, I probably wouldn't have eaten. I was going to be with my wife and my daughter, end of story. I wasn't going anywhere.

I didn't realize it then, but my little vigil in the delivery suite was an echo of what my mother had done after the kidnapping at Michael Reese Hospital. She, too, stayed in her room around the clock, refusing to leave in case her child was miraculously returned. The difference was that she *had* let her baby out of her sight, just for a moment, and that was all it took for him to vanish.

Now, more than four decades later, I was the one who refused to leave the room. I was rewriting my mother's history to give it a happy outcome.

—⁓—

There was no longer any question in my mind after Emma's birth—I *had* to know the truth about who I was. But I realized that what I'd been telling myself—that it was for Emma and Michelle—wasn't true. It was also very much for me. If I had any hope of being a good father to my daughter, I had to figure out why I'd lived my life the way I had. Why I'd slipped in and out of relationships, assumed different roles, planted no roots. The thought of ever leaving Emma—of drifting away from her like I'd done with so many other people—was terrifying. I didn't ever, ever, ever want to leave her.

So I had to become more self-aware, more honest with myself.

After all, refusing to leave Emma's side at the hospital was evidence that the kidnapping had indeed left a deep imprint on my soul. It was still affecting how I behaved, all these years later. It wasn't anything I could keep dismissing as not important. In fact, it was gravely consequential to my life. I had to know—why was I the way I was? Why did I do the things I did? Was it how I was raised?

Or was it something in my blood?

All of these questions couldn't be answered until a larger question was asked.

Was I really Paul Joseph Fronczak?

One of the reasons I'd never actually tried to learn the truth was that I believed learning it would be hugely expensive. Within twenty or so years after the kidnapping, advances in genetic testing made it possible to prove blood relationships. But it took many more years for the testing to become affordable. I knew that if I could somehow get samples of my parents' hair, I could send them to a lab for testing and finally learn the truth. But that kind of testing was costly—several hundred dollars, maybe more. Before Emma, I'd let the price of testing scare me away from doing it. Or at least that's what I told myself.

After Emma, that changed. I still didn't want to confront my parents about my identity, but I knew I had to do something, so I decided to get their hair samples without them knowing it. Michelle and I cooked up a plan. My parents flew to Las Vegas for a visit, and we waited until they went to Sunday mass before going into their bedroom and lifting loose hairs off their pillows. We put the hair samples in a baggie, and I hid the baggie in my bathroom cabinet, behind a bottle of Listerine. I intended to send out the samples just as soon as my parents flew back home, but after they left I found I couldn't do it. I kept the baggie in the cabinet for several days.

It's too expensive, I told myself.

But really, it was too scary.

Then one day, Michelle and I went to a CVS pharmacy to pick up a prescription. I looked at a shelf behind the pharmacy counter, and what I saw there made me stop in my tracks. It was a row of small boxes all labeled IDENTIGENE DNA PATERNITY TEST KIT. "Admissible in Court," the label declared. I asked to see a box and read the instructions, and learned that all the test required was a simple saliva swab. The cost of each test was less than thirty dollars.

I no longer had an excuse. The truth could be mine for the price of a nice lunch. Even so, I put the kit back and went on with my shopping.

I thought about the test kit every day for the next three weeks. Finally, I went back and bought three of them. It was early summer, and my parents were coming for another weekend visit to spend time with Emma, whom they adored. I had to make something happen on that trip. It had gotten to the point where I could hardly think about anything else.

But when my parents arrived for the visit, I felt dread. Like a child who did something wrong and knows his parents will soon find out. I simply couldn't imagine asking my mother and father to revisit their nightmare. It was something I hadn't dared talk to them about for decades, and I *still* didn't dare. I pictured their stunned, hurt faces, and I imagined their deep disapproval of my wish to dredge the whole mess up again. Asking them seemed impossible. I looked for any chance to mention the tests to my parents, but every time I thought I had an opening, I chickened out. Michelle kept urging me on, with looks and pats and pep talks. But I couldn't do it.

Friday came and went. So did Saturday. Sunday began to slip away. An hour before I was supposed to drive my parents to the airport, I saw my mother sitting at my kitchen table, talking to Michelle.

My father was standing behind her, drinking something. It was a light, casual moment.

Suddenly, I heard my own voice.

"Hey, Mom. Did you ever wonder if I was really your son?"

Just like that. It was out there. I braced myself for anger and shouting, but instead my mother calmly looked at me and smiled.

"Of course, we thought about it," she said. "But there was no way for us to know."

"Well, what if there was?" I said. "What if there was a way to know for sure? Would you want to know?"

My mother looked at my father, who said nothing. Then she looked at me.

"Yes, I guess we'd like to know," she said.

I couldn't believe it. "Hold on," I said and rushed to the bedroom to get the Identigene kits. Before my folks had a chance to process what was happening, they were sitting with me at the kitchen table, three DNA tests open in front of us.

My mother went first. Hesitantly, she swabbed the inside of her mouth with a swab stick. Then it was my father's turn. Typically, he hadn't said a word about taking the test. He just followed my mother's lead. I watched as he swabbed his mouth and handed me the stick. Very carefully, I put it in its little plastic tube. Then it was my turn, and I went through the same procedure. When we were done, I scooped up all three tests and whisked them away. I was practically giddy.

Remarkably, my parents had agreed to be tested without so much as an argument. The moment had been loose, almost jokey. Like it was all a fun little family project. I'd expected the encounter to be unbearably heavy, but it had been the opposite. We'd dealt with this massive, crushing, long-buried secret as easily as if we'd been deciding where to go for dinner.

But on the drive to the airport, my parents got quiet. It was a thirty-minute ride, and we took it in total silence. Not a word. At the airport I kissed them good-bye and watched them walk through the gate. I felt closer to them than I probably ever had before. But I also felt uneasy.

Sure enough, a few hours later, my cell phone rang. It was my parents' number in Chicago.

"Paul, we thought about it," my mother said, "and we don't want to do the test."

It wasn't really a surprise. I'd kidded myself about how easily the evening had gone. In fact, nothing had changed. I waited to hear my mother's explanation of why they didn't want to do it, but it never came. She simply said again, "We don't want the test. We don't want to know." Arguing would be pointless. I told my mother I loved her, and hung up.

But even then, even then, I knew I'd send the tests in anyway.

How could I not? The burning question of my life was on the verge of being answered, and I was supposed to forget about it and go back to the way things were? I began to feel angry that my parents had forced it to be this way—forced me to choose between what they wanted and what I needed—but in fact I didn't even see it as much of a choice. After so many years I finally had the tools I needed to learn the truth. They were in my possession. I controlled them now. There was no way I wasn't going to use them.

I had the three DNA tests all packaged up and ready to go. I kept them in the drawer of my desk, and right after my call with my mother I went to look at them. There was something awesome, something powerful, about those three little boxes. The next morning, however, I walked by my desk without reaching for the kits. I figured I could mail them some other time. I did the same thing the following morning, and the morning after that. Every night, I woke up from a restless sleep thinking about the kits. But every morning, I passed them by.

That went on for two full weeks.

Michelle was torn, too. She wanted me to know the truth, but she also felt I shouldn't go against my parents' wishes. I told Michelle I had the same reservations, but that wasn't true. I was okay with disregarding my parents' wishes. The reason I didn't send out the tests was fear.

I was afraid of what would happen when I learned the truth.

One morning, no different from other mornings, I woke up, showered, and got dressed for work. I ignored my desk, as I had every day for the last two weeks, and walked right past it. Only this time, I stopped. I stopped and went back. I opened the drawer and took out the three kits. Without telling Michelle, I walked out the front door and crossed the street to a mailbox. I opened the mailbox lid and held the three kits just above the opening. I held them there for a while. All I had to do was let go and drop them in.

Just let them go.

And then I did it—I let go.

But the boxes didn't go in. They got stuck in the slot.

I reached in and pushed them down, forcing them through, until I heard them rattle to the bottom. I let the lid slam shut and I stood there for a few more minutes, staring at the big blue mailbox.

Then I turned around and walked back home.

9

FTER EMMA WAS BORN, I took a job as the assistant director of admissions at the Art Institute of Las Vegas. Michelle and I had talked it over, and we agreed I needed a more stable job than acting. Just as I could never understand how Michelle stayed in her job as a teacher year after year, she couldn't understand why I hadn't found something and stuck with it. So I took the job at the institute. It was reasonably fulfilling work, and I was happy with it. I had a wife, and a daughter, and a job. I was a family man now.

Yet once I pushed those three DNA kits into the mailbox, my focus began to drift. I knew it would take about two weeks for the results to come in, and in that time it was hard to think about anything else. At home, Michelle and I didn't talk about it much. Without the results, there was nothing to discuss. So we just waited.

I was at my desk at the institute one afternoon, going through some paperwork, when my cell phone went off. I'd programmed it to sound like an old telephone ring, raw and noisy, and when it rang I was startled.

"Mr. Paul Fronczak?" a male voice asked.

"Yes."

"I'm calling from Identigene," the man said.

I swear, I could hear my heart begin to beat faster right through my chest. This was it. Literally the moment of truth. A movie popped into my head—*The Conversation* with Gene Hackman. That's something I automatically do in moments that are emotional or surreal—I identify with a movie character going through something similar. As if what's happening is actually part of a movie, not real life. This time I was the moody surveillance expert Harry Caul, his whole life hanging on a few spoken words.

"First, I need to ask you some questions," the Identigene rep said, before taking me through a security protocol. He began by asking why I'd chosen to do the test.

"I'm trying to figure out who I am," I said.

There were more questions: my address, home phone number, date of birth, a private pass code. Then, silence. One beat. Two beats. Three beats.

"We have the test results," the rep finally said. "There is no remote possibility that you are the son of Dora and Chester Fronczak."

No. Remote. Possibility.

In that instant, everything stopped. Time froze. I thought I'd prepared myself for whatever the answer would be, but clearly I hadn't. I was in shock. I was confused. I was hurt. My thoughts were swirling. With those few words, my whole life became a lie. My birthday. My background. My ethnicity. My name. Everything, all of it, false. Nothing was real. Nothing was true.

I was living someone else's life.

I got off the phone quickly and sat at my desk with my head in my hands. I don't cry often and I hadn't expected to cry, but I did. More than anything I felt sad, deeply sad, as if my heart had been broken. And after that, I felt a kind of panic. A question screamed in my head: *What now?*

I picked up my cell and called Michelle. She could tell I was in shock, and she tried to say something to console me.

"Paul, it's okay," she said. "It's all going to be okay."

"But I don't know who I am."

"Yes, you do. You are Paul. You are Emma's father. You are my husband. That is who you are."

"But I don't really know."

There was nothing anyone could say to help. The emptiness was too great. The reality was too harsh.

For a long time, I'd been the child with two names.

Now, suddenly, I was the man with none.

PART TWO

LAS VEGAS

10

WHEN I WAS SEVENTEEN, my father said I had to get a job at the factory where he worked. One morning, he took me with him to fill out an application.

We drove in his big Buick LeSabre to South Western Avenue, where the Foote Brothers Gear and Machine Company had its main plant. The company, my father told me, had a proud history. When George C. Foote started it in the 1860s, it made shaft hangers and pulleys. During World War I it made parts for America's first military tanks. My father's job was building transmissions for Apache helicopters. None of that sounded interesting to me at the time, and I didn't want to work there, but I didn't have any say in the matter.

The factory itself was cavernous and cold. The smell of oil and the racket of grinding machines were overwhelming. Everywhere I looked, men with smudged faces and uniforms wrestled with giant gears and slabs of metal. As my father walked me through the dreary main floor, I had the feeling I was in a really dangerous place. *This is a nightmare*, I thought. *This is hell.*

I knew right then I would never work in a factory like my father.

I filled out the application, but I never heard back about the job. I didn't learn why. Maybe the position went away. Maybe my father realized factory work wasn't for me.

But after that trip to his workplace, I began to feel sorry for my father. I'd spent ten minutes there and I couldn't wait to leave. My father had spent *his whole adult life* trapped inside it. Yes, the factory provided him with a steady income, a new car every few years, nice clothes for his family, an annual vacation, a good house. But at what cost? There was no excitement in that factory. No stories, no adventures. Nothing my father could look forward to. There was just the endless clang of churning, soulless machines.

That was not what I wanted for myself.

Whether my father realized it or not, his decision to take me to work that day had a profound effect—it showed me what I didn't want to do with my life. In fact, I wanted the opposite of my father's life. I didn't want the routine, the mundane, the ordinary. No, I needed to know there was always a chance of something extraordinary happening around the corner. I needed to be on adventures. I wanted to jump in and out of new skins, just like I'd done when I was a kid.

So that's what I did when I grew up—I went from job to job, role to role, place to place. I moved to Las Vegas, the transient city. City of tumbleweeds.

And then I turned forty-five, and I had a child, and inevitably my life slowed down. I broke my promise to myself and I fell into a routine.

And, to my surprise, I didn't mind. In fact, I liked it. A routine meant my life was normal. It meant I'd stopped running, stopped chasing. And that felt good. And if something was missing, if some itch wasn't being scratched, well, then, so be it. I had, at last, found a role I could play for the long haul. I'd slipped into my own skin.

And then—

One phone call changed it all. One swab of spit turned everything upside down. Something extraordinary *did* happen to me—I learned my life had been a lie.

And this presented me with a choice.

A role more thrilling than any I'd ever played was suddenly there for the taking. It promised excitement, but it also promised chaos. It all but guaranteed disruption. It was the firecracker with the short fuse, the blindfolded jump off a cliff.

The adventure of a lifetime—solving a mystery almost fifty years in the making.

The mystery of my own life.

My choice was this:

Either I could walk away from it. Or I could embrace it.

In the end, it wasn't really a choice at all.

—⁓—

The actual test results from Identigene were brutally clinical. The woman I knew as my mother, Dora Fronczak, was listed as my "alleged mother," and was "excluded as the biological mother of Paul J. Fronczak." This meant she didn't carry any maternally derived DNA present in my body. Her Parentage Index, or the likelihood that she was my biological mother, was zero. The same was true of my "alleged father," Chester. The results included a lot of numbers I couldn't decipher, but the bottom line was that several different genetic systems were tested, and my parents didn't match me in any of them. It was cut-and-dried.

I drove home that night in a fog. At the front door Emma ran up to greet me, and I gave her a big, long hug. Michelle stood behind her and looked at me in a sympathetic way that said, *Can you believe this?* but also *I'm so sorry.* We both knew we had entered strange new territory. The phone call from Identigene had shifted something big and fundamental in both our lives.

The first question I asked her was "Do I tell my parents?"

I honestly didn't know if I should. They had a right to know, for sure, but they'd specifically told me they didn't *want* to know.

"If you had been the real Paul, you could have told them," Michelle said. "But they don't need to know, so why hurt them?"

She was right. And anyway, I wasn't in any hurry to tell my parents I'd submitted their samples. I didn't feel guilty about it, I just didn't want to have to deal with their anger. Mostly, I was too confused and anxious to worry about them. I'd been handed explosive information about my past, and I had no idea what to do with it. I couldn't even figure out what my first step should be. The reality was that I'd been mistaken for a kidnapped baby, but that mistake had happened nearly fifty years earlier. It was history now, old and forgotten, and how do you wade into that?

Instead of answering my questions, finding the truth had only led to a million more. And finding the answers to *those* questions, it seemed to me, would be like trying to talk with ghosts.

Still, I couldn't just ignore what I'd learned about myself. I knew from the very start that I'd have to do *something*.

"I want to pursue this," I told Michelle that first evening.

"Okay," she said. "But I don't know where it's headed."

"Me neither," I said. "I guess we just have to dive in."

It was a tentative beginning.

But in the days that followed, my perspective changed and my resolve strengthened. When I first got the call, my reaction was to bemoan my own loss of identity. I made the results about me. But it dawned on me that I wasn't the only victim of this terrible mistake. I wasn't in this thing alone.

The DNA test results instantly created a new mystery—where was the real Paul Fronczak?

The sad truth was, he hadn't been found. He hadn't been returned to his family. He was still missing, still unaccounted for. As far as we knew, he had never escaped the clutches of those who carried him out of a hospital and into a nightmare. Nothing had been made right for him. Nothing had been solved.

And so, consciously or not, I began to bond with him. A real and meaningful bond. He was someone I'd never met or even thought about all that much. A shadowy figure, neither boy nor man, neither alive nor dead.

Nevertheless, we were partners now.

We bonded in our victimhood. We'd both been horribly wronged. The real Paul was ripped from his family, while I, presumably, was abandoned by mine. Before either of us was even two, we'd both been dramatically uprooted. Then we'd been cast into our separately fraudulent lives, both of us doomed to a personal isolation we had no hope of understanding.

We were flip sides of the same tragic coin—the taken and the left behind, the wanted and the unwanted. The real Paul and the fake Paul.

Now, almost half a century later, we were connected again, by a DNA test.

When this connection became clear in my mind, in the days after the test results, I felt an immediate sense of relief. I felt less alone. Whatever lay ahead for me also lay ahead for the real Paul. My answers were his answers, too. Any action I took going forward would not be solely for my benefit. It wouldn't even be *primarily* for my benefit.

No—my reason to go forward was finding the real Paul.

Everything clicked after that. It all made more sense. Very quickly, I convinced myself that nothing else mattered. And when I did, the first step became clear. In order to solve the mystery, in order to find the real Paul, I had to go public with my story.

—w—

Michelle and I were sitting together in our TV room, talking about what we should do, when a name popped in my mind.

"I think I know the guy who can help us," I said.

I went on my iPad and searched for George Knapp.

George was a well-known reporter and news anchor for a local Las Vegas station, KLAS-TV. He had a fascination with aliens, just like I did. In fact, George had broken a big story about Area 51, the remote U.S. Air Force testing facility 83 miles from Las Vegas that many believe was where government officials stored the debris from a UFO crash in Roswell, New Mexico, in 1947. George told the story of Bob Lazar, a physicist who claimed to have worked at Area 51 on a project to reverse-engineer alien technology. In someone else's hands, the story might have been seen as preposterous. But George's report made national news, and he won a United Press International award for his coverage. His curiosity about aliens is what led me to him.

Still, I didn't know if he'd be interested in telling my story. My gut told me he would be, because it involved an infamous crime and it had surprising twists and turns. My hope was that George would do a story, and that the publicity would bring in fresh clues and leads that could help us crack the mystery of the kidnapping. It was the quickest, easiest way to get the word out and get some answers. Surely, after nearly five decades of stony silence, there had to be someone out there who knew what had happened to the real Paul. Surely someone would step forward.

That was my hope, anyway.

On October 21, 2012, a week after I got the test results, I typed out an email to George Knapp on my iPad.

Hello. I was identified by the FBI as Paul Joseph Fronczak, the kidnapped baby from Michael Reese Hospital in Chicago, IL, April 26, 1964. I was abandoned in Newark, NJ, on July 2, 1965, and found in a stroller outside a variety store. I was placed in an orphanage. When the FBI learned about me, I was put in a foster home and given the name Scott McKinley. I have just discovered that I am not Paul Joseph Fronczak. I need help to find out who I am, and I welcome any assistance you can provide. Thank you.

Fifteen minutes later, I got an email back from George.

"I want to meet you," it read.

We set up a time for the following Monday. I drove to the KLAS-TV studio on Channel 8 Drive, just off the Las Vegas Strip and across from the Wynn casino resort. George was waiting for me in the lobby. He struck me as a formidable guy. He'd won two Peabody Awards and nineteen Emmys, so I knew he was a crack investigator, but he also looked the part of an old-school journalist. He had a shock of silver hair, a strong jawline, and pale blue eyes that firmly held your gaze. His smile was warm and modest, and he looked both weary and wise—like someone who had seen a lot and done a lot. Most of all, he gave the impression you could trust him with anything.

George led me to a conference room and had his cameraman, Matt, join us. There, I told them my story. The kidnapping, the clippings in the basement, the years of doubt, the DNA test. George stopped me once or twice with a question, but mostly he just listened and shook his head. When I was done, he jumped out of his chair.

"This is unbelievable!" he said. "We've got to get this on the air right away!"

It was exactly what I wanted to hear. I felt a surge of excitement, of hope.

"Let's find Paul!" I said. "Let's get some answers!"

At that moment, I fully believed the solution to the mystery was right around the corner. That it would be solved in a month, maybe two. I was convinced someone had to know what became of the real Paul, and I was sure the TV report would flush them out. After that meeting, there was no turning back. The mission had begun.

—⟅⟆—

George and I spent the next several weeks preparing the report. We submitted Freedom of Information requests to the FBI, trying to get our hands on the original case files (we never got a response). Then a KLAS news crew came to our house and shot footage of Michelle and me in the kitchen talking about the case. Emma stood next to us and told the cameraman about her trip to Target while he was taping us. We tried to shush her, but it didn't do much good.

I also went back to the KLAS studio to tape a sit-down interview. I wore a pale blue dress shirt with a starched collar, and a striped tie, but no jacket. I wanted to look believable and respectable, but I didn't want the interview to be too serious. I even cracked a few jokes as I described how surreal it all felt. Maybe it was a defense mechanism. Maybe I just didn't want to wallow in the darkness of it all.

George picked an airdate for the report—April 25, 2013. It was the day before my forty-eighth birthday, or what I'd *thought* was my forty-eighth birthday but no longer was.

There was only one thing left for me to do: talk to my parents before the report aired.

Michelle had been urging me to get it over with and call them. She knew I wasn't looking forward to it, and she didn't want me to put it off too long.

"Paul, you have to tell them," she'd say.

"But how? How am I going to tell them?"

"You just have to call them and tell them. They're your parents. They raised you. You can't not tell them."

I knew she was right, but I couldn't imagine the phone call. I couldn't see myself saying the words. My father was a little hard of hearing, and my mother heard only what she wanted to hear, so the thought of breaking the news to them over the phone filled me with dread. I kept postponing it, until there was only one day left before the report was to air. If I didn't tell them soon, they'd end up finding out they weren't my real parents from a friend who'd seen the report, or even from a reporter, and not from their own son. My relationship with them was at stake.

Finally, I sat down at my computer and typed out an email. My reasoning was that an email would give my parents time to gather their thoughts and process the news before having to respond to me. To tell the truth, an email was the best I could do.

When I finished writing it, the night before the report, I sat at my desk and reread it several times, so I wouldn't have to press send. After a while, I knew it was time to let it go, and I did. It zipped eighteen hundred miles across a time zone, until it settled in the old computer my parents kept in the den. I addressed it to both of them, but I wrote it directly to my mother, because I knew she'd be the one to read it.

Dear Mom and Dad,

I am writing this email to you because this is something very important, and I feel that if I try to speak with you over the phone, you will not fully understand or listen. First, I am your son, and always will be. You and Dad have been wonderful parents, and have shaped me into the person I am today. I love you both and that will be forever.

The DNA test results came back and it turns out that I am not your biological son. I am not the kidnapped baby that you had stolen from your arms on April 27th, 1964. This means that the real Paul Joseph Fronczak may still be out there, alive, not knowing who he is. This also means that I do not really know who I am, how old I am, my genetic background or heritage.

I know that this is hard for you, but this is also about me at this point in our lives. I have been struggling with the fact that I want to know if the real Fronczak baby is still alive, and what happened to him. I also want to find out who I am, and why I was abandoned in Newark, NJ, back in 1965.

These questions were getting the best of me, so I sent our story to a remarkable, award-winning journalist here in Las Vegas, George Knapp (do a Google search on him). Mr. Knapp was intrigued by the story and wanted to meet with me. We spoke for awhile, and he said he would like to run a story on the case. Mr. Knapp is not like the newspaper men you and dad had to deal with back in 1964. He is a professional with a specialty in investigative stories and reporting.

My goal for being a part of this story is based on two separate goals—I want to find out if the real Paul Joseph Fronczak is alive and what happened to him, and I want to find out who I am, and what happened to me. This is an unsolved case, and with today's media and technology, we might just be able to solve it.

Wouldn't you and Dad like to know what really happened, and who I really am? Like I said, I love you both and you have been wonderful parents. I am not doing this to hurt you or discredit the fabulous job you both did in raising me. This is just about finding out the truth.

I hope you and Dad understand, and would like to help with this story. I would really love for you and Dad to maybe even meet with Mr. Knapp. CBS News is going to run the story on April 25 here in Las Vegas. I hope the story will then go national; that would be the only way to possibly solve this terrible crime that took place almost 50 years ago.

I hope you and Dad will be with me on this, and be a part of the process. This is very important to me, and having you and Dad with me every step of the way would be the greatest thing I could hope for.

Thank you for all you have done for me in the past, and for the rest of our future together.

Your loving son,
Paul

I didn't expect to get an answer right away, or even that night. I figured I might hear from my mother the next day, sometime before the report aired.

But I didn't. No email, no call. The day after the report, I still hadn't heard from my parents. The fantasy that had been forming in my head—that my mother and father and brother and I could all embark on this journey together, like some great family adventure—suddenly seemed silly. Another day passed without any word. I was a wreck. I was waiting for the world's biggest shoe to drop.

Four days after I sent the email, while I was at home with Michelle, my phone rang. It was my parents' Chicago number.

"Hey, Mom," I answered, trying to sound casual.

"How could you do this to us?" my mother said, her voice full of anger and hurt.

"Do what?"

"I can't believe you did this. We told you not to do it. I'm sorry we weren't good enough parents for you. I'm sorry you felt you had to do this."

"Mom, I just want to find Paul," I said. "I want to do this for you."

Then my mother yelled into the phone.

"*You have ruined our lives. Now we have to relive the nightmare again. Why would you do this to us?*"

I heard the phone drop, and I heard someone pick it up.

"Dad?"

"You're an asshole," my father said calmly. "You should have left this buried."

Then he ended the call.

11

MY PARENTS' REACTION was a shock. I hadn't expected them to be that angry. I'd always felt intimidated by them, and I could never stand to let them down. But now, I hadn't just disappointed them, I'd betrayed them. I had, to their thinking, ruined their lives. And that felt terrible. To me, there was nothing negative about what I was doing. How could there be? I was trying to find my parents' real son! But clearly they didn't see it that way. Clearly, I had hurt them.

I told Michelle about the call, and she was rattled, too. It was as if my father hanging up on me suddenly made things real. I couldn't deny that, by pursuing my search, I was gambling with relationships I already had. I was risking things that really mattered to me and my family. Personally, I could find a way to handle my parents shunning me, but what about Michelle and Emma? My folks doted on Emma, and she was so happy whenever they came to visit. Had I just ruined that relationship for her?

I tried calling my mother back a few times, but she never picked up. Michelle called, too, and once or twice she got through. I listened as she argued my side: Paul just wants to know where he came from. Paul wants to know who abandoned him and why. He doesn't want to hurt anyone. He just needs to know the truth. I hoped Michelle might be able to budge my parents a bit, but, to be honest, I didn't expect she would. I knew that when my folks got mad about something, they could dig in and stay mad for a long time.

Up until my parents' reaction, I had been naïvely optimistic. I was certain the mystery would be solved quickly, with no damage to anyone. But already, that was no longer true. The journey was going to be more perilous than I'd thought. I hoped my parents would change their minds one day, but if it came to it, I had to decide if I was prepared to never speak with them again in order to pursue my search. So was I? Was I ready to give up the parents I had to find the ones who didn't want me?

Part of me wishes I could say I wasn't. But the truth is, I was. To me, learning the truth was more important than just about anything.

—⁂—

George Knapp's report aired on KLAS-TV on April 25, 2013. I was at work at the Art Institute when it ran, and my supervisor let everyone gather in the conference room so we could watch it together.

"You ever have that feeling when you were a kid that you must have been switched at birth or something, or that aliens had dropped you off because you couldn't possibly belong to your own family?" George asked at the beginning of the report, trying to convey the absurdity of my situation. "Well, for Paul Joseph Fronczak, it's more than a fuzzy feeling. Tomorrow is supposed to be his birthday, but he's just recently learned he has no idea when he was actually born, that his parents aren't really his parents, and that he hasn't a clue where he's from or who he is."

And then it was me on the screen, in an old home movie—a little boy hopping around the front yard in blindingly white shorts and shirt. Sad, operatic music played underneath the grainy movie. "I don't even know how old I am," I said in a voice-over. "Or who I am, or what nationality. All those things you just take for granted." A bit later it was Michelle's turn, and in a serious tone she said that finding my true identity "is important to our family." The report closed with George asking the public for help—clues, tips, leads, anything.

The next day, I telephoned George to do a segment on his live national radio show, *Coast to Coast AM*. I was on for two hours and I hit all the main points of my story—the kidnapping, the sense of estrangement, the lifetime of drifting, the DNA test. I fielded questions from listeners and I begged anyone with any information to come forward.

Later that night I checked the Facebook page George had helped me set up. We called it "Who Is Paul Fronczak?" I truly believed useful information would come pouring in. But the first message I read wasn't a clue, it was a criticism.

"Frankly, just so Paul knows, his adoptive family *is* his real family," a woman named Kathryn wrote. "His DNA-relatives are strangers. Most likely, his abandonment was some sort of a desperate, dysfunctional lone-mother scenario where the gift was that she gave up her son. What did Paul miss? Most likely a very dysfunctional life. And now his parents are suddenly faced with the fact that their child is still lost and they stopped looking for him. That will only result in loss, grief and guilt for them."

The next message, though, was consoling. "I was adopted, and I know what you mean by not having things in common with your adoptive family," wrote a woman named Linda Grace. "I always had things I loved that they had no interest in—horses, gardening, fishing. I finally found all of my blood relatives and they love these things as much as I do. I prayed every night that I be put in touch with my family, and now I am praying for you, also. God willing, Paul, someone will have the answers you seek."

Linda's message was more important than she'll probably ever know. It showed me there were people out there who understood what I was going through. The loneliness and displacement I felt weren't mine alone; others felt them, too. I quickly looked up the statistics for adoptions in the United States, and I learned that in any given year, there are about 135,000 children who are adopted, with more than 400,000 others in foster care.

For a long time, I hadn't known I was part of that group—the people unwillingly separated from their biological families. Now that I knew I was, it felt good to know I wasn't alone.

—⁓—

George's report was picked up and re-aired by a TV station in Chicago. Within days, my story was everywhere. The Facebook page filled with requests from TV and radio producers, some as far away as Australia. We got calls from representatives of all the major networks—CBS, NBC, ABC, CNN. A handwritten letter from Barbara Walters showed up at our doorstep. A producer for Anderson Cooper called me several times. I heard from Matt Lauer, and I was told NBC could have a plane pick me up and whisk me to their studio at a moment's notice.

One evening when all this was happening, I drove home from work and saw several people standing outside our house. I immediately knew they were reporters. I spoke with them and convinced them to leave, but the next evening one of them was back. He knew when I'd be getting home from work, and he wanted another shot at me. I drove past the house five times, waiting to see if he'd leave. Finally, he did.

The media staking out my house was another surreal echo of what had happened to my parents back in 1964. They'd been hounded by newspaper reporters for several days after coming home from Michael Reese Hospital, during what was surely the darkest time of their lives. It was an ordeal they never recovered from, and for the rest of their lives they kept a determinedly low profile. In a way, they spent the bulk of their lives hiding out.

That's why they were so angry with me now. That's what my mother meant when she told me, "Now we have to relive the nightmare again." Their greatest fear was having reporters re-invade their lives, ask more questions, force them to relive an event they desperately wanted to forget. I'm not sure I ever appreciated how terrifying it had been for them to have people staking out their house until reporters began staking out mine.

But they weren't hounding just me. As my parents had feared, a fresh batch of reporters descended on them and reenacted the ghastly vigil of fifty years earlier, cornering them as they left their home and asking for their deepest feelings about the sad case of their son. And, once again, my father did his best to shield his wife and shoo the reporters away.

"We're not commenting on anything, no thanks," my father said as he rushed my mother into the car—grayer and slower than a half century earlier, but surely every bit as angry about the intrusion. "We're fine, but that's it."

It was painful for me to think of my parents being bothered this way. Yet I was the one who had brought it on. The first time around, my parents hadn't invited the publicity. But this time, I had. I'd gone out of my way to get it. And I'd done it despite my parents' many pleas not to. If I could have, I'd have made it so no one hounded my parents, but that wasn't something I could control. The only way to be sure my parents would be left alone was to drop the search altogether, and it was already too late for that.

Not long after George's piece re-aired in Chicago, I got a call from a woman named Lora Richardson. She identified herself as a special agent of the FBI. She told me the bureau was interested in my story, and we set up a time for her to come by the house. She showed up with another female agent, and we sat down in the living room to talk. One of the agents had no cold-case experience at all, while the other was just about to retire. I got the feeling their visit was just cursory, but I put that feeling aside. The agents took a liking to Emma and didn't mind that she insisted on being in the middle of whatever was happening. I answered a few basic questions about my past and my parents, and then I took another DNA test for them.

I hadn't given too much thought to this particular repercussion of going public. I understood that the kidnapping in 1964 was a federal crime, and that by proving I wasn't the real Paul Fronczak, I was, in effect, reopening a long-closed case. I just hadn't dwelled on the law enforcement side of things.

In fact, there is no statute of limitations in kidnapping cases. Charges can be filed at any time after the alleged crime, even fifty years later. When I was handed over to the Fronczaks in 1966, the FBI more or less dropped the case—and the kidnapper was never found. The thinking, I'm guessing, was that, yes, the perpetrator of an infamous crime was still at large, but at least the victim was safe and sound. But now, I'd proven that nothing about the case had been resolved. In theory anyway, the victim was still out there. The kidnapper was still at large. No justice had been served at all.

It wasn't exactly the FBI's finest hour.

Still, did they really want to reopen the Paul Fronczak case? Did the original evidence and case files still exist? Surely there could be only a handful of relevant witnesses still alive, and how useful could their aging memories be? I wondered if the FBI would simply wash its hands of the case, citing the improbability of making any fresh headway.

Then I got another call from Special Agent Richardson. The call was about the original FBI case files.

I learned that ten boxes stuffed with paperwork and evidence had indeed been slated to be destroyed. They were put in storage to await the shredder, or maybe the incinerator, I don't know. And by all rights, the boxes should have been destroyed many, many years ago.

But they hadn't been.

Through some bureaucratic slipup, the boxes had stayed in storage. When the FBI went looking for them, there they were—reams and reams of reports and statements and photos undisturbed for half a century. Had they been destroyed, it would have been that much harder for the FBI to reopen the case. But, somehow, they survived.

I was excited to hear the files still existed. I'd had to make do with a couple of shoe boxes filled with old clippings, but here was a huge window into the seminal event of my life. There had to be something in those files that had been missed the first time around, some evidence that could be more thoroughly analyzed with new technology. I allowed myself to believe the files might provide us with some kind of road map to finding the real Paul.

But I was being naïve again. The files could very well provide such a road map, but there was no "us" in the equation. If the FBI decided to reopen the case, I would have no access to the old files. It would be an active criminal investigation, and one in which I wasn't the primary victim. The kidnapping itself had nothing to do with me. The FBI's goals would be to find the kidnapper and find the real Paul—not help me discover who I was. It didn't matter that finding the real Paul was my priority, too. The FBI didn't need me to do its job.

In early June 2013, the FBI announced publicly that agents had located the original files, which spokeswoman Joan Hyde called "a lucky break." Still, no decision had been made about reopening the case. It took the bureau two more months to reach that decision.

On August 8, Joan Hyde told the *Chicago Tribune*, "It was deemed appropriate to take a fresh look at the evidence we have and possibly re-interview sources that are still around." Some physical evidence, Hyde confirmed, might indeed benefit from modern testing.

It was official. The FBI was back on the case. In August 2013, the Baby Fronczak abduction became the oldest kidnapping cold case in U.S. history to be reopened.

12

THREE WEEKS AFTER the KLAS-TV segment, I got a Facebook message from someone named CeCe Moore.

> Hi, I am a professional genetic genealogist who works closely with adoptees and others who do not have knowledge of their heritage. I am willing to donate my time to provide assistance in interpreting a DNA genealogy test. Please contact me to discuss your options.

CeCe explained she was currently working on the Benjaman Kyle amnesiac case. Kyle was a middle-aged man who was found beaten and unconscious behind a Burger King Dumpster in Georgia in 2004. He had no ID or driver's license, and when he awakened he couldn't remember his name or social security number. Doctors diagnosed him with dissociative amnesia, which meant he couldn't remember much of anything about his life before the attack.

Several different groups, including law authorities and TV producers, tried to solve the mystery of Kyle's identity, but none could. That's when CeCe stepped in. I would later learn that she cracked the case and connected Kyle to his biological family. But, at the time, all I knew was that she was working on it.

I messaged CeCe and said I'd be in touch. But I let the contact drop. There were so many messages coming in, so many different things happening, and I just didn't follow up with her. My priority was still finding the real Paul, and I was still optimistic all the publicity would help the case be solved quickly.

Besides, I didn't know what a genetic genealogist was.

——⁂——

That would soon change. My radio interview with George Knapp also caught the attention of Matt Deighton, the public relations manager for Ancestry.com, and Matt sent George an email:

> I'm with Ancestry.com and I think we can help with this mystery. We have just launched a new DNA test that checks more than 700,000 locations on your DNA. We've had a lot of success connecting adopted people back to their family and I'm confident we can help Paul. We have more than 2 million 4th cousin matches in our system already. We'd like to offer a test to Paul to help him solve this mystery. If it doesn't work, he hasn't lost anything.

The offer was exciting. Matt worked for the world's biggest family history service, and he believed he could help me find out who I was. Still, I was skeptical. I didn't know much about building family trees, but I knew my tree had exactly one person on it—me. The rest was emptiness.

Was it really possible to fill in all the lonely branches, given a starting point of basically nothing? I didn't see how. The only real clue to where I came from was where I was abandoned—in a city in the Northeast. It was reasonable to assume my biological family lived somewhere in that area. Also, you could take a good guess at my age. But beyond that, what was there to work with?

Still, like Matt said, I had nothing to lose. I agreed to take the DNA test, and Matt sent me a kit. When it arrived, I filled a small vial with saliva and sent it back. Not much later I got a message on the Ancestry website that my sample didn't have enough DNA in it to process. The problem, I learned, was that I had put *too* much saliva in the vial. I guess I'd been a little overeager. I retook the test, and this time, I got it right.

These were my first timid steps into the world of personal genomics. Pretty quickly, I came to understand that a tiny vial of saliva was my best chance at learning who I was.

I began reading everything I could about genealogy—the study of families and the tracing of their history and lineages. The business of building family trees. Humans have been mapping their lineages for centuries; the Chinese philosopher Confucius, for instance, has a family tree that dates back 2,500 years. But it was two events in the 1970s that changed the field forever—the TV show *Roots*, which inspired millions to explore their own family histories, and the advent of the internet, which began the process of making it fairly easy to do so.

Early on, the study of DNA was mainly helpful in the field of medicine. Next, it became a tool for law enforcement. Today, it has spawned an industry—personal genomics. Individuals tracing their roots to better understand who they are. As one Ancestry.com executive put it, the collection and analysis of genetic samples "is a unique opportunity to study human evolution, migration patterns, ethnic diversity and the history of the species."

And all of these big, sweeping discoveries about ourselves and our origins begin with microscopic molecules called deoxyribonucleic acid—DNA. These are the molecules that store our biological information and determine how we develop and function. The DNA in our cells bands together to form chromosomes, which are duplicated when cells divide. Mapping all this genetic activity can tell us who we are and where we came from.

What the folks at Ancestry.com do is compare one person's 700,000 DNA letters, or bases, against the 700,000 DNA letters of hundreds of thousands of other people, in search of a single letter that matches. The analytical tools required to do that didn't exist a decade ago. But now they did, just in time for me. "Genetic self-knowledge," the Ancestry.com executive declared, "is critical for all of us, not only for understanding our past, but also as we move into the future."

This made sense to me, and gave me a new name for what I was searching for—genetic self-knowledge.

My conversations with Matt changed a lot of things. For one, he got rid of my skepticism about what personal genomics could accomplish. His enthusiasm was contagious. Matt was drawn to the field when he was a young boy in Utah, watching his mother write dozens of letters to possible relatives in order to build a family tree. In college he took a class in family history, and he was hooked. Matt explained how the number of people who have submitted DNA samples to Ancestry and other family history companies exploded a few years ago, increasing the number of discoveries dramatically.

For instance, Matt worked with a lot of foundlings who, like me, didn't know their real families. Thanks to the boom in DNA samples, he was pretty much solving a case a week. Matt made me hopeful that my family history might not always be the black hole I feared it was.

Matt was also the one who shifted my priorities, by making the search for my own identity at least as important as my search for the real Paul. He turned my focus around. Yet while I agreed to do whatever I could to help Matt discover who I was, I also asked that he help me with finding the real Paul. My connection to the kidnapped child was very real, and I had vowed never to give up on him. Matt explained that in order to find the real Paul, he needed an extraordinary piece of luck—he needed the real Paul, whoever he was, to have submitted a DNA sample to Ancestry. "There is a chance," Matt told me, "but it's slim." Still, he agreed to help.

There was one other hitch—Matt also needed DNA samples

from my adoptive parents, the Fronczaks, to run through his database. I'd sent the samples they gave me to Identigene, but Identigene wasn't allowed to hand them over to anyone else without permission from my parents. And I knew my folks would say no to Identigene, and no to me.

My parents did provide DNA samples to the FBI, and I assumed the FBI would run their samples through any number of databases, but I couldn't know for sure that they would. The FBI had no obligation to update me about their investigation, and they rarely did. I was out of the loop. But I didn't want to just sit on my hands and wait for word from the FBI anyway; I wanted to conduct my own investigation. I wanted to try to find the real Paul myself. And in order to do that, I had to get a Fronczak DNA sample to Matt.

With my parents certain to say no, I was left with only one option. My brother Dave.

—◊◊◊—

We'd never been close or chummy; if anything, we'd been adversaries. I found him condescending, frowning and shaking his head whenever I did something he deemed distasteful. We didn't have one thing in common that I can think of—not one. After our big fight, the one where I pulled out a clump of his hair, we basically shut each other out.

The irony of that incident dawned on me years later: I'd pulled out Dave's hair, literally yanked out a DNA sample, and now I was trying to do it once again.

Dave and I did have a couple of thawing moments. One time, he and my parents came out to visit me in Arizona. I had a BMW motorcycle back then, and I offered to give Dave a ride. He surprised me by accepting. He climbed aboard and put his arms around my waist, and we took off. I gave it some gas and we ripped down an empty street. Looking back, I think Dave may have admired my adventurousness, or at least envied it a bit. And that motorcycle ride was one of the only times—maybe *the* only time—when he joined me in an adventure, even if it was just a few fast miles on a bike. That moment felt different from any other we had shared, and it felt good.

I think that was the closest we ever felt to each other.

Later, when Dave graduated college, he called and asked if we could get together. He had something to tell me. We met at a downtown Chicago bar called El Jardin, which had the best margaritas in town. I was managing a lighting store outlet, and I swapped lighting fixtures for free food and drinks. El Jardin was very much my turf. But when Dave walked in, I felt an immediate wave of sympathy for him. I wasn't sure why.

We sat down, and, over drinks, Dave told me he was gay. I wasn't surprised; I sort of already knew. I'd never really thought about it, I'd just assumed it. It was one of the things that drove us apart—while I was bringing girls around and indulging with abandon, Dave was hiding his own sexuality. I was glad he'd come out with it now. I put my hand on his shoulder and tried to be as supportive as I could.

"I'm going to tell Mom and Dad next," he said, in a way that made it sound more like a question than a statement.

"Just do it," I said. "They'll be okay with it."

But they weren't. When Dave told them, they shut him out. They didn't talk to him or see him for a year. It was a foreshadowing of the banishment that awaited me. My mother would call me sometimes and ask, "What did we do wrong with David? Why is he this way?" I spoke up for Dave, but I didn't try to shake my parents off their views. They were staunch, lifelong Catholics, and they believed what they believed. They had to make a decision—side with their son, or side with their faith. They chose their faith. It couldn't have been easy for them, and it was certainly hard for Dave. It took a year, but eventually my parents let him back into the fold.

I didn't tell Dave about submitting my parents' DNA test before the KLAS-TV report aired, but I told him afterward. I said the most important thing for me was finding my parents' real son—and his real brother. He said he understood why I'd done the interview. A couple of weeks later, I emailed him and asked if he'd submit a DNA sample to Ancestry.

"No problem," Dave emailed me back. "Feel free to have it sent to me."

I was heartened by my brother's support, which felt like a lifeline after how my parents had reacted. But when I called Dave to ask about the test, I could tell from the start of our conversation that something had changed. His tone was sharp and blunt, like my father's. He even sounded like my father.

"How could you do this to Mom and Dad?" he asked. "After all they've done for you? You should drop this immediately."

I told him I couldn't do that.

"Well then, fuck you," Dave said, and hung up on me, just like my father had.

My brother and I didn't talk again for the next three years.

—⁂—

In the Provo, Utah, offices of Ancestry.com, Matt Deighton enlisted one of his top genetic researchers—Crista Cowan—to work on my case. Crista was essentially born into the business. Her family was unusually interested in genealogy long before she showed up. When she was a young girl, her father took her to Salt Lake City every summer so they could spend hours at the mammoth Family History Library, poring through archives and writing letters to possible relatives. When she was twelve, Crista's job was to help her father input data into a computer, using a rudimentary DOS-based program.

"I liked the detective work," Crista later told me. "I liked fitting puzzle pieces together."

At Ancestry, Crista set up a rolling, wall-size whiteboard in the hallway just outside her third-floor cubicle, near the windows that gave her a clear view of Mt. Timpanogos. In the center of the whiteboard, she printed a name—Paul Joseph Fronczak. Then she added some branches that fanned out from the center but had no names on them.

My family tree now existed, and it was all empty branches.

There was one other broad clue to who I was—my biological ancestry result. This was an approximation of which of the world's many regions my ancestors hailed from—AFR (sub-Saharan Africa), or MEA (the Middle East and North Africa), or MED (Italy, Spain, Portugal), or SCA (Finland, Denmark, Sweden) or somewhere else in the great wide world. We're talking about ancestors who walked the planet thousands of years ago, so not exactly my immediate family. Still, the DNA test I had taken with Identigene promised to reveal *something* about my past, and that was exciting.

It turned out I was 94 percent European, and 6 percent sub-Saharan African.

Like I said, this was a very broad clue. It's been proven that every person living in Europe today is related in some way to *all* of the child-bearing Europeans who were alive in the ninth century. Basically, the test confirmed I am part of one of the biggest families on earth—the family that is *everyone* whose ancient ancestors once roamed the 4 million square miles of Europe.

Ancestry, however, would be digging deeper than Identigene. I had to wait six weeks for my DNA to be analyzed, and in that time I felt more anxious than ever. Suddenly, I wasn't afraid I wouldn't find any answers; suddenly, what scared me was what I *might* find. I'd started a process that, theoretically, could lead me to the truth of my identity—to the reality of me. But what if, as I got closer to that truth, I didn't like what I saw? What if the personal costs of the search proved too burdensome? Could I shut the whole thing down?

I supposed I could, but signing up with Matt and Ancestry felt like a surrendering of control in a way. My DNA was in the system now, wending its way back in time. If finding my real family was possible, then was it inevitable, too? I had the feeling of being swept up in something I couldn't stop.

On June 20, 2013, I received an email with the preliminary results of my DNA test. The Ancestry analysis revealed that 94 percent of my DNA traced back to Europe, 5 percent to West Asia, and 1 percent to Africa. That was roughly the same determination reached by Identigene—that my ancestors hailed mainly from Europe. But then I got the first true surprise of my search.

I am Jewish.

I'd been raised Catholic, by parents who came from a long line of Catholics, in one of the most Catholic cities anywhere. I was deeply steeped in Catholic traditions. We went to mass, we took communion, we prayed to Jesus—that's what we did and that's who we were. But no—that's not who *I* was. Ancestry compared my DNA to the DNA of some three thousand people who came from the same global region as my ancestors, and in this way determined that 37 percent of my genetic ethnicity was European Jewish.

Just like that, one of my fundamental beliefs about myself had been proven false.

It was an amazing discovery, to be sure, but I can't say it was life-changing. Over time, it might prove to be. Over time, it might become the most significant truth I learned about myself, I don't know. But back then, because I was more focused on finding the real Paul, the information was more interesting than truly revelatory. It was something to file away about myself. Something to deal with later. A starting point.

But there was more. Matt told me the initial analysis had revealed something else. Something more significant.

A relative.

A *blood* relative.

"We have identified a possible cousin," Matt said.

13

HER NAME WAS FRANCES KIRBY—Fran, to those who knew her. She grew up in the Sheepshead Bay area of Brooklyn, on Avenue Y. Her father, an American GI, and her mother, who'd enlisted in the British Army, met at a London train station during World War II. It was Fran's mom, Miriam, who got her interested in family history by telling her stories about their relatives. Later, a cousin in England gave Fran stacks of family documents dating back to the 1700s. Fran and her husband, Larry, joined Ancestry in 2013 to start building their own family tree.

As soon as Fran joined the site, her DNA was compared to the DNA of everyone else on Ancestry, including mine. And we matched. There was a high probability that, somehow, Fran and I were related. The initial analysis predicted we were anywhere from fourth to sixth cousins, though our actual relationship could be even more distant. But almost certainly, we shared an ancestor somewhere. I had an actual blood relative.

Which meant, at least, that I wasn't an alien.

I felt a real charge when I heard about Fran. She was someone I could reach out to, talk to, get to know—she existed. My family was out there. The truth, perhaps, wouldn't be too far behind. But the more I learned about the match, the more I had to control my excitement.

In fact, everyone who signs up with Ancestry gets an average of *seventy-six* matches with people who are likely fourth cousins or better. Eventually, I would have more than five hundred such matches. A fourth cousin is a fairly distant relative—all it means is that you share a set of great-great-great-grandparents. There is one degree of separation between you and your brother or sister, but the relationship between you and your fourth cousin involves ten degrees of separation. That is ten people between you—in my case, ten unknown people. Think about it—how many fourth cousins can you name?

What's more, with a relationship that distant, Fran could turn out to be a third cousin, but she could also be a fifth or sixth cousin—a *really* distant relation. Yes, there was a high probability that Fran and I were related in some way. But what did that actually mean? Most fourth cousins are complete strangers to each other, even though they're related. And even first cousins—even brothers and sisters— can be strangers, too. So what did it mean to be part of someone's family tree?

Was I looking for my family, or just my closest family? Or *any* family?

I wasn't sure.

Still, matching Fran was important, because she was another building block. Through her, we might be able to find closer relatives, and fill in some of those empty branches. Take a step toward putting names on the two branches that mattered most—my biological parents.

But first, we needed to find Fran and get her to agree to help us. The day we got the match, I sent her a message on the Ancestry site. I told her I had no idea who I was or who my family was, but I wanted her to send me information about her family anyway.

Not until I got her response did I realize how fishy my message sounded.

Hi. I'm a little reluctant to send any personal info. But I would like to help you
if I knew this was all for real. Thanks, Fran.

I asked Fran to google my name, so she could see the George
Knapp report. "I'd like to help you," she replied after watching it, "but
still a little skeptical. How do I know it's you on the video?" Finally, I
asked Matt Deighton to contact her, so she'd know I wasn't a scam artist. I learned this is one of the biggest hurdles to building a family
tree—convincing strangers to share personal details with you. The
DNA test identifies a match, but much of the rest is raw detective
work—letters, phone calls, pleas for help, poring through photos. You
have to be skilled at persuasion to get anywhere in the field of personal
genetics.

Once Fran was on board, Matt and his researcher Crista got to
work. Their plan was to put together a list of grandparents that con-
stituted a common ancestry for fourth cousins. To do this, they needed
to go back four generations and try to identify sixteen crucial people—
Fran's sixteen great-great-grandparents. From that pool, Matt explained, "we will be able to narrow down the family members and give
you a second cousin—or closer."

The good news was that only one of the eight sets of great-great-
grandparents had to be the right set. So the very first set we found
could be the set that unlocked the whole mystery. "But it's also possible
that we find seven sets, and it's the eighth that is the key," Matt explained. "This is still a gamble and it's all up in the air, but we're going
to give it a shot."

Crista helped Fran build out her family tree, and very quickly
identified two sets of great-great-grandparents. The next step was
finding some of Fran's first cousins and testing their DNA. That's
when the team hit a roadblock. Fran did have a first cousin who lived
in the United States, but all the others lived elsewhere, some in En-

gland, some in South Africa. To find them, convince them to take DNA tests, send them the kits, and get the results back was incredibly time-consuming. The processing time for a single DNA kit was six to eight weeks. Just chasing one first cousin could take months.

That wasn't the only problem—Fran's unique ancestry was another roadblock. All four of her grandparents were immigrants. Her father's family traced back to Galicia, a historical geographic region in Eastern Europe, while her mother's maternal family hailed from England. To make some sense out of these far-flung threads, Matt and Crista would have to piece together a lot of family history from official documents: birth certificates, marriage licenses, things like that. But they encountered what they called an "accessibility of records issue"—a difficulty finding reliable family documents overseas. It wasn't impossible, it was just very slow going.

The final hurdle was Fran's Jewish ancestry. The fact that both of us were Jewish, Matt explained, actually made things more complicated.

That was because of something called endogamy, which refers to a pattern of marrying within the same ethnic, cultural, religious, or tribal group, due to customs and laws. One of the problems with Jewish genetic genealogy is that the gene pool of European Jews dating back twenty generations has been clouded by marriages between cousins and other relations, often because a Jewish community was so small, and there were no other options. In an endogamous culture, according to the International Society of Genetic Genealogy, "people will be related to each other in a recent genealogical timeframe on multiple ancestral pathways, and the same ancestors will, therefore, appear in many different places on their pedigree chart."

In other words, someone you think might be a third or fourth cousin might actually be a sixth or seventh cousin. People can be related in several different ways without even knowing it. Another name for this phenomenon is pedigree collapse—with certain groups, you can run out of unique ancestors, and it just becomes harder to build an accurate tree.

So Fran and I both having Jewish ancestry didn't make things any easier.

Still, Fran jumped right in and quickly lined up two first cousins who agreed to be DNA-tested. One, from her father's side, lived in upstate New York; the other, from her mother's side, was in England. If one of them matched with me, we would know which ancestral line to pursue, and we could cut down the pool of common ancestors by 50 percent. If neither of them matched, we'd have to continue the slow process of building out Fran's family tree, branch by branch. The DNA kits went out, and we waited.

In the meantime, Fran and I traded emails and talked family. She told me her mother had died just a few months earlier, and she asked me how my adoptive parents felt about my search. I explained that they'd shut me out. "My mom feels there is no way we'll find her bio son, so why even bother?" I wrote. "I feel just the opposite." Fran was supportive, and urged me to keep going. "I hope we are close family!" she wrote. I told her I hoped so, too.

Eventually, the test results for Fran's two first cousins came back.

Neither one was a match.

It was a setback, to be sure, but it wasn't the end of anything. It just meant Matt and Crista had to keep plugging away at Fran's family tree. Fran was the only real lead, and there wasn't much else that could be done. Just keep digging, and hope a closer match somehow popped up.

In the fall of 2013, I traveled to New York City with Michelle and Emma so I could finally meet Fran face-to-face. I decided it didn't matter if she was my third or fourth or seventh cousin—she was family. We were related, and that was enough for me. It wasn't like I could pick and choose between relatives. Fran was the first one I had the chance to meet, and I didn't want to miss that chance.

We got together in a hotel. Fran was there with Larry, her husband of forty-four years. *Forty-four years!* Now that was a relationship that didn't need testing to define. Fran and Larry were lovely, wonderful people, and we talked for about an hour, about nothing and everything. Two strangers getting acquainted. As I sat there talking to Fran, I tried to feel the importance of the moment—I mean, I tried to really *feel* it. After a lifetime of not knowing where I belonged, I was finally sitting next to a flesh-and-blood relation. I was no longer alone on an island. And that had to mean something. That should have been *huge.*

And it was, in a way, but I can't say it felt monumental. It felt good, but that was it. Maybe I'd built up the moment too much in my head, I don't know. It had nothing to do with Fran, it was just that I'd invested so much in discovering my true identity, and this was only a small step in that direction. I'd hate to think that my determination to learn the truth about myself made me miss meaningful, emotional moments along the way, but maybe that's what happened. In any case, I think Fran was going through the same thing. We both realized the significance of the moment, but in the end we were still just fourth cousins. And neither of us seemed too sure what that meant, exactly.

Over time, it proved more difficult to build out Fran's tree than anyone expected. I would eventually learn that, due to the inability of DNA analysis to account for pedigree collapse, the degree of closeness between Fran and me was probably exaggerated. We were definitely related, it just wasn't that significant a connection. At least not on paper.

Still, Fran Kirby was the first person I met—other than my daughter, Emma—who I could say with any certainty shared a blood-line with me. And no matter how you look at it, that was no small thing.

—◊◊◊—

Early on in my search I got a voice mail from Angela Williamson, who worked for the National Center for Missing and Exploited Children. The center is an investigative resource created by Congress in 1984, after the separate, infamous abductions of two six-year-old boys, Etan Patz and Adam Walsh. Angela's title at the center was a mouthful—Biometrics and Unknown Victim Identification Projects program manager. She was offering to have the center help me in my search.

I happily agreed, and Angela told me to reach out to the NCMEC Call Center to register my case. "Tell them you have been in contact with me," she instructed, "and say that you are an 'unidentified living person.'"

Just like that, I had a new classification. I wasn't just a foundling anymore. I was also an unidentified living person. Not a UFO—a ULP.

Angela explained the center would put my DNA sample into the National Missing and Unidentified Persons DNA Database. "This enables your DNA to search against DNA samples provided by families who are missing children," she explained, "and your parents' DNA to search against DNA from unidentified children." Unfortunately, the center first needed to prove I wasn't related to the Fronczaks by running their own DNA tests. Which meant not only submitting my DNA sample but getting my parents to submit theirs, too. And I already knew how that would turn out.

In the end I sent in my DNA, but that, too, seemed kind of pointless. My sample would be useful only if someone was working with NCMEC to search for me. I'd been abandoned on a city sidewalk nearly fifty years earlier. What were the chances anyone anywhere was actively trying to find me?

—\m/—

My expectation was that George Knapp's report would flush out important tips and lead to a quick resolution, but things didn't work out that way. Most of the messages that came through the Facebook page weren't tips or leads but rather shots in the dark.

Several people noticed that in boyhood photos I resembled James Dwyer Bordenkircher, a child who went missing from his home in North Lake Tahoe, California, in 1965. Many of those who followed the case believed James had drowned in a lake; others, that he was lost in the woods. Still others believe he was abducted. Nearly fifty years later, people were wondering if I could possibly be James Bordenkircher. Theoretically, it was possible—I'd been abandoned in New Jersey one month after James disappeared in California. But when I was handed over to the Fronczaks, my photo ran in lots of national newspapers. Had I been James Bordenkircher, someone would have noticed.

Plenty of people thought I looked like Brett Favre, the Green Bay Packers quarterback. There was a resemblance, but I definitely wasn't Brett's long-lost brother. Another person who messaged me asked for more information to help in her own investigation of my case. "What color are your eyes? What color was your hair as a child? As a young adult? Do you have Cushing's Syndrome? You look like you could have Welsh blood, especially with the heavy jaw." A nice man named Fred messaged me and told me he was a dowser—one of those people who use a divining rod to locate things underground. "Never used Facebook, this is the first time," Fred wrote. "I feel you were born Aug. 7, 1964 at 2:57 a.m. in Philadelphia. I also have an opinion on the stolen Paul if you're interested."

A majority of the messages, though, were simply encouragements. People wishing me luck, sympathizing, urging me to keep my spirits up. A lovely lady named Laura sent me poignant words of advice:

> So many of us, people our age, are searching for a piece of us that's missing. Maybe everyone is? Maybe all of us say, 'Really, *who am I?*' Paul, I wish you luck and *strength*. But I am going to tell you that finding the truth of who you are resides *inside you*. It will be good to know your real birthday. It will be good to solve the mysteries. But after all is said and done, that "feeling" of not knowing who you really are may not go away. In the end, none of the labels matter—name, birthdate, heritage. *You are you.* The only you there is. And once you feel that, you will know what I mean.

I thought a lot about Laura's words, and they seemed pretty wise to me.

Still, nothing was going to get in the way of my search for the real Paul, and the real me. The slowness of everything—weeks and weeks of waiting for DNA test results—made me realize that George's local TV report wasn't enough. If I really wanted to unearth strong leads, I had to share my story with a lot more people. I had to go national.

Fortunately, there was so much interest in my story I had my pick of national outlets. I talked it over with Michelle, and we agreed that we would work with a major TV network to get my story out. Michelle was starting to understand, same as I was, that nothing was likely to be resolved anytime soon, and, like me, she wanted the case to crack as quickly as possible. Mainly so that I could find the answers I needed, but also so that we could get back to being an ordinary family.

In the end, we decided to go with ABC and their news show *20/20*. Barbara Walters won us over. When we met in New York City,

Barbara told us about the daughter she'd adopted in 1968. She seemed to be sensitive to the issues of people who'd been separated from their biological families. Plus, Barbara became Emma's new best buddy. They hit it off so well, Emma climbed right into her lap and sat there like they'd known each other for years. Afterward, Emma couldn't stop telling people about her new friend Barbara.

We flew to New York City to tape interviews for 20/20. They devoted an entire hour to my story and, later, a second hour. I eventually learned those two episodes were 20/20's best-rated episodes in two years.

The first report told the full story of the kidnapping and my abandonment in New Jersey, as well as of my DNA test earlier in the year. In a voice-over, Barbara noted how my parents had missed so much in their young son's life—his first steps, his first word, his first everything. My parents declined to be interviewed for the show, but they did provide a short formal statement.

> We wish Paul well in his search, and we continue to cooperate with the FBI in search of answers.

Still, I was certain they would watch the episodes, and I made sure to say, "My parents raised me and they did a great job." I meant it when I said it, and I wanted my parents to know that's how I felt. The sad part was that I had to tell them through a national TV show.

I noticed something else during the first 20/20 taping. I noticed that, while I felt completely swept up by the process of sharing my story on national TV, Michelle didn't. She was part of the story, for sure, but in terms of the search for my identity, she was only a peripheral part. She was on the outside of it, even during the taping. As I was hustled here and there, the center of everyone's focus, Michelle was always secondary. I may have expected that Michelle and I would work together on everything, but that was naïve of me, too. While I dug deeper and deeper into the search, it fell to Michelle to take care of our family's normal, daily needs—child care, dinners, scheduling—all while working a full-time job herself. There was no way she could ever feel as involved in the search as I did.

I should have realized that what was fueling me wasn't doing the same thing for my wife. I should have realized that, bit by bit, my attention was being drawn away from the family I had and toward the family I hoped to find. But I just didn't see it that way. It wasn't like I was disregarding my family entirely; I was still very involved in our household. I truly believed I could find the real Paul and learn my identity *and* be there for my family. But Michelle didn't believe that was possible. It was as if she thought of my interest in the case as more of a hobby than anything else, and she wanted to limit the amount of time I devoted to it. But for me, it wasn't a hobby—it was a passion. It was everything. And I faulted Michelle for not being as passionate about it as I was.

The truth was, she was scared.

A friend of mine who saw the *20/20* report told me that as he watched Michelle and me sitting together in our kitchen, talking to Barbara Walters, he felt a strange uneasiness—as if he was watching two people pulling in different directions. But I was too caught up in the excitement of the moment to understand what he was trying to tell me.

—⁓—

When the *20/20* reports aired, in late 2013 and early 2014, everything ratcheted up. The pace, the pressure—everything. Suddenly we were getting emails and even late-night phone calls from a stream of people who thought they could help solve the case. One woman was convinced that an actor on the soap opera *Days of Our Lives* was the real Paul, and kept writing and calling to push her theory. Someone else told me about a black market baby-smuggling ring in Chicago in the 1960s, and linked both me and Richard Nixon to the ring: "I know this sounds completely crazy, but I have reasons to believe that Nixon's daughter Tricia may have become pregnant in 1963. I think you should look into the possibility that you may be her son. You look like Tricia, and if you've heard her speak, you might recognize the timbre of her voice, and her manner and patterns of elocution. Please check it out."

I got several messages from a man who was certain thanatology was the key to solving my case. "Thanatology is the study of death and dying, and there is amazing stuff hidden here," he explained. "The year 1964 was a leap year, and April 27 was the 118th day of the year, 38 days from March 20, the real equinox. The Cubs lost to the Phillies on the 26th, 5 to 1. The moon may have been in the 7th sign, Libra. Dan is the seventh son of Jacob. All these things lead to something called snake, over Mother, attachment, death instinct. Okay, I've said too much."

Some of the voice mails we received at home were dark and muddled and unsettling. People with wild theories, people speaking in hushed tones. Sometimes I would answer the phone and find myself talking to one of these creepy callers. We knew to expect a few crackpots, but knowing that anyone could reach us and interrupt our lives created a lot of anxiety.

Even so, I rarely hung up on anyone. I was patient and probing, and I didn't dismiss any theory out of hand. I didn't want to let a real lead slip away. Watching me get up from the dinner table to talk to yet another odd caller bothered Michelle more than I realized. She didn't like seeing me get so easily pulled into dark conversations with strangers or, even worse, people who might have malicious intent. Understandably, she felt our family was being exposed to something that was potentially threatening.

"What if the kidnapper is still out there?" Michelle asked. "What if they're afraid of being caught, and they see us on TV, and they know where we live? What if they come and try to take our kid?"

"I can't just stop," I said. "I can't just quit looking."

"Paul, this scares me. People are paying attention to us. And the person we're looking for, the kidnapper . . . this is a bad person."

"A tragedy happened to my parents!" I said. "How can I just let it go? We have to find the real Paul."

Michelle didn't ask me to give up the search—not yet, anyway. She was just trying to let me know how frightened she was. But by then, a thought had already formed in my mind. I didn't say it out loud to Michelle, but I believed it.

This is bigger than us, I thought. *This is bigger than anything.*

And there was something else—I was enjoying myself. I was *into* it.

Even the strange theories and the calls from weirdos—for me, they were all part of the process. Part of the *adventure.* I found nearly everything about the search exhilarating. The side of me I'd suppressed in order to lead a more normal life—the side that craved excitement and loathed routine—had been awakened. And I welcomed that. I was fielding new tips, chasing down leads, dashing off emails, scouring the Web—I was Paul the detective. And that, pure and simple, was *exciting.* And at the end of it all, I expected to find the prize I'd craved for so long—the truth about who I was.

Why would I want to stop all that?

—⁂—

In the summer of 2013, I received a remarkable tip. It came from a thirteen-year-old girl.

The story was sketchy, but the details were astonishing. 20/20 had created an age-progression image of what the real Paul might look like today. The young girl watched the report and noticed her father looked like the image. Not just a little—a lot. She also knew her father had been adopted under mysterious circumstances. So she played amateur detective and started searching in her house for possible clues.

She was looking through a bedroom dresser drawer when she found something hidden beneath a pile of clothing. It was an old, yellowed newspaper article, about something that happened a long time ago.

The article was about the Baby Fronczak kidnapping.

14

⌒⁓⌒

THE YOUNG SLEUTH emailed me in June 2013. "Paul, if I'm right, I have *loads* of information for you," she wrote, "but first I don't want you to tell anyone about this. Not your parents, not even your wife. My name is Jenny and I am 13. I highly believe my father is the real Paul."

She wasn't the first person to tell me she thought she knew who the real Paul was—lots of people sent me baby photos of relatives they believed were exact matches with the Baby Fronczak photo (most weren't really even close). But Jenny's letter was uniquely urgent and dramatic. She had compared current photos of her father to photos of Chester Fronczak in 1964, and "the resemblance," she said, "is *unbelievable.*" She told her mother about her suspicions, and together they confronted her father. But he didn't want to believe them, "because if I'm right and the stolen baby is in our house," Jenny wrote, "so is someone that was part of the kidnapping plan—my grandmother."

Jenny laid out her theory. In the 1960s, her grandmother—who lived with her and her parents—had several miscarriages. Her grandmother's parents, she explained, were powerful people fully capable of getting their hands on a baby somehow. Jenny figured her great-grandmother kidnapped Baby Fronczak and gave her to Jenny's grandmother, explaining that the baby had been adopted. But no adoption records were ever found. What's more, her great-grandmother's facial features, and the features of the woman in the 1964 police sketch of the kidnapper, "are identical," Jenny wrote.

She also believed her grandmother had found a newspaper story about the kidnapping in 1964, and accused her parents of the crime. "They told the doctor she was crazy, and she was put on medication," Jenny wrote. "My grandma always told us that she would just sit there snapping green beans, but she never told us why she was on the medication." Only after she couldn't get any good answers out of her grandmother did Jenny start her sleuthing.

In her grandmother's room, she found some old film canisters. One of them was marked "First Birthday." Jenny watched the old home movie, which showed her father's birthday party. It looked like a typical home movie, except for one inexplicable thing. In the early parts of the movie, the boy's birthday was being celebrated in April.

But in footage that was spliced in, the party was happening in October.

For unknown reasons, Jenny's father had two birthday celebrations six months apart. Jenny concluded that someone had switched his birthday from April 1964—the month the real Paul was kidnapped—to October 1964.

"God, this is so much scarier when someone you know, who is sitting on the couch with you, might be a criminal," Jenny wrote. "I'm doing some more snooping today and I'll email you if I find anything."

That snooping led to the discovery of the newspaper clipping about the kidnapping. To me, it seemed impossible it could be a coincidence. Why in the world would Jenny's grandmother have kept an old clipping about Baby Fronczak in her dresser drawer for so long? But there was more. The next thing that happened was astounding.

As soon as Jenny's grandmother learned the clipping had been discovered, she disappeared.

—◦◦◦—

It was like something out of a pulp-fiction thriller. Jenny's grandmother just up and left, taking nothing, telling no one. She simply vanished. Had she fled because the truth was finally out?

Still, there were holes. For one thing, there was no Chicago connection. Jenny and her family lived out west. Then Jenny's mother, who'd begun emailing me, too, told me she'd found a card addressed to her husband's parents. The card was dated February 1964, and it was postmarked Chicago.

"It's a sympathy card," Jenny's mother explained. "We don't know who it's from."

A little more research revealed that Jenny's grandmother and her husband had a sixteen-month-old daughter who died in February 1964—two months before the Baby Fronczak kidnapping.

As I traded emails with Jenny and her mother, I allowed myself to believe I'd found the real Paul. How could it not be him? The strange home movies, plus the uncanny resemblances, plus the missing grandmother, plus the sympathy card—this had to be it. The next step was convincing Jenny's father, Will, to take a DNA test, the results of which could then be compared to my parents' samples by the FBI. But, understandably, Will was skeptical.

I waited to hear back from Jenny and her mother about the test. I urged them to show Will the TV reports about my case, so he'd understand the gravity of the search. Eventually, I got on the phone and spoke with him myself. I told him about my situation, and he told me about his. Like me, Will had questions about his identity. Like me, he wanted to find out who he really was. We were both struggling with similar demons. He was a deeply private man, and he was caught in the middle of a difficult situation, but it was clear to me he wanted to help if he could. He wanted *answers*. Finally, he agreed to take the test, and submitted a sample to the FBI.

I was at home with Michelle and Emma when I got a call from Will. I held my breath as I answered it. He had heard from the FBI. The results were in.

The DNA didn't match. Will wasn't the real Paul.

The news was crushing. I slumped down on a chair. I'd been so sure. I thought we'd solved it. So many things pointed in our favor. But DNA doesn't lie. The truth was the truth. The real Paul was still out there somewhere.

I struck up a nice friendship with Will, and he and his family came out to Las Vegas to visit even after the test results. They still wanted to meet me.

Emma and I joined them for lunch, and Emma got along great with Will and his daughter Jenny. Afterward we all went for ice cream at a nearby parlor. Will and I kept talking about how surreal our situations were. It was a strange thing to bond over—a terrible crime, a disappearing grandmother, inscrutable pasts—but we bonded anyway. I eventually learned Jenny's grandmother had gone to live with her ex-husband, but I never found out why she had the newspaper clipping, or what was up with the home movies.

Some answers come at you cold and steely in the form of DNA percentages. Some answers, you never get.

—␣␣—

"Hi, my name is Kim, and I want to provide you with some information that may be of interest to you."

So began a message from Kimberly Ingrassia, who watched the

20/20 report in November 2013 and marveled at what she saw. The show featured home movies of me in the days after I was handed over to the Fronczaks—movies that showed a young boy jumping around his new front yard, oblivious to all the attention on him. Kim knew who that boy was.

"I am the daughter of Janet Eckert Ingrassia, and the granddaughter of the late Claire and Fred Eckert," Kim wrote. "My grandmother and mother ran the very first adoption home established in the state of New Jersey. Babies were placed in their care until an adoption took place. You were one of these babies."

I was astonished. Kim's mother, Janet, had been the one who cared for me for nearly a year after I was abandoned on a sidewalk in Newark in 1965. What's more, Kim's message included a note her mother had written for me.

"You were an adorable baby!" Janet began. "You were brought into our home towards evening time. You were carried in secretly from the public. The State did not want anyone to know you were placed in our home. They had suspicions you were the Fronczak baby. You had a blanket over your head, and we peeked under the blanket to see you, and you smiled. Your eyes were so big."

The information was amazing. Here was a witness to a crucial time in my life—a time I had no memories of. A voice from almost fifty years ago, suddenly clear again. My past, rushing forward to catch up with me now. And the details in Janet's note—they were remarkable. She told me how I liked to play with blocks, trains, and airplanes. She told me how I was baptized in a little white dress the Eckerts had for me. "You were our special baby," Janet wrote, "because we knew we would not have you for long."

In the home movies of me running around the Fronczaks' front lawn, I'm wearing a white jumper suit. It was Janet and her mother who bought that suit for me, so I would have something nice to wear on the day they gave me to my new parents. It cost them a full month's pay.

"I am sorry I cannot give you all the answers you want," Janet wrote. "But I just want you to know that, for the little time you were with us, you were deeply loved in the Eckert home and held a special place in our hearts. I know my parents are looking down at you from Heaven, and smiling."

She ended the letter with "God bless you, my Scott."

—⁓—

Janet's note was a window into a world I hadn't known I'd been a part of—a world of tenderness and open affection. From Janet's telling, my time with her family was happy, almost idyllic: me swimming in the backyard pool; me running down the driveway to greet her father when he came home from work; me eating cake with my fingers. The Eckerts repeatedly telling me how much they loved me, and me answering with a beaming smile. These were astonishing things to discover about myself. The contrast to my childhood with the Fronczaks was stark.

I also learned about the name I had prior to my time with the Fronczaks—Scott McKinley. My assumption was that some anonymous state official had chosen it just to fill an empty line on a form. But Janet told me her mother had picked that name out for me.

I understood that I had a third name—the name I was given at birth. But I wasn't anywhere close to learning that name. And Paul wasn't really my name, either. I'd just taken it over from the boy who was kidnapped. It *became* my name, but it had been picked for someone else. But now I learned that someone who loved me picked the name Scott just for me.

And in an instant, it dawned on me. In my search for my real family, I'd found a different family I'd never known I had. A *third* family. Our time together had been brief, but nearly fifty years later Janet could still summon the love she felt for me. She could still remember tiny details of my days with her. She still called me "my Scott."

Less than a year isn't a very long time, but is it long enough for strangers to become a family? From Janet's letter, it sure sounded like that's what happened when I showed up on their doorstep, covered by a blanket.

I contacted Kim and told her I wanted to meet her and her mother. They still lived in New Jersey, where Janet's parents had run their adoption home. They'd sold the house in the borough of Watchung where I'd spent those many months, but I reached out to the owners and asked if Janet and I could stop by and have a look. I wanted to see if I could go back in time, and maybe even remember some of these sweet moments in my life.

Janet hadn't seen me since the day I was given to the Fronczaks, but when we finally met she hugged me and cried as if we were long-lost friends. Janet had been only seventeen years old when I was brought to live with the Eckerts, but she worked right alongside her mother, Claire, and spent as much time with me as anyone. Her then-boyfriend—who became her husband—had been there in 1965, too. Janet introduced us, and he said he remembered me well. Janet said we had bonded, even though I'd been frightened the first time he entered the house. "Everyone gravitated to you," Janet said. "We all did."

After talking for a while, the three of us went to the Eckerts' former home in Watchung. It was a big, beautiful house, with a lovely footpath and a lush backyard. The owners were extremely nice and let us walk around. Janet pointed out all the special places she remembered—the spot where they kept my crib, the living room where I used to sit on her father's lap and fall asleep.

"You were very happy here, Scott," she said.

We spent about an hour in the house, going over their memories. I soaked it all up, hoping for a twinge of remembrance. But nothing rang a bell. The house was just a house, the stories unfamiliar. More than anything, I wanted to remember those happy days. I ached for the tiniest flashback, the smallest seed of memory. But, other than Janet's kind words, there was nothing to hold on to.

Still, I felt I was with someone who genuinely loved and remembered me, and that was a beautiful feeling. Even though I didn't recognize the boy in Janet's story, I still felt happy for him—happy that he'd found such a loving and caring environment after being left on a sidewalk. Whatever dark forces had led to his abandonment, at least he'd been cared for by people who were clearly kind and good. Perhaps that transition period had been more instrumental for the boy than anyone realized. Perhaps it had even saved him.

Toward the end of our visit, Janet took my hand in hers.

"Scott, my parents did not want to let you go," she said. "They wanted to keep you. They wanted to adopt you. They did not want to see you leave."

I didn't know what to say. If what she was telling me was true, it would change the way I perceived my history—boy is abandoned, boy is given to a family that wants him. There had been another step in between—a step that could have led to an entirely different life for me. I'd been abandoned, yes, but I wasn't unwanted—someone *had* wanted me.

Which meant I'd been taken from a family who already loved me, and given to a family who wanted me only because they thought I was their son.

But what if I hadn't been linked to the Fronczak kidnapping? What if Newark Detective Joseph Farrell hadn't played a hunch and compared a photo of me to the birth photo of Paul Fronczak way back in 1965? If I'd been just another anonymous foundling, like all the other babies who wound up with the Eckerts, would I still be Scott McKinley today?

And what sort of man would I be?

Impossible questions with no answers.

Hearing the Eckerts had wanted to adopt me made me both happy and sad—happy that I'd been so loved, but sad, perhaps, that I'd lost out on that life. My parents are deeply good people who did their very best in incredibly challenging circumstances, and they gave me a wonderful home and loved me. In so many real and meaningful ways, I am their son—period. But I couldn't help wondering if my crippling sense of not belonging, of being an outsider, might never have arisen had I stayed with the Eckerts.

Then again, who can say—it might have been even worse.

I spent a few hours with Janet and her husband before getting back on a plane to Las Vegas. I liked her a lot, even though our connection wasn't one I could feel with any depth. Our visit had been moving and warming, but it had also been a little eerie. It felt strange to be called Scott. It increased my sense of not knowing who I was. It was like the movie *Sliding Doors*, where a woman travels two different life paths, all because, in one scenario, she catches a certain train, and in another she doesn't. Is our destiny so precarious it can be entirely reshaped by a single, insignificant event?

Do we become who we are because of mere chance?

Again, I had no answers, only more questions. But that was the way my search was going. The mysteries only deepened.

—⟋⟋⟍—

By the time the 20/20 report aired, I'd been working with Matt and Ancestry for several months. They were plugging away at Fran Kirby's tree, but progress was slow. Still, I felt like they were doing everything they could do on the DNA front. And they were.

But *I* wasn't.

CeCe Moore, the genetic genealogist who'd contacted me a few days after George Knapp's piece, was also working on my case. I'd made the mistake of not following up with her, but then ABC invited her to come on board. CeCe told me there was something more I could do to increase the chances of finding a genetic solution to the mystery of my identity.

Because I was working with Ancestry, I'd been entered into the company's database—but *not* into any DNA databases run by competing companies. In fact, there are three major DNA testing companies—Ancestry, Family Tree, and 23andMe. They are the CBS, NBC, and ABC of the industry. At the time, one of the companies claimed to have genotyped—or analyzed the DNA sequences of— around 300,000 people, and another claimed about 650,000. The third was just below 100,000. That was more than a million possible matches in total. However, Ancestry uses only its own database. They fish only in their own pond. So by using just their database, I was missing out on hundreds of thousands of potential matches.

CeCe offered to work on my case pro bono and immediately get my DNA into all three databases. This time, I was smart enough to say yes.

I'd soon learn that CeCe wasn't just any genetic genealogist. She was one of the field's leading professionals, and an expert in the analysis of DNA for unknown parentage cases. And the more I looked into CeCe's background, the more I realized how little I knew about DNA analysis. It's a seriously confusing field, even if you're interested in that sort of thing, which, just a year earlier, I hadn't been. Still, if CeCe believed DNA would be the key to uncovering my identity—and she did—then I felt I should try to learn a little more about it.

Here are the basics, starting with a cell—the smallest structural unit of an organism. Each of us has somewhere in the neighborhood of several dozen *trillion* cells. And in the nucleus of each cell, DNA molecules are packaged into chromosomes. Each cell has twenty-three pairs of chromosomes: twenty-two of them are called autosomes, while the twenty-third pair determines our sex (females have two X chromosomes, males have an X and a Y). The autosomes contain genetic information from both of our parents and most of their ancestors—a real jumble of data, but also a fairly comprehensive genetic record.

In the last century, and particularly in the last twenty-five or so years, we've figured out how to analyze DNA and make meaningful use of the results. There are three main types of DNA tests—a Y-DNA test, which tracks the Y chromosomes passed down from father to son; an mtDNA test, or mitochondrial DNA test, which traces DNA passed down from mother to child; and an autosomal DNA test, which analyzes DNA from both parents and suggests someone's total ancestral heritage. The autosomal tests offer the most matches with other people's DNA, and can reach back through about seven generations, or roughly two hundred years.

New and improved autosomal DNA tests have been a kind of breakthrough in the field—and CeCe Moore was part of that breakthrough. She was involved in the beta testing for all three autosomal DNA tests on the market, and she's considered an innovator in their use. She's a consultant for the TV shows *Finding Your Roots* and *Genealogy Roadshow*, and she's helped many hundreds of adoptees find their birth families. CeCe is also a hugely popular blogger under the name Your Genetic Genealogist, and she leads a team of genetic sleuths called the DNA Detectives.

"I believe very strongly that everyone has equal rights to their heritage," CeCe later told me. "I'm passionate about reuniting families."

I asked CeCe what sparked her interest in genealogy. It started when she was young and discovered a book written by a distant cousin, outlining the family's ancestral line. Seeing her own name listed in the book filled her with wonder. Later, she began devouring Nancy Drew novels. "I loved the detective work, the math, the fitting things together," she said. When her niece got engaged, CeCe created an ever-expanding family tree as a gift. After that, she never looked back.

I felt extremely lucky to have CeCe in my corner. Not only was she a DNA wizard but she was also a lovely person. Kind, friendly, and giving. She lived across the Mojave Desert from me, in Southern California, and she had a son who was just about the same age as Emma. I'd never stopped being hopeful, but a lack of good leads and the slow pace of DNA analysis chipped away at my gung-ho spirit. CeCe joining the team gave me fresh hope.

With her help, I entered my DNA into the other two major databases in early 2014.

—⁂—

Even the most proficient genetic genealogist will tell you that every DNA case relies on the same unpredictable X-factor—luck.

In the Hudson River town of Beacon, New York, in December 2013, a man was given a unique Hanukkah gift by his family—an Ancestry DNA kit.

The man, in his fifties, owned a kayak company, as well as an apparel business that had been in his family for three generations. He was a big, strapping guy who volunteered as an EMT for the Beacon Ambulance Corps and served as a ski patroller for the Thunder Ridge Ski Area in Patterson. He'd always wanted to know more about his family, so the Ancestry kit was the perfect present. The man took the DNA test, and sent it in.

A few weeks later, in January 2014, I logged on to Ancestry.com to check my match results, as I did every morning. Pretty much every day, there were no new significant matches. I'd gotten used to that. But on this day, there was a message waiting for me in my in-box. It was from the man in Beacon—Alan Fisch.

"I just received my DNA results, and it matched us as second cousins," Alan wrote. "I would like to talk to you to see how we may be related."

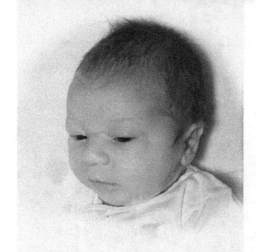

LEFT: The real Paul Fronczak in a hospital photo taken shortly before his abduction in April 1964.

ABOVE: The Fronczak kidnapping led to a media frenzy—and the biggest manhunt in Chicago history.

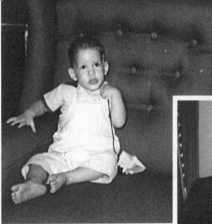

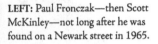

LEFT: Paul Fronczak—then Scott McKinley—not long after he was found on a Newark street in 1965.

RIGHT: Paul with Dora and Chester Fronczak and FBI officials in an FBI office in 1965.

LEFT: Paul and family at his baptism in Chicago's Saint Joseph and Saint Anne Catholic Church in 1965.

RIGHT: Young Paul in a photo taken by the Fronczaks shortly after they took custody of Paul.

LEFT: Paul in the early 1980s, before he began the search for his true identity.

ABOVE: Paul with his father Chester and his brother Dave in a 1980s family photo.

ABOVE: Paul played in several bands in his twenties, but couldn't share his passion for music with his family.

RIGHT: Paul in his twenties on one of the many motorcycles he has owned.

ABOVE: Paul meeting the team of genealogists, led by CeCe Moore (second from left), in 2016.

ABOVE: Genealogist Michelle Trostler in front of the "wall of stickies" she assembled for Paul's case.

ABOVE: Paul meeting some of his relatives for the first time in a Pennsylvania restaurant in 2015.

RIGHT: Paul poses with Lenny Rocco on the day they met in 2015.

LEFT: Paul and Lenny Rocco, a doo-wop singer, performing together for the first time in 2015.

RIGHT: Paul looking through old family photos with Joy and Sandy Rocco in 2015.

LEFT: A pregnant Marie Rosenthal with her daughter in the early 1960s.

RIGHT: Paul approaching a trailer in New Jersey in search of a relative in 2015.

LEFT: Paul visits his parents' gravesite in a southern New Jersey cemetery in 2015.

RIGHT: Paul in an empty lot in Atlantic City during an underground radar sweep in 2016.

LEFT: Paul searching for human remains in an Atlantic City lot in 2016.

LEFT: Paul in 2016 on the spot where he was abandoned in 1965, outside what was then McCrory's department store.

ABOVE: Paul with his wife, Michelle, and their daughter, Emma Faith.

LEFT: Paul with his daughter, Emma Faith. "She's the reason I needed to find the truth," Paul says.

15

A POSSIBLE SECOND COUSIN MATCH—that was big. If Alan Fisch and I were indeed second cousins, that meant we shared a set of great-grandparents. And only one *great* was far less daunting than three. The connection didn't seem all that ancient to me. It was just three generations back. If we could get Alan's family tree and work backwards from his parents, we might be able to find the common ancestor who would lead me to my own birth parents.

Over at Ancestry headquarters in Provo, Crista Cowan also noticed Alan pop up as a possible second cousin match for me. It was an exciting moment. Since my family tree was essentially nonexistent, having Alan's tree would allow her to search for commonalities and possibly find even closer cousin matches. Crista immediately searched to see if Alan had added his family tree to the site.

But he hadn't. There was no tree at all. And that was unusual. Most people who signed up with Ancestry did so because of an interest in genealogy, and had likely already built out a partial family tree. But Alan hadn't. There was nothing there.

When I got Alan's message, I tried to find his family tree, too, but I couldn't. So I messaged him back and asked for his help.

"How do you think we match?" I asked.

Alan's response was a kick in the gut.

"I am adopted," he wrote. "I don't know any of my blood relatives."

There was no family tree, because Alan didn't even know who his parents were. He was, like me, a virtual clean slate.

I was stunned. It seemed unfair, almost impossible. My closest DNA match yet, and he was as clueless about his heritage as I was. What were the chances of that?

Still, if Alan was adopted, there had to be official adoption records. Maybe we could learn the identities of his parents that way. But Alan told me his adoption records were sealed. "I don't know much," he admitted. "All I know is that my birth mother is from Philadelphia and she was sixteen when she had me."

That was strike two—no access to his records.

There had to be something else there, I told myself. Some other way to identify our blood connection. *He's the guy*, I found myself thinking. *He has to be the guy who helps me solve this.* "If we are second cousins," I messaged him, "this could be a major breakthrough in my life. If you have a moment, please google Paul Joseph Fronczak and let me know what you think."

A short while later, after he'd watched the first *20/20* report, Alan responded.

"This is really something," he wrote. "Here is my home number. I want to learn as much as I can about my birth family and heritage."

You and me both, Cousin.

—⚬⚬⚬—

I wasn't the only one who matched with Alan Fisch.

Clear across the country from me, in Philadelphia, Aimee Gourley—formerly Aimee Rinaldi—checked her Ancestry account in early 2014 and saw Alan's name. He was listed as a possible third cousin.

Aimee and Alan exchanged messages, and she learned he was adopted. She also learned he was Jewish, and his birth mother lived in Philadelphia. To me, those two bits of information didn't seem helpful.

But to Aimee, they did.

That's because Aimee had something I didn't—a remarkable oral family history handed down to her by her grandfather Albert Rinaldi.

Long before the boom in amateur genealogy, Albert Rinaldi had enchanted his young granddaughter with vivid and colorful tales of her ancestors. Not just a few stray details, but living, breathing stories.

"He knew everything," says Aimee. "He was an awesome source of family history. He and I would walk around cemeteries and look at grave sites together. He would take me down memory lane and fill me in on all the old family stories. It was really neat."

Albert's stories were even more valuable to her because of how private most immigrant families were. "A lot of families didn't even put out obituaries because they didn't want their family history known," she says. Fairly often, women who married into immigrant families were quickly lost to the records, showing up nowhere. Finding a male ancestor was hard enough, but finding his wife might be impossible.

But not for Albert Rinaldi—he knew who was married to whom.

Not surprisingly, Aimee caught the genealogy bug and signed up with Ancestry to build her own tree. One day, she was contacted by a man named David. "We are a second cousin match," David wrote. "Can I look at your tree?" Aimee learned a bit more about him, and quickly got the feeling she knew where he fit in. "He messaged me one day and said his mother never knew who her father was," Aimee recalls. "So he never knew who his biological grandfather was. All he knew was his grandmother had been a nurse in New York."

When she heard that detail, Aimee took a chance.

"Did your grandmother's name happen to be Cody?" she asked.

David was sitting in a dentist's chair at the time, and nearly knocked over the tray of instruments.

"OMG!" he messaged back. "I'll call you when I get out of here."

Aimee knew the name Cody because her grandfather had told her a story.

The story was about Albert's brother, who had a child with a nurse from New York named Cody. From that one detail, Aimee was able to help David fill in a good part of his family tree. She was even able to send him a photo of his biological grandparents together in Coney Island. "There they are, this happy couple in a little roller-coaster car," she says. "David couldn't believe it."

When the Alan Fisch match came up, Aimee agreed to help him figure out his ancestry. Right away, she had a strong feeling she knew who he was, too.

First, there was the fact that he was born in Philadelphia. Aimee's roots traced back to the Philadelphia area, too. Then there was Alan's Jewish heritage. His DNA test showed Alan was 79 percent Jewish.

That should have been a major problem, because Aimee's family was primarily Italian, with only 2 percent Jewish ancestry. Based on that discrepancy alone, it didn't make much sense that Aimee and Alan could be related. The only way it would make sense was if there had been a crossover—a Jewish person wandering into Aimee's family tree. But that would have happened long ago, and identifying the crossover could be difficult.

Except that Aimee already *knew* about the crossover. She'd heard about it during one of her walks through the cemetery with her grandfather.

"He told me about his uncle marrying a Jewish woman," Aimee says. "And this was *way* back. My grandfather was born in 1914, so his uncle was *really* old. But my grandfather knew the story, and he told it to me. And from that one little memory, I knew there was a Jewish connection there."

Now, all she had to do was build it out. But Aimee is a pharmacy technician and a busy mother of three, and she could work on Alan's tree only in whatever free time she could find. Bit by bit, the project got pushed to the back burner. The connection was there. The tree could be built.

It just wasn't going to happen overnight.

—⁓—

By then, I understood that a large part of my search involved waiting. I understood it, but I hated it. Alan Fisch entered the picture eight months after I'd gone public with my story, and my fantasy about a quick resolution had long since been shot down. But it was still difficult dealing with the long lulls. Progress in the DNA world is measured in weeks, even months, not days. Even a breakthrough like Alan Fisch is really just raw material for a long and grinding discovery process that might or might not prove fruitful. So I knew I had to be patient, but that had never been my strong suit.

If several days went by without any news or developments, I'd get aggravated and irritable. The longer the lull, the more distant and pre-occupied I'd become. Michelle noticed it, too. She saw how a small bit of good news could lift my spirits and make life seem nearly normal again, and how a stretch of dead silence could shut me down completely and fill our house with gloom.

Because I was so bad at waiting, I took to the internet and immersed myself in every detail of my case. If I couldn't do anything else, at least I could do that. We had a small room on the second floor of our house that we used as an office, and I'd go there and open my laptop and google "Paul Fronczak" to get started. I did that every day. I'd look for any new mentions and stories and sites—*anything* that was even vaguely related to my search.

At first, I worked only after Emma went to bed, punching in new search topics and reading about cold cases and answering emails until two or three in the morning. Eventually, I started opening my laptop when Michelle and Emma and I were sitting around and talking and watching TV. Physically, I'd be there with them. But mentally, I was somewhere else. I don't think I realized how withdrawn I often was, and I'm not sure I could have stopped being that way, but there's no doubt that it was unfair to Michelle.

For one thing, Emma is a demanding child. A sweet, beautiful, wonderful, lovable, magical little girl, but demanding. She is inexhaustible, and she doesn't like playing alone, so she requires attention. As a teacher, Michelle was around children quite a bit. But Emma was the first child I'd ever spent a lot of time with, and I was unprepared for how much work was involved in raising her.

Even before I discovered I wasn't the Fronczak baby, Michelle and I argued a lot about Emma. But after I withdrew into my search, more of the burden of handling her fell to Michelle. She began to feel like my search might have actually been a welcome distraction for me. As if I'd given myself a hall pass, excusing me from the hard work of parenting.

"Paul, you can still do the search, but you can't do it morning, noon, and night," Michelle said. "We need you, too."

"I can't just stop," I said—the same answer I always gave.

"Where does it end, Paul?" Michelle asked. "What happens if you do find out? What then? Will it be over, or will you just keep going?"

"I don't know. I just need to find out first."

"You already know enough to know they didn't want you. If they wanted you, they wouldn't have done what they did. What more do you need to know?"

Sometimes, I didn't even answer her questions. I felt like Michelle didn't understand how damaging it was not to know your identity. At the same time, Michelle felt like my identity was already known—I was her husband and Emma's father first and foremost. *That* was the identity that mattered. We were a small family of three, but we were a family, and Michelle was fighting to preserve it. She didn't want to lose me to an unending search for something that might not be there.

In her mind, I was becoming obsessed.

In mine, I was doing what I needed to do for the sake of my family.

One night, Michelle and I had a pretty good fight about it all. I was frustrated and angry, and so was she. Michelle did a lot of yelling, and I argued back, though I'm not much a yeller. I don't really like to raise my voice. We went back and forth for a long time and got nowhere. At the end of it, Michelle just seemed weary and sad. She sat down on our bed and let out a sigh.

"You're doing to your family what your family did to you," she said. "They abandoned you, and you're abandoning us."

I didn't say anything back. I just hoped she wasn't right.

—᙮᙮᙮—

Both CeCe Moore and Crista Cowan dove into the task of building Alan Fisch's tree. They worked separately, with different approaches, but they were both relentless. Everyone had the feeling Alan might be a big breakthrough. I might not have always sensed it, but there was a new urgency to the process, now that I had a second cousin match.

CeCe was in constant contact with both Alan Fisch and Aimee Gourley, helping them fit all the pieces together. She wanted Alan to submit DNA samples to FamilyTree DNA and 23andMe. She believed his DNA signatures would help her locate more cousins to fill out both our trees. She sent him a kit, and he quickly mailed back his swab. Meanwhile, I made plans to meet Alan. I wanted to look him in the eye, shake his hand, size him up. I wanted to see if I'd feel a spark of recognition.

Luckily, Alan was every bit as excited about our newfound connection as I was. "Everywhere he went he'd tell people, 'I'm finally going to get to meet my parents,'" says his wife, Randi. "He believed this was the link to his family."

We made arrangements to meet in New York City, about an hour from where he lived. Alan would bring his wife, and I would bring mine. It would be a mini family reunion—or, more accurately, a family *union*. The whole thing was thrilling. Alan and I were about the same age. We got along well in our phone calls, and I felt like we could become friends. I could picture us at barbecues together.

Then we got more good news.

Alan's adoption records were sealed tight, and every time he'd tried to get them, he'd failed. He and Randi petitioned New York's Dutchess County to unseal them on medical grounds, but the request was denied. The Fisches contacted a lawyer, but they soon realized the battle to open the records would be long and costly—probably north of five thousand dollars. They never gave up, but they were running out of options.

Then producers for *20/20* took a crack at getting the records unsealed, and they succeeded. It didn't even take very long. The power of a major TV network, I guess. Just two days before I was set to fly to New York to meet Alan, I learned his adoption records would be opened in about a week. The records would likely reveal the identities of his birth parents, which would greatly speed up the process of building his family tree. It was an exhilarating moment, both for Alan and for me. Our mutual dream of finding our families had never seemed more reachable.

On February 12, 2014—the day before Alan and I would meet in New York City—I got a call from Randi. I assumed it was about some detail or other of the meeting.

But it wasn't. She had terrible news.

Alan Fisch was dead.

16

H E'D WOKEN UP and had trouble breathing. Randi came home from work and found him on his knees, struggling for air. He didn't want to go to the hospital, but Randi insisted. His daughter Jenna rode with him in the ambulance.

At the hospital, Alan was in good spirits. He told everyone in the ER that they had to fix him up quickly because he was going to New York City to meet his new cousin in a couple of days. Every nurse and technician heard his story.

The doctor who examined him found an occlusion—a blocked blood vessel—in his lungs. Alan was given clot-busting medication and spent a quiet night in the hospital. But the blood clot was moving, from his lungs to his heart.

The next morning, Alan had a heart attack and passed away.

There were no warning signs. He'd seemed healthy. He was active and energetic. But because he was adopted, he didn't know his medical history. He had no way of knowing what was inside him, waiting to happen.

Only much later did Randi learn that two other members of Alan's biological family had died under similar circumstances.

When Randi called me from the hospital, I thought I had misheard her. Alan passed away? It didn't seem possible. It made zero sense. Alan was young. He was coming to meet me in a day. He was excited. I'd just heard his voice, heard him laugh. He was *here*, a part of this, right alongside us all. And suddenly he wasn't.

I didn't know what to say to Randi. I could hear the shock in her voice, the disbelief. I told her I was sorry and I tried to say something more that would help her, and maybe help me, too, but I couldn't form a thought, much less a sentence. We were in a conversation neither of us could comprehend.

I got through work that day, somehow. Later, as I drove home, a gold and amber brightness bathed the windshield. It was a spectacular sunset. More intense, more alive than usual. It made me think about Alan, and how he'd never see a sunset again. The old saying—we're not promised tomorrow. I felt a wave of sadness and I pulled over and cried. I'd never met him and I didn't really know him, but I felt his loss. I felt pain for his wife and for his children. I thought of Emma losing me, and it was unbearable. What must they have felt?

And the grim unfairness of it—how could Alan get so close to his goal, and not be given the chance to grab it? And had it even been a worthwhile goal? Alan couldn't have known he had so little time left, but had he known, would he have spent a single precious second of it chasing after his biological family? Wouldn't he have devoted all his energy, all his being, to the family right in front of him—the family who loved him, and whom he loved?

On the day Alan passed, Randi Fisch told her children she was canceling the trip to New York City. Without her husband, there was no reason to go. But Alan's children—Jason, Jenna, and Jessica—felt otherwise. They didn't want their father's dream to end this way.

"Dad would want us to still go," Jason said to his mother. "Let's do it to honor Dad. Let's do it to make his wish come true."

So it was that Randi and Jason drove down to Manhattan to meet me. We got together in a hotel room, and we sat on a sofa and talked. There was a lot of crying and head shaking. We talked about the kind of man Alan was, and about the impossibility that he wasn't sitting there with us. Jason, a tough, square-shouldered kid, declared that he and his family wanted to stay involved in the search for Alan's birth parents. Alan's passing only made them more determined to learn the truth. I thought they showed incredible bravery, and I was moved by their strength and their love for Alan.

I think it was only then that I truly realized something—if Alan and I were related, so were Jason and I.

Jason became the second blood relative I'd ever met.

A few days later, Alan's adoption records were unsealed. He missed seeing them by less than a week. Alan's birth certificate did indeed list the name of his biological mother, Melinda.

The space for his father, however, was blank.

That was a setback, but with any luck we could learn the identity of Alan's birth father from Melinda. She still lived in the same area in Philadelphia where she'd lived when she was sixteen and had Alan. No one knew how she'd react to learning she'd be tracked down—or to hearing the son she gave up was dead. We all had our fingers crossed.

Sadly, it didn't help. Melinda flatly denied she was Alan's mother, and refused to take a DNA test. No matter how hard she was pushed, and no matter how conclusive the evidence to the contrary, she stuck to her story—the birth certificate was wrong, she wasn't the mother, go away. CeCe found her brother and asked him to take the test, but he, too, said no.

Still, Alan Fisch, at least, had tested his DNA before he passed.

Then CeCe heard back from 23andMe, the company that had tested Alan. His sample, she was told, was unusable. He'd likely submitted too much saliva, just as I had when my first Ancestry test failed. All I had to do was send in another sample. But with Alan, we got only one shot, and it failed.

No father. No mother. A failed DNA test. I didn't want to, but I couldn't help but personalize what was happening. The tragedy was Alan's death, and everything else was trivial by comparison. But for the first time, I felt like events might be conspiring against me. As if, on some level I couldn't understand, I wasn't supposed to learn the truth of who I am.

On Sunday, February 16, 2014, Alan Fisch was buried in the Beacon Hebrew Alliance Cemetery, in Fishkill, New York. His loved ones sat shivah in his home at sundown. The family asked that, instead of flowers, people donate to the Beacon Volunteer Ambulance Corps. Randi still visits Alan's resting place often, and she passes the cemetery every day on her way to work.

"We miss you," she'll say aloud as she drives by. "We miss you a lot."

I learned something about Alan Fisch a few weeks after he passed. I learned he was a drummer. He started playing when he was young, and he still had a drum kit in his basement that he liked to bang on every now and then. He even taught his young grandson how to play.

Alan loved music. He had it in him, in his genes, in his blood. Just like me.

—◊◊◊—

Aimee Gourley hadn't forgotten about Alan Fisch. As busy as she was, she found time to triangulate Alan's DNA matches to try to find the right connection. She traded hundreds of emails with CeCe Moore, comparing their research and bouncing theories off each other. She also stayed in touch with the Fisch family, especially Alan's daughter-in-law, Erica, another genealogy buff.

In mid-February 2014, Aimee got a call from Erica.

"I want to let you know that Alan passed away," Erica told her.

"Oh, no!" Aimee said. "Oh, I'm so sorry."

Perhaps Erica guessed that, now that Alan was gone, Aimee would be dropping the case. But that's not what happened.

"I'm not giving up," Aimee told her. "We're going to find Alan's father."

In fact, Aimee already had an idea where Alan's dad might fit into the tree.

She started with the assumption that she and Alan could be connected on either of two lines on her paternal side—the Rinaldis or the Roccos. Then she remembered one of her grandfather Albert's stories—the one about his uncle John Rocco marrying a Jewish woman named Sarah Tuckojenski sometime around the turn of the century.

That was the Jewish connection that explained how Aimee—who had less than 2 percent Jewish ancestry on the Rinaldi side—and Alan, who was 79 percent Jewish, could be related. Her connection to Alan had to be on the side with the singular Jewish crossover—the Rocco side.

One of her grandfather's old stories, told on one of their cemetery strolls, had echoed out of the past to help Aimee now, in her search for Alan's birth father.

Still, Aimee had to prove her Rocco theory was correct, which meant finding living Rocco relatives to take DNA tests. She shared her research with CeCe, and together they narrowed the field of possible candidates. Who made sense? Who fit the profile? Who was the right age to be Alan's father?

In March 2014, Aimee, CeCe, and members of the Fisch family got on a conference call. The goal of the call was to share developments and come up with names of relatives to test. One person emerged as a good candidate—a man named Lenny Rocco. His grandparents were John and Sarah Rocco, and he was in his seventies. CeCe researched him and discovered he grew up in Philadelphia, not far from where Alan's birth mother grew up.

"I think Leonard Rocco is very likely a close relative," CeCe wrote in an update not long after the conference call. "Leonard's father, Thomas, also married a Jewish woman, and they all grew up in Philadelphia, which makes them strong candidates to be Alan's close family."

—∿∿—

A week after Alan passed, I got an email from someone named Sam Miller. Sam was a successful software salesman living in Dallas; he'd been the thirtieth employee in Ross Perot's data company. He was about my age, and he had a wife and kids. He wrote to tell me that he'd seen the 20/20 report about my case, and was shocked by the age-progression photo-image of the real Paul Fronczak.

Sam said he looked *exactly* like the photo.

But it wasn't just the resemblance that led him to believe he might be the real Paul. Like me, he was born and raised in Chicago. He went through life believing his mother and his father, who died of pancreatic cancer when Sam was three, were his birth parents. Then, after his mother died, he developed a serious kidney problem and searched for a cousin who could help him understand his family's medical history.

"Can you tell me about my mom's kidney problem?" he asked the cousin.

"What kidney problem?"

"I think my mother and my aunt had the same kidney disease as me."

"Wait a minute," the cousin said. "You mean your mother never told you you were adopted?"

It was a thunderbolt, but only at first. The news led Sam to cycle back through his memories, looking for all the signs he'd ignored. He didn't look at all like his brother. As a child he would recoil when his mother tried to hug him. He always felt like the odd man out in his family. When he was sixteen, he woke up in the middle of the night, turned off the house alarm, stood in the backyard swimming pool, and looked up to the heavens.

"Am I an alien?" he asked aloud, pleading for an answer. "I don't belong here. Please come take me home."

I knew how he felt. I understood the question. I understood the feeling of being part of something else, something that wasn't your life.

But there was more. Sam discovered his adoptive mother had gone to great lengths to make it look like she'd actually given birth to him. She walked around with a pillow beneath her dress to make her look pregnant. She wore the pillow to the hospital on the day of the adoption, and left it there when she brought Sam home. "One day you weren't here," his brother told him, "and the next day, you were."

Finally, Sam dug up his baby pictures, and compared them to the lone hospital photo of Baby Paul.

"It was jaw-dropping," Sam says. "The photos were identical. I felt like I'd been hit in the head with a fry pan."

Sam called ABC and the FBI.

—⁓—

There was yet another wrinkle. Sam Miller was dying.

When he was twenty-seven he'd been diagnosed with adult poly-cystic kidney disease, and now his kidneys were failing. If he didn't get a transplant, he would likely die. The possibility that he could be the real Paul was like a last-second life raft.

"I thought, *This could be my biological family! This could be my big break!*" Sam says. "My daughter and son were terrified of losing me, and I was resigning myself to not being there to see them graduate college. But maybe I didn't have to die. Maybe this was my chance. I looked at the age progression and I thought, *This has to be me. I have to be the real Paul.*"

Sam and I exchanged emails, and he kept me posted about the FBI investigation and his failing health. I could tell it was an extremely emotional time for him and his family, but I also learned that Sam is an upbeat person who deals with difficult situations by finding the humor in them. When he was in the hospital and sliding further and further downhill, he'd throw fake cockroaches across his room just to frighten the nurses.

I was pulling for him—pulling for him hard. I wanted him to be the real Paul, and I wanted him to live. I imagined my parents leaping into action and helping their real son battle his disease. The circumstances fit—a Chicago upbringing, odd behavior by his mother, the same feelings of estrangement I had. Plus, he really did look uncannily like the age-progression photo. I mean, it might as well have been a photo of Sam. So why couldn't he be the real Paul? Weren't we due a lucky break?

Before Sam heard back from the FBI, the ABC producers stepped in. CeCe Moore arranged for Sam to take a DNA test, while ABC petitioned the state of Illinois for Sam's birth certificate, believing any discrepancy in the listing of his birth mother might bolster the case that he was stolen from the hospital. ABC cameras were filming when Sam got a call from an Illinois State official.

Sam was told his birth certificate listed his biological mother.

There was no discrepancy, no mystery to it. He had a real mother, and she wasn't Dora Fronczak. Plain and simple, he wasn't the real Paul.

Then CeCe got Sam's DNA test results back, and she called him to tell him that they, too, proved he wasn't Paul. Sam had trouble believing it. He'd been so certain. His resemblance to the age-progression photo, he told CeCe, "is really haunting me. Are you sure I'm not the real Paul?" CeCe gently explained how she knew beyond a doubt that he wasn't.

"I was crushed," Sam says. "I kept thinking what a wonderful thing it would be for the Fronczak family to finally find their son. I'd wanted it to be me, but that's just not the case."

Sam's condition worsened. He went on dialysis. Once again he resigned himself to dying. But then—another twist.

There was no record of anyone with the name of the biological mother listed on Sam's birth certificate. She had never existed. The certificate was fake.

Sam got a call from an FBI agent, who told him, "You still could be the kidnapped baby. Don't talk to anyone anymore. We want to swab you."

Two FBI agents pulled up to his house in a giant SUV. An agent swabbed his cheek and warned him again not to talk to the press anymore. Then they drove away.

Sam had new hope, and possibly new life.

Several days later, he got a call from the FBI.

"We have the results," an agent told him. "You are not Paul Fronczak."

—∞—

It was another devastating moment for Sam. I felt bad for him, and bad for my parents. It was hard to get so close to being able to give my parents an answer—to deliver to them the son they'd lost so long ago—and then have it all go away in an instant. The same pattern was playing out again: a steady buildup of optimism, followed by a quick, devastating crash. Hope, then despair, then more waiting.

I stayed in touch with Sam, and I hoped the publicity he received would help him find a new kidney. In fact, several people did phone in and offer him a kidney, but some didn't match, and others eventually changed their minds. One woman told Sam she wanted to do something great with her life, and saving him by giving him a kidney was the greatest thing she could think of. The woman tested, and she was a match. Sam allowed himself to be hopeful once again. But at the last minute, the woman's family talked her out of it.

"I got my affairs in order," Sam says. "I got ready to die."

Then something remarkable happened.

Sam's insurance agent interviewed a young man for a job with her agency, and told him she didn't think the position was right for him. "You just seem interested in a lot of other stuff," she said. The young man, an Iraq War veteran, didn't disagree, but said he wanted to work there anyway.

"God is telling me to take the job," he said. "And God is telling me that I need to save someone's life with a kidney."

The agent was shocked. She'd never met the man, and he knew nothing about Sam Miller. Yet here he was offering up a kidney.

"What blood type are you?" the insurance agent asked.

He had the same blood type as Sam, too.

The young man got tested and turned out to be a match with Sam. He gave him his kidney, and Sam is still alive today.

"I'm not out of the woods yet, and I don't know how long I'll be around, but I'm here now and that's what matters," Sam says. "My kids tell me they've never seen me happier."

Sam's ordeal and his good nature had a big effect on me. He was literally dying, yet he stayed upbeat and never stopped chasing his goal—to get a kidney and stay alive for his family. All that mattered to him was his family. He may have felt like an alien once, but he didn't anymore. He'd found his home, and it was wherever his wife and children were.

—⟶⟶—

I wanted to feel that way, too. I wanted to feel like my need to learn my identity and my desire to be a good husband and father were connected—that I was doing what I was doing *because* of my family. But it didn't always feel that way. My search was actually pulling me away from them.

Yet even though I could see it happening—could see my family straining at the seams—there was no way I could stop what I was doing. Something inside me, urgent and insistent, kept pushing me forward, pushing me to solve the mystery.

You need to know where you came from, this voice would say. Otherwise you'll be a vagrant all your life.

The highs and lows of my search only made things worse. The setbacks were getting more hurtful, the obsession more consuming. I was on the computer all the time, day and night. At work, I couldn't concentrate. I had less time for Michelle and less time for Emma. Still, I couldn't be pushed off my position—that nothing was more important in my life than learning who I was, and learning what happened to the real Paul. I needed Michelle to understand this, but she felt the cost of the search was too high. When things got really strained between us, we agreed to see a marriage counselor.

For me, that meant having the same argument, except somewhere else.

"I wish you would just walk away from this," Michelle said in one of the sessions. "Just stop it. Just. Stop."

But I don't think she really expected me to stop. Not deep down. By then, we were nearly one year into the search. She had to know there was no turning back.

—⁓—

Meanwhile, CeCe was busy building Alan Fisch's tree, trying to figure out how he and I and Aimee Gourley were connected. CeCe and Aimee decided she should DNA-test her father, and he came up as a match for both Alan and me.

Still, CeCe had to pinpoint the ancestral line that Alan and Aimee and I all shared in order to find closer living relatives to test. She focused on two sets of Aimee's great-great-grandparents—Generosa Rinaldi and her husband, and Thomas Rocco and his wife. The Rinaldi line and the Rocco line—somewhere along one of these lines were the answers I was looking for. But each line represented hundreds of possibilities. Somehow, CeCe had to narrow the search.

With Aimee's help, she did just that, focusing on the line with the singular Jewish crossover—the Rocco line. That allowed CeCe to target Aimee's great-grandfather John Rocco and his four children, Bertha, Jean, David, and Thomas.

One of those four children had a son who lived in Philadelphia—the same place where Alan's biological mother, Melinda, lived.

The son was Lenny Rocco.

Aimee and CeCe found Lenny Rocco's Facebook page, and also a website for Rocco Mixed Martial Arts, a boxing and fitness business run by Lenny's son. They found photos of Lenny from his younger days, tan and shirtless and chiseled and hammering a heavy bag. They found a photo of young Lenny singing with a doo-wop group. On YouTube, they found a recent video of Lenny crooning "Up on the Roof" while scenes of him sparring in a boxing ring played. Lenny had a full head of black hair and he looked like Frankie Valli. His voice was beautiful.

He also had a strong and prominent jaw. Much like mine.

17

LENNY ROCCO WAS A SOLID LEAD, but there was a snag. There always was.

CeCe and Aimee put together a document trail that traced the paternal Rocco line back to the Salerno region of Campagna, in southern Italy. CeCe was convinced that if Alan Fisch was Lenny Rocco's son, then Alan's son, Jason, would carry an Italian Y-chromosome signature. She tested Jason on his Y chromosome—but the results showed all of Jason's Y-DNA haplogroup matches were from Eastern Europe, not Italy.

That was a problem. As far as CeCe knew, there was no historic Y-chromosome crossover from Eastern Europe to Italy for Jason's particular Y-DNA signature. It didn't fit any pattern that she knew of. CeCe asked Bennett Greenspan, the CEO of FamilyTree DNA, if he'd ever seen Jason's Y-chromosome signature in a male from southern Italy, and Bennett said he hadn't, either. CeCe pored through academic journals and found no evidence that Jason's haplogroup subclade had *ever* been found in Italy. There was simply no known or documented historic migration that had carried Jason's particular Y-DNA signature from Eastern Europe to Italy.

In other words, based on the Y-DNA, it didn't seem likely that Lenny Rocco could be Alan's father.

Still, CeCe wanted to DNA-test Lenny to be sure. She'd wanted to test him since she discovered he grew up in Philadelphia. But she needed to be careful with how she used the few remaining DNA kits she had left. CeCe had been paying for the first few kits out of her own pocket, and had received a donated kit from 23andMe to test me with. Later, her friend Bennett Greenspan offered to donate more kits. Still, her supply was limited. Before she sent one out for Lenny Rocco, she needed more research to point toward him.

—⁓—

Around this time, after months of working on my case on her own, CeCe held the monthly meeting of a group she cofounded, the North San Diego County Genealogical Society—specifically their DNA Interest Group—at the Georgina Cole Library in Carlsbad. After the meeting, she went for drinks at BJ's Restaurant and Brewhouse with two women from the meeting she'd become friendly with. One of them was Michelle Milledge Trostler.

Michelle grew up in Palo Alto, across the street from the birthplace of Silicon Valley—the tiny garage where Bill Hewlett and Dave Packard built their first audio oscillator in 1938. Her parents were both computer programmers at Lockheed Aerospace. Michelle earned a B.A. in sociology and women's studies at the University of California, San Diego, and added a master's in sociology. Then she quit the field and wound up at Sun Microsystems during the infancy of cloud computing. She was a marketer with the brain of a techie, adept at synthesizing and applying huge chunks of information. "I love crunching data," Michelle says. "I know it's dorky, but I love an orderly spreadsheet."

She was also passionate about genealogy, which required some of the same skills. When she was young she learned she was a direct descendant of Benjamin Franklin (he was her sixth great-grandfather).

Her family even had some of Ben's old furniture in their house, and often lectured her with Franklinisms like "A penny saved is a penny earned." The Franklin connection spurred her love of genealogy, which eventually landed her in the DNA Interest Group with CeCe. From their interaction in the class, CeCe could tell Michelle knew her stuff.

At another meeting of the group in 2014, CeCe talked about my case. "It was amazing," says Michelle. "It was like a jigsaw puzzle with a million pieces, and most of the pieces are missing. No mother or father. No definition for the maternal side versus the paternal side. No real idea of what's going on. It was like the greatest puzzle of all time." Michelle asked CeCe if she could help her with my case, and when CeCe said yes, she jumped right in.

The other woman having drinks with CeCe and Michelle at BJ's was Carol Isbister Rolnick, who lived a few minutes from Michelle.

Like Michelle, Carol had a young son and daughter. When Carol broke her leg several years earlier and couldn't drive, Michelle gave her lifts to their sons' baseball practices. The boys became buddies, and so did they. A Wisconsin native, Carol had an interest in genealogy that stretched back to her youth, sparked when she read her grandfather's memoir. She had a background in marketing and had spent some twenty years working as an event planner. But after two decades she was burned out and ready for a new career challenge. She tested her autosomal DNA to learn more about her family history, and began attending the monthly DNA Interest Group meetings in Carlsbad. At the first meeting she went to, a dynamic speaker—CeCe Moore—changed her life.

"It was like the skies opened up," she says. "I just got it. I could relate to everything CeCe was saying. I understood it and I wanted to know how I could be part of this dynamic new field. How I could become a genetic genealogist. Right then I decided I wanted to do this for a living."

Carol brought her friend Michelle Trostler along with her to the meetings. She was as eager to work on my case as Michelle was, but then her husband lost his job, and Carol's career change was put on hold while she went back to work as a marketer for a local burger chain, Islands. Her passion for genealogy, though, never waned. She kept going to the DNA Interest Group meetings, and she pitched in to help Michelle and CeCe with my case whenever she could. Eventually, she worked on my case pretty much every day.

Twenty-seven hundred miles away, in Maryland, a woman named Allison Demski was working as a "search angel," a volunteer who does non-DNA research—census records, property deeds, registries, certificates—on DNA-based cases. Like so many people, she built her own family tree when she was younger and got hooked. She worked as a volunteer paramedic and became a foster parent for many children, most of whom were born addicted to drugs. She had a busy, bustling life—she and her husband are the parents of three children, and she also runs a medical transcription business. Still, somehow, she found time for her passion.

Allison signed up with a private Facebook group called Search Squad—volunteers who assist adoptees in finding their birth families. She helped nearly a hundred adoptees learn the truth about their heritage. "It was incredibly emotional and powerful work," she says. "Every case has its own little nuance that makes it special. And along the way these people become like family to me."

Eventually, Allison began doing DNA analysis, too. One day, CeCe Moore joined a Facebook discussion of one of Allison's cases. They clicked and started working together, with Allison joining CeCe's DNA Detectives team. Before long, Allison was helping build some family trees on my case. When Allison joined the team she brought a host of invaluable research and analysis skills, as well as an uncanny adeptness at calling people and convincing them to take DNA tests.

So it was that four remarkable women—CeCe, Michelle, Carol, and Allison—became *my* search angels. They weren't getting paid, and they had to squeeze their complicated DNA crunching into already packed schedules. They were all mothers of young children, and they often had to find an hour or two in between baseball and soccer practices and games. Sometimes they did their work late at night, sitting up in bed with their laptops, or in another room so they wouldn't wake their husbands. Sometimes they put my case ahead of family obligations. Michelle Trostler found a quiet corner to work on my case toward the end of her grandmother's memorial service. Communicating mainly through Facebook messages, they never stopped digging, never stopped building, never stopped trying to make the puzzle fit.

Incredibly, and to my great fortune, I'd happened across four women who cared about my case every bit as much as I did, and maybe even more.

—⁂—

The team's strategy with my case was triangulation. Triangulation means determining the location of a point in a territory by measuring its closeness to the sides of triangles overlapping in that territory. The more family trees the team could gather and compare, the better chance they had of pinpointing where I fit into the great big jumble of people.

It was grueling, laborious work. Michelle devoted herself to inviting all of my DNA matches to share their trees with me. I had a thousand matches on one site alone, and at least another thousand in the other two company's databases. The vast majority of those were distant and not likely to be helpful, or even were false hits, but the team was taking no chances. So Michelle sat down and individually invited each match. She found that if she really pushed it she could do about one hundred invites an hour, and she didn't stop until every name on the list was checked.

But that was just the beginning of the process.

Convincing people to share their family trees is difficult, and a little persuasion is often required. So Michelle found many of the candidates on Facebook and sent them messages encouraging them to help out. Sometimes a match would be anonymous, hidden behind a nondescript Ancestry username—JohnSmith339, for example. Michelle would then search other websites and genealogy blogs for the same username, and try to identify the person that way.

"I'm a genetic genealogist working with your match, Paul Joseph Fronczak," Michelle wrote in her messages to the invitees. "Paul was abandoned at 18 months in a shopping mall in Newark, NJ. We are looking for his birth parents. We are making progress, but we need your help. You are a 2nd to 4th cousin match for Paul, and that is the best he has."

In the end, only about 20 percent of my one thousand matches agreed to share their family trees. But that was a really good start. It allowed CeCe and Michelle to begin studying the new trees for names that reappeared. CeCe had notebooks full of surnames and ancestral couples that repeated in the trees of my matches, and spreadsheets with thousands of shared DNA segments mapped to my chromosomes. Meanwhile, Michelle covered an entire wall in her home office in Carlsbad with yellow and white stickies bearing the names of possibly relevant matches. "The little stickies were matches and the big ones were definite ancestors," she says. "The wall looked like something you'd see in a psycho's house."

I'm not sure I understood how hard CeCe and Michelle were working on my behalf until later, when I got a good look at their research. For instance, I learned that in May 2014, they got a big break when Ancestry.com introduced a feature allowing users to attach my DNA numbers directly to the trees of other users, as long as they were granted temporary editor status, rather than spend three to five hours building that tree from scratch, which was what they'd been doing.

I hadn't realized that scrutinizing each of my potential matches took hours and hours and hours. Multiply that by two hundred trees and you get a sense of what the search was like. Their devotion—and sheer stamina—was remarkable and humbling.

Michelle, by her own admission, became just about as obsessed with my case as I was. Before she started working with CeCe, Michelle was diagnosed with Lyme disease. The effects were crippling. She was deeply fatigued, and most days it was all she could do to crawl out of bed. Still, when the opportunity to join CeCe and work on my case arrived, Michelle didn't hesitate. "I was still extremely sick with this life-sapping disease, but I could sit at a desk and punch a keyboard, so it was perfect," she says. "I wanted to prove to myself that I could still do something worthwhile with my life."

The deeper she dove into my case, the more consumed she became. She wound up spending less time with her husband and children—"I ignored them," in her words—to keep triangulating family trees and inch closer to a solution.

"Why are you doing this to your family?" her husband asked her one night. "You're not even getting paid!"

"I have to do this," Michelle replied. "We have to find Paul's parents. We are getting closer."

That was an argument I understood well.

Sometime around the middle of 2014, with both CeCe's team and Crista Cowan at Ancestry working on my case, the quest to solve the mystery became a kind of race. No one really talked about it, but I could tell it was happening.

It wasn't that CeCe and Ancestry were rivals—in fact, they work together quite often. It was that genetic genealogists are a meticulous, goal-oriented breed. They devote great amounts of time and energy to finding a single connection—a single name out of millions—and, understandably, they take great pride when they succeed. Think of how you'd react after several months of searching a haystack and finally finding the needle. As weeks turned into months and leads came and went, the search for my birth parents became more urgent, more intense for everyone. An unasked question hung in the air.

Who—if anyone—would get to the finish line first?

—⁊⁊⁊—

In the spring and summer of 2014, CeCe and Michelle spent weeks pulling in more and more family trees. I'd get a message from someone willing to share their tree with me and forward it to them. Michelle took people's DNA data and added it to a massive spreadsheet. People who shared the same segment of DNA were arranged into groupings. CeCe's spreadsheets and Michelle's stickies multiplied.

My Ancestry page produced a bunch of potential matches from Tennessee. Michelle triangulated all the Tennessee hits and attached my DNA to their trees, looking for any ancestors who matched any of my other DNA matches. Two Tennesseans—Thomas Bean and his grandmother Betty Towle Bean—were both good matches for me, and had a well-built family tree. CeCe and Michelle attached my DNA to their tree, expecting to see shared ancestor hints.

But none emerged, and that was baffling. The only conclusion was that the tree was somehow incorrect. They dug deeper, trying to see precisely how I was connected to the Beans. Then they found a segment on chromosome 15—one of the twenty-three pairs of chromosomes in humans—that was shared by the three of us. This is what it looked like on a spreadsheet:

COMPARISON TO PAUL FRONCZAK	CHR	START POINT	END POINT	cM	#SNPs
BTB (grandmother of TB)	15	29,000,000	63,000,000	45.2	7550
TB	15	30,875,030	61,043,338	35.7	68395
BTB	15	65,000,000	91,000,000	29.4	4920
TB	15	76,197,344	89,012,705	17.5	93396

This mass of numbers meant that Thomas, his grandmother, and I shared genetic information on chromosome 15 starting at about 29 megabase pairs (a unit of length that measures the size of segment matches on DNA or RNA) and ending at about 63 megabase pairs.

In other words, we were definitely related.

These specific points of connection allowed CeCe and Michelle to see who else matched our chromosome 15 segment. The more people who matched us at that exact segment, the more likely it was that one common ancestor would emerge.

An Ancestry user named graycan came in as a 35 Mbp to 50 Mbp match—but graycan's family tree didn't provide any common ancestors, either.

A woman whose father was an American soldier and whose mother was Korean matched us at the same segment, but she couldn't help because she didn't know the identity of her father.

A user named dehill33 matched us, too, but he didn't know who his great-grandfather was, preventing Michelle from tracing our connection any further back. When you can't move backwards on a tree anymore, genealogists call it a brick wall. The mysterious Tennessee ancestor who connected all of us was hiding behind that wall.

A few more people who matched us at that segment popped up, and together they formed what Michelle called the East Tennessee Mystery Group. She and CeCe spent months and months making phone calls, sending emails, comparing trees, and ruling out matches, all trying to find the single connecting link. Solving the Tennessee mystery, they believed, could solve the Fronczak mystery, too.

—⁂—

In Philadelphia, Aimee Gourley stayed on the Lenny Rocco lead. She knew from her grandfather Albert that the Roccos had settled in Philadelphia and Atlantic City. So she called her cousin Tony, who'd spent time with the Rocco clan when he was younger. Tony remembered going to Atlantic City to visit his aunt Bertha Rocco and her husband, Augie, a saltwater taffy maker. He remembered Bertha yelling at Augie because he took Tony to his shop to teach him how to make the taffy.

Tony also knew about Lenny Rocco, and he confirmed that Lenny grew up in South Philadelphia—and likely went to the same high school as Alan Fisch's birth mother.

The same high school. Could that be just a coincidence?

Aimee also remembered her grandfather telling her that his uncle John Rocco was a boxer who fought under the name Tommy Murphy. John's 1932 death certificate listed his occupation as "bodybuilder." She knew Lenny Rocco was in the boxing business, so that was another connecting factor—maybe boxing was in the Rocco blood.

A single thought formed in Aimee's mind: *Lenny is Alan Fisch's father.*

Aimee shared her Lenny Rocco research with CeCe, and also with Crista at Ancestry. Crista had seen Aimee pop up as a match for me, and she called her and helped her build out her already impressive family tree. With Aimee's help, Crista was hoping to tell the full story of the great-great-grandparents—Antonio Rinaldi and Maria Rocco—who connected Aimee and me. Ship manifests and other documents showed that Antonio emigrated from Italy to the United States in 1891. Maria came in 1898. Both were teenagers, and both were part of what's called a chain migration—family members coming over separately across several years.

In 1900, Antonio and Maria got married in Philadelphia, uniting the Rinaldis and the Roccos. One of the men on that line, Lenny Rocco, was the man CeCe and Aimee identified as their leading candidate to be Alan Fisch's father.

Now it was time for Aimee to reach out to Lenny and ask him to take a DNA test. But Aimee didn't feel right calling Lenny out of the blue; she wasn't an experienced caller like Michelle or Allison. Instead, Alan's daughter-in-law, Erica, made the call.

When Erica reached Lenny, she came right out and told him Alan Fisch might be his son.

"Uh, I don't think so," Lenny said.

Erica asked if he knew Alan's birth mother, Melinda. Lenny thought about it.

"I knew her from the neighborhood, yeah," he finally said. "I was at a party with her once. So yeah, I guess it's possible."

Finally, would Lenny agree to take a DNA test?

There was a really good chance he'd say no. Not everyone is

thrilled to hear about a child they never knew they had. Some people would just as soon make the whole matter disappear.

But Lenny didn't feel that way.

"Sure," he told Erica, "I'll take the test."

Crista, who unlike CeCe had a large supply of DNA kits, sent one to Aimee to give to Lenny Rocco.

—⟋⟍—

The Fisches made plans to drive down to Philadelphia to meet Lenny Rocco face-to-face. On a Saturday, Randi and her children stopped first to meet Aimee Gourley at Aimee's mother's house, about an hour north of Philadelphia. The next day, they drove to see Lenny at his daughter Lenai's place. They knocked on the front door, and a gracious Lenai led them inside.

A few seconds later, they saw Lenny Rocco.

Broad shoulders, thick build, receded eyes.

And Lenny fixed his gaze on Alan Fisch's son, Jason.

Broad shoulders, thick build, receded eyes.

"I knew that very second we were related," Lenny would say.

Before they could be certain they were family, Lenny and Jason hugged as if they were.

The Fisches gave Lenny the DNA kit, which he soon sent out.

If Lenny did indeed prove to be Alan's father, that meant that my second-cousin connection to Alan would likely make me a first cousin once removed to Lenny. Lenny would become my closest known relative—someone I shared as much as 6.25 percent of my DNA with. Lenny and I would be family! Indisputable relatives!

The thought of that was breathtaking.

What's more, identifying Lenny as the connection between Alan and me would theoretically clear a straight path to identifying my birth parents. If Lenny was my first cousin once removed, one of his aunts or uncles should lead directly to my mother or father. By testing any of Lenny's other first cousins, I could find my mother's or father's name. I could find out where I came from, and what happened to me fifty years ago.

It could actually be that close.

Weeks passed without word about Lenny's test. Aimee waited and waited, hoping her hunch proved correct. Every day, she logged on to Ancestry.com to look for any new matches on Lenny's page. But his page never changed.

Until, one morning, there was a change.

It was right there in black and white. Simple and official.

Lenny Rocco appeared as the father of Alan Fisch.

18

IT WAS A TURNING POINT. Alan's name popping up beneath Lenny as his son was like a spotlight being turned on in a dark room. Still lots of blackness, but suddenly a lot of clarity, too.

CeCe Moore saw Lenny's name turn up and shook her head. All her instincts had told her that Lenny was the one. Way back in early 2014, before anyone was even focused on Lenny, CeCe was right there with Aimee Gourley in believing he was the crucial link. But in the end, she simply couldn't go against what the science seemed to be telling her.

"The [Rocco/Fisch] Y chromosome *isn't* Italian," she marveled in another Facebook message after Lenny was revealed to be Alan's father. "Somehow an Eastern European Y chromosome got into Central Italy!"

It was the first time the DNA had ever misled CeCe this way.

The Alan Fisch–Lenny Rocco connection was a historical anomaly. Long, long ago, someone in the Roccos' direct paternal line carried an Eastern European Y chromosome to central Italy. It could have been a single person, centuries ago, taking a lonely voyage across Europe and down into Italy—a previously undocumented trek that wound up shaping my ancestral history.

For all its hard science, genetics is still the story of restless humans on the move.

"I wish I hadn't let the Y-DNA dissuade me from the Rocco line," CeCe wrote in an email to me. "I was focused on it until then. Aimee and I were writing back and forth about it almost daily."

I felt bad for her. By then, CeCe had invested more than a year of her life in my case. She'd spent hundreds of hours poring over numbers, floating theories, pushing for more tests, calling in favors, filling notebooks, producing spreadsheets—and yet, because she didn't have an unlimited supply of DNA kits, she didn't test Lenny Rocco right away.

And now that Aimee had helped the team at Ancestry prove Lenny was Alan's father, CeCe felt certain it was only a matter of time before Ancestry—a big company with vast resources—cracked the case open. She saw the next steps in her head, and she knew they saw them, too. The race that no one overtly acknowledged had, CeCe feared, been won.

Still, CeCe and the team didn't let up for a moment. In fact, they doubled down. After the Lenny Rocco discovery, everyone went into overdrive. There were still a lot of people to be found, names to be added, DNA tested. Nothing had been solved yet. Lenny was a key piece, but he wasn't *the* key piece. Someone in time, a ghost long gone, was still hiding behind the brick wall.

And someone here now had to find them and drag them to daylight.

—⁂—

When I saw Alan's name beneath Lenny's, I went straight to YouTube to watch Lenny sing "Up on the Roof" again. Here was my cousin—*my cousin!*—crooning the Drifters hit on the roof of a gym in Philadelphia. "Lenny Rocco and the Rocks Present . . ." the video opens, to scenes of Lenny throwing jabs in a ring, still fit and barrel-chested in his seventies—a true tough guy. As I watched the video, another movie scene popped into my head—Robert DeNiro shadowboxing in *Raging Bull*. Lenny was like the older Jake LaMotta, a little bruised and battered but still kicking. And somehow I had wound up in his smoky, sweaty world.

But then, in the video, Lenny Rocco sings, and his voice is tender, almost a falsetto, floating above the synthesized beats.

At night, the stars put on a show for free
And, darling, you can share it all with me!

I was mesmerized. The guy could sing. He was stuck in a long-ago era, the 1950s, and some people might have found the whole thing cheesy, but not me. What I saw was a man singing his heart out, not caring if anyone was listening.

Lenny Rocco loved music. He had it in his blood.

Just like me.

I dug up what I could on Lenny. He'd been a doo-wop singer, and he'd had a couple of original hits. In the late 1950s he formed a group in Philadelphia called Lenny Rocco and the Rocks, with Barry Pouls (bass), Freddy Faulkner (falsetto), Bob Gardiner (baritone), Ross Matico (second tenor), and of course Lenny—lead singer. Their first recording was as a backup group for Rocco's wife, Sandy, the sister of his bass man.

The group put out a single in 1960—"Bon Bon" on the A-side, "Pistol Packin' Papa" on the flip. A year later came a hit song—"Sugar Girl"—followed by "Number One DJ," which Lenny composed on the spot in the recording studio, and which was his biggest hit. After just a few singles the Rocks broke up, and Lenny and his bandmate Freddy became a duo. He wrote and recorded another hit—"We Had a

Quarrel"—with a group called Robin Hood and his Merri Men, and later joined another group called the Casuals.

Lenny shows up on lots of doo-wop websites—a footnote to the history of the genre, but part of that history nonetheless. I found an old black-and-white photo of Lenny with his original bandmates, all in matching striped vests and slicked-back hair. They're just goofy, happy teenagers. Lenny's head is thrown back, his mouth wide open, singing to the heavens. I didn't know why he never became famous, but I did know his voice wasn't the problem. Lenny was a singer. His voice was beautiful.

And I wanted to play my bass guitar with him.

Lenny agreed to take the DNA test just before Christmas 2014, and the results came back early in the new year. That was a hopeful few weeks for me. Lenny was a piece of good news—he broke the lull. And that allowed me to relax just a bit, and try to be more present for my family.

—⁂—

It's hard for me to say if I succeeded. There was still a lot of tension between Michelle and me—still the same arguments about Emma and my availability. At best, I was constantly preoccupied, my attention never fully on my family. At worst, I was a shell of a husband and father. I may have been a bit less absent in those few weeks, but I was still a kind of ghost in my own home.

Even the news that Lenny was Alan's father—a huge victory in my eyes—wasn't something I could share with Michelle. She was happy to hear it, and happy for me, but she also believed that no answer would ever be enough—that every answer would only lead to more questions. And that, pretty much, was true. Michelle hoped that one day I might learn what I needed to know to finally stop searching and fix what I'd broken—our little family. She just didn't see that day on the horizon. Wherever I needed to get, I clearly wasn't there yet, and there was no telling when—and if—I'd ever get there. And so Michelle was weary—tired and scared and weary. The victories that kept me going only made the search seem more endless to her.

I understood that. I just didn't know what to do about it. I needed Michelle to be more supportive. And she needed me to be more involved with her and with Emma. There was no way both of those needs could be met. So the tension and the fighting continued.

In January 2015, I began sleeping in the guest room of our home.

—∾—

No one was more anxious to learn if Lenny was Alan's dad than Aimee Gourley. It had been her hunch, her grandfather's stories, and her sleuthing, together with CeCe's expertise and endless work, that had drawn Lenny out. So this was personal to her. She wanted to be right more than anything, because that meant a broken family could be put back together. A father could meet his son. Aimee considers herself a modest, private, quiet person—Zen-like, almost. But in the days when Lenny's test results were still out, she was a wreck. Sick to her stomach with nerves. "Sweating bullets," she says.

When the results came back, and Alan's name showed up under Lenny's, Aimee had the same thought as CeCe—Lenny should lead straight to my parents.

But she also understood that a lot more people had to be tested, and a lot of those people wouldn't want to do it. We'd gotten lucky with Lenny, but we couldn't count on that luck continuing. The answer was closer than ever, but someone still had to nail it down.

When the Fisches drove down from Beacon, New York, to meet Lenny and give him a DNA kit, Aimee couldn't go with them; she had another obligation. But now that Lenny had been proven to be Alan's father, Aimee started planning a big family reunion. She called Lenny's daughter Lenai, who lived ten minutes from Aimee's sister Kimberly, and they agreed to meet for coffee at a Starbucks. One coffee turned into several, and they sat trading stories for three hours.

Aimee asked Lenai to tell her about the Rocco clan.

"Well, a lot of them aren't really speaking at this time," Lenai said. "Not everyone is in touch."

Then Aimee zeroed in. CeCe had coached her and helped her understand what Lenny's match with Alan meant to my case. She knew Lenny's grandfather John Rocco had four children—Bertha, Jean, Thomas, and David—and she knew that one of them, Thomas, was Lenny's father. As CeCe had explained, that meant that Jean, Bertha, or David held the key to finding my identity (it couldn't be Thomas, because if he were my father, Lenny and I would be brothers or half brothers, not cousins). What, Aimee asked Lenai, could she tell her about Jean, Bertha, or David?

Lenai had the most to say about David Rocco.

"Not a nice person," she said. "He would make your blood run cold."

Aimee had heard this before, from her grandfather. "David Rocco is one of those characters you don't want to mess with," he told her. David was a boxer or a bodybuilder, and probably a gangster, too. Aimee got a sinking feeling about David Rocco. She didn't want our months of searching to lead back to him.

With Lenai's help, Aimee organized the Fisch-Rocco family reunion in March 2015. Around fifty people said they would come. That weekend, there was a big snowstorm on the East Coast, which knocked out some of the people who'd planned to fly up from Florida. A death in the family on Aimee's side kept some others away. But even so, thirty or so people gathered for brunch at a beer and burger place called TJ Smith's in Warrington, Pennsylvania, not far from Lenai's house.

It was a noisy affair. Lots of hugging, lots of stories, several toasts. But it wasn't conducive to serious conversations, so afterward Aimee and ten or twelve others went to Lenai's house for coffee and cake. There, Aimee pulled Lenny Rocco aside.

"So how about this Paul Fronczak thing?" Aimee said.

"That is something," Lenny said. "How can we help this guy?"

Lenny was friendly and open. He wanted to pitch in. He seemed genuinely touched to be meeting a grandson, and lots of other relatives, he didn't know he had. Aimee asked him to tell her about his uncle David Rocco.

"Oh yeah, Uncle David," Lenny said. "He was a character."

Dark stories about David followed—that he'd been a hit man for a local union in Atlantic City; that he'd gone to prison at nineteen; that he'd killed a man there. A scary, scary guy, Lenny said. Not all there in the head. And something else. Lenny squinted and looked away, searching his mind for a memory.

"Okay, I was little when this happened," he said. "I don't really remember it. I just remember we weren't supposed to talk about it. We were told not to bring it up. My parents told me to never mention it."

"What was it?" Aimee said.

"There were twins in the family," Lenny said. "David had these twins. And there was something wrong with them, and David gave them up. He got rid of them. And we weren't supposed to talk about it. So no one brought it up."

Aimee got another sinking feeling. These twins were long gone and unlikely to ever be found. If one of them was my father, we'd never be able to prove it. The mystery might never be solved.

—ᴍ—

CeCe heard the same stories about David and the twins. So did Crista at Ancestry. Everyone had the same concern. If David had fathered twins in his early twenties, fresh out of prison, and given them up for adoption, they weren't likely to show up on any tree we'd been looking at so far. The twins could have gone anywhere. Still, David's criminal past and forfeiture of his children made it plausible that he was somehow connected to another shameful act—my abandonment in 1965. "I am interested in David's line the most," CeCe wrote in the Facebook message to the team. "He did prison time and gave up twins for adoption. They are the most likely suspects."

Her secondary target was David's sister Bertha, and the team began tracing her line, too.

At the same time, CeCe and the team kept plugging away on the Tennessee connection. Michelle Trostler, in particular, spent endless hours building up the family trees of people in her East Tennessee Mystery Group. None of it was easy. The possibility of undocumented children going back a few generations was always there. Maybe someone had given a child to a neighbor to raise. Maybe there had been an unofficial adoption. Maybe there had been an illicit affair, leading to what genealogists called an NPE—the dreaded non-paternity event. The further back you traveled in time, the harder it was to be sure of anything.

Still, Michelle diligently built out her trees. She kept digging, kept connecting names. Patient, yet meticulous.

"Sometimes you have to spin your wheels to get anywhere," Michelle says. "That's who I was. I was the wheel spinner."

—ᨠ—

On February 1, 2015, a new match appeared for me on Ancestry. Her name was Ruth Manis, and she was from Tennessee. Ruth was listed as my predicted second cousin.

A second cousin. An important match. Our first really good lead in a while.

Allison saw her first when she logged in to my Ancestry account that morning. She quickly called CeCe, who went online and tried to log in to my account, too. She typed in my password, but her log-in attempt was blocked. She tried again, and again it failed. She tried a third time, but no go. She was locked out of my account.

In fact, Ancestry had asked me to change my password that morning. I wasn't sure why, and I didn't ask. I just did it. Ancestry is a big company, and they were helping me for free, and I didn't want to get in their way. Whatever they needed me to do, I'd do it. The switch must have happened right after Allison logged on, and right before CeCe tried and failed.

I didn't consider that I'd be locking CeCe and the team out of my account. Or maybe I did, but I assumed they'd get back in somehow. In any case, my cell phone soon rang. It was Michelle Trostler.

"We're locked out," she told me.

I explained what Ancestry had asked me to do.

"Paul," Michelle said, trying to stay calm, "I've been working on this case for a year. A lot of my work is written inside your account: names, relationships, notes, DNA—it's all in there. A year's worth of work. And now I'm locked out. You need to get me back on."

I gave Michelle my new password. CeCe and the team might not have been a big company, but they were working hard and working for free, too. I needed them to keep doing what they were doing.

—ɯɯ—

Everyone pounced on Ruth Manis. With a little luck, a predicted second cousin can solve a case fairly quickly.

CeCe called Ruth and told her my story, and Ruth was happy to help. We learned she was a lovely lady with a southern drawl who'd received an Ancestry kit for Christmas and decided to give it a go. She was excited about it, but not exactly computer savvy. For instance, Ruth was using an AOL browser, which wasn't supported by Ancestry. CeCe asked her to transfer her DNA segment data to the FamilyTree DNA site so she could see the segment data not visible on Ancestry. Then CeCe crossed her fingers.

"The sweetest lady," CeCe told the team on Facebook. "Not a techie, though, so I hope she can figure it out."

If CeCe couldn't find any connection to the New Jersey–Philadelphia area in Ruth's tree, the plan was to trace her family back to her four sets of great-grandparents, then test living descendants on those four lines to see on which branch Ruth and I connected. If Ruth and I were truly second cousins, we would share a set of great-grandparents. And if we could pinpoint which line I was on, we could conceivably connect me to a first cousin—or closer. My Tennessee connection could be more than a back door to the solution—it could be the best way in.

There was a new urgency now. CeCe and Allison hurriedly began building out Ruth's tree, moving forward in time from her great-grandparents. The team spent three months lining up and calling potential testers. They never told the testers they were working with me; they didn't want to scare anyone away with all the publicity surrounding my case. They just said they were working with an adoptee who was a strong second cousin match with Ruth Manis. They anticipated that second cousins who were older would be more likely to say no, and many of them did, so they pushed harder with cousins who were younger and less skeptical.

Allison, in particular, was tireless. Early on, she found a potential second cousin tester who was proving difficult. The cousin seemed to want to help, but was stalling on taking the DNA test. Allison finally got tired of waiting and sent a message to his daughter.

"Woohoo!" Allison messaged the team. "The daughter just called me! I told her if her father wasn't interested in testing, she could do it as well. She thought it was 'super cool.'"

Eventually, the father did agree to take a test—then had second thoughts and threatened to back out. He wanted reassurance that he wasn't going to be framed by some unknown child he never knew he had. CeCe called him and told him the "child" in question—me—was fifty years old. That did the trick, and the father submitted his DNA test.

One tester down.

Next, Allison rooted around another great-grandparent line and sent Facebook messages to four descendants. She found more potential testers on another line and sent out six Facebook messages and left three voicemails. "I am going to take a shower finally today," Allison messaged the rest of the team. "Someone will probably call as soon as I get in." One of them eventually did call back, and agreed to test.

Two testers down.

The pace was relentless. Allison, CeCe, and Michelle all routinely stayed up well into the night, searching for testers and contact numbers. When CeCe would finally call it quits on the West Coast, Allison would just be getting up on the East Coast and pick up on CeCe's research. "I am sending all of you vitamins so you don't get sick," Allison wrote in one message to the team.

Through many tens of hours of more work, Allison found a third potential tester.

Three down, one to go.

Around this time, Michelle's friend and neighbor Carol Rolnick officially joined the team. If Michelle was the wheel spinner, Carol was the dog with a bone. She found an older second cousin in rural Indiana, and got on the phone with him and his wife. They seemed to want to help, but they weren't sure and they hemmed and hawed.

"Do you have anyone in the family who is interested in genealogy?" Carol finally asked.

"Sure, my nephew," the husband said.

"Great, can I talk with him?"

A week later, Carol connected with the nephew, who said he'd be happy to help. Carol called Allison, who handled all the shipping and handling of CeCe's donated DNA kits, and asked her to overnight a kit to the nephew in Indiana. The sooner he got it, the less chance he'd get cold feet.

The team kept pushing. A few days into the Ruth Manis phase, Michelle sent the team a message on their Facebook thread.

"Okay guys, I just got a call back from my doctor, who says I need to take myself to urgent care or the ER," she wrote. "So I'm going to get dressed and come back and send out one more message and then I gotta go to the hospital."

"Why are you going to the ER?!?" CeCe asked.

"Doctor says go. Pretty bad abdominal pain. Can't walk."

Michelle stayed in touch from the ER and relayed the diagnosis—she had acute pyelonephritis, a kidney infection that was a complication of Lyme disease, and she needed IV antibiotics. Still, she couldn't wait to get back to searching for live testers.

"I will do the IV bag," she wrote, "then hopefully I'm out of here."

A different possible second cousin match popped up on 23andMe, and CeCe scrutinized eleven families looking for a link to Ruth's four sets of great-grandparents. But no children in these eleven families were a match. "Could be a wild goose chase," CeCe wrote—meaning the match might have the wrong surnames on his tree. CeCe wondered if her own dense notebooks and Michelle's wall of Tennessee stickies might prove helpful—could any of those names match the names of the various branches of Ruth Manis's family tree? In fact, many did, and the team scanned these matches for patterns. Specifically, they needed to find someone from a rural area of Tennessee who'd somehow hooked up with a Jewish partner from the New Jersey–Pennsylvania area, and then had a child. They needed to tie a Tennessee match to Alan Fisch and Lenny Rocco, and thus to me.

"I keep waiting for someone on Ruth's tree to end up in NJ and jump out at us," CeCe wrote hopefully. But so far, no one had.

"Go to bed," Carol pleaded with CeCe. "My kids have early release tomorrow so I can work on this in the afternoon."

But CeCe didn't go to bed. Instead she stayed up with the rest of the team, wondering if there was a dreaded NPE in Ruth's tree and debating whether the Tennessee connection needed to have Sephardic Jewish ancestry versus Ashkenazi ancestry. Their debate went into the wee hours.

—w—

By the spring, after weeks and weeks of intense research and hours of cajoling phone calls, the team finally had the four testers they needed. Almost certainly, one of them had to match my DNA. CeCe pushed her contacts at FamilyTree DNA to speed up their already quick work on the tests.

The results for one of Allison's testers came back first. They matched Ruth Manis's DNA, as expected. But they did not match mine. Strike one.

Another set of results came back, and that tester, too, wasn't a match.

The two final sets of results weren't far behind. Since Ruth and I were predicted second cousins, one of them *had* to match. Nothing else made sense. One of them *had* to be it.

But—

Neither one was a match.

None of the four second cousins the team had found, representing each of Ruth Manis's four great-grandparent lines, shared DNA with me.

After the fourth negative test, CeCe, Michelle, Allison, and Carol jumped on a conference call. So much work—months of work—and nothing to show for it? There was cursing. There was disbelief. There was anger and frustration. The team had always understood that Ruth might not actually be my second cousin. But they sure hoped that she was. Instead, the four negative results implied that Ruth was actually a third cousin who happened to share an abnormally high percentage of DNA with me.

That was a setback. A significant setback. Being third cousins meant Ruth and I shared great-*great*-grandparents—one generation further back. And that meant the team needed a pool of *eight* living descendants to test—one for each line of Ruth's great-great-grandparents. In other words, they had to find *four more testers* on top of the four they'd already tested. And that could take several more grueling weeks of research, phone calls, mailing DNA kits, and waiting for results.

"What is it with this case?" a dejected Michelle asked on the conference call. "This crazy case!"

19

BUT THEN IT was back to the search. That's how their minds worked—what's next? Where do we look now? In the conference call, CeCe decided to switch the team off Ruth Manis for the moment—no one was anxious to spend weeks finding four more testers—and put together a list of action points. Logical next steps. The most important one was refocusing on the Rocco line.

The team knew that since Lenny Rocco was Alan Fisch's father, and Alan and I were second cousins, that meant that Alan and I shared great-grandparents—John Rocco and Sarah Tuckojenski. It was time to figure out exactly how I was descended from them. The focus was on John and Sarah's four children—Bertha, Jean, Thomas, and David.

Thomas Rocco was ruled out because he was Lenny Rocco's father—since Lenny and I were cousins, not brothers, Thomas couldn't be my father, or even my grandfather.

One of the remaining three, David Rocco, was the tough character everyone had warned us about. David had married a woman named Shirley Ostroff, but they had no children—*except*, perhaps, for the mysterious twins Lenny told us about. The twins that were given up for adoption. CeCe's plan of attack was to find a living tester on Shirley Ostroff's line, to see if I was descended from one of those twins. Lenny Rocco had told her he thought I looked like Shirley's side of the family, and if that was true, I would be descended from both David Rocco (his DNA matched mine through Lenny) and his wife. Which would mean David and Shirley were likely my grandparents.

Which would mean that one of the long-gone twins was one of my long-gone parents.

Carol contacted the Philadelphia Division of Vital Records and dug up the marriage certificate for David Rocco and Shirley Ostroff. She needed it to confirm the names of Shirley's parents, since there were several Ostroff families in the Philadelphia area in 1946. Once she learned Shirley's parents' name, she built the tree forward looking for a living relative—and she found Shirley's great-nephew Josh Ostroff. Carol called him, and luckily he was pleasant and eager to help. But he told Carol someone else had recently contacted him and asked him to take a DNA test.

Carol's heart sank. The Ancestry researchers had beaten her to the punch, she thought. Her team was a step behind.

"Who called you?" Carol asked.

"Some gal from the U.S. Navy."

The U.S. Navy? The woman who called Josh turned out to be CeCe's friend and colleague, and CeCe contacted her to find out the details. She learned that Josh's great-grandfather's brother had perished in the Pacific during World War II. The Navy had a repatriation of remains program that required them to find living relatives of fallen soldiers to test. That's how they'd found Josh Ostroff. Incredibly, Josh was sitting at the intersection of two vast mysteries for which his DNA was the key!

The good news was that the team might not be a step behind after all.

—⁂—

Josh Ostroff took a DNA test, and CeCe put a rush on the results. Meanwhile, she asked Carol to turn her attention to the two remaining descendants of John Rocco—his daughters, Bertha and Jean.

Carol called the Atlantic City library and found an obituary for Bertha Rocco. The obit mentioned her two sons, Gilbert and Leonard. Then Carol used a little hack—she called the cemetery where Bertha was buried and asked for the contact person associated with her grave site. The cemetery gave her a name—Leonard Rosenthal—and a very old phone number in Florida.

That had to be Bertha's son Leonard, but Carol had no idea where the last name Rosenthal came from. All she knew was that Bertha's husband was named Augie Cipressi. She looked through 1940 records and found Bertha Rosenthal listed as the head of her household. Two sons, Leonard and Gilbert, were also listed—but no husband. Could this be the right Bertha?

It could be if Augie was Bertha's *second* husband, and if Bertha had a first husband named Rosenthal, who no one knew about.

Carol kept going. She was in Palm Springs at the time, on vacation with her husband and children, and she worked quietly in the living room at night so as not to wake anyone. Every now and then her husband would yell, "When are you coming to bed?" Carol would always yell back, "Soon."

"Gotta sign off, since I'm supposed to be having fun with the family," Carol wrote to the team on Facebook, "but you know I'll be checking my phone every two minutes to see what's up."

Carol found an obituary for Gilbert Rosenthal that said he'd been survived by his wife, Marie, and their three children—Karen, Linda, and Fred. Using public records, the team was able to determine that the oldest child was born in 1961, and the youngest in 1965. Barring an extramarital affair, that meant Gilbert couldn't be my father—there was no slot for me in his family. But the only way to know that for sure was to find one of Gilbert's children and get him or her to take a DNA test.

Across the country in Maryland, Allison was helping Carol dig around for records. She did a search for Gilbert's three children and learned that Karen was deceased. A bit later, Carol found Karen's obituary.

ROSENTHAL, KAREN R. 47—of Galloway, passed away Saturday, May 1st, 2010 suddenly at Jefferson University Hospital, in Phila., PA. Miss Rosenthal was born in Atlantic City on January 9, 1963, the daughter of the late Gilbert and Marie Rosenthal. Dear sister of Linda and Fred. Aunt of Josh and Julia. Close friend of Stephanie and the gang at WAWA store # 702 in Somers Point, where she had been a long time employee. Her service and interment are private and at the convenience of the Family.

Karen Rosenthal was gone at the age of forty-seven. That left only Linda and Fred as potential testers.

Carol and Allison found an address for Linda near Atlantic City, but no one could find a working phone number. Instead Carol focused on Gilbert's son, Fred. A Google search turned up his phone number, and Carol gave him a call. She reached his wife, who explained that Fred worked nights. The best time to call him was around noon. The next day, during Carol's lunch break, she went down to the parking lot, sat in her Toyota RAV4, and called Fred again.

This time, he answered. Carol explained why she was calling, and a little bit about my story. Fred was friendly, but guarded.

"You're very convincing," he told her, "but I'm a skeptical person and this feels like a scam. And I can't figure out why you're trying to scam me."

"No, no, this is totally legit," Carol said.

"Where can I read more about this case?" Fred asked.

Carol gave him the address of CeCe's website, The DNA Detectives. The site featured a video about my case. Looking it over ought to convince Fred of the legitimacy of Carol's request. Or at least that's what she hoped.

Next, she went on Facebook and shared the news about Fred with the team.

"Gave him the website and your blog to look up," she wrote. "Will follow up with him to see how he is feeling. He typed in the URL when we were talking, so I'm hoping he's checking us out at the moment."

"Thank you so much Carol!" CeCe responded. "We are migrating the site today to GoDaddy, hopefully it won't go down at all, but it might."

In fact, CeCe's website did go down for maintenance—precisely when Fred Rosenthal tried to find it.

Instead of a polished, informative website, he got a message to check back later. The timing was terrible. When Carol called Fred back, he didn't answer. She tried him a few more times, but he never picked up. She left messages, but none were returned. The last plausible tester on Gilbert Rosenthal's line had been lost.

—\~\~—

Then Josh Ostroff's test results came back. Josh was our tester from the line of Shirley Ostroff, the wife of David Rocco. If his DNA matched mine, I would be a Rocco descendant through David.

The test results showed that Josh's DNA did *not* match mine.

CeCe called to tell me the results. On one hand, it was a relief. I'd heard only bad things about David Rocco, and I also understood that pinpointing my connection to his wife, Shirley, would be difficult, given their chaotic life.

On the other hand, it was another dead end. Another line of investigation slammed shut. It felt like we were running out of options.

But there was still Jean Rocco—the fourth child of John Rocco and Sarah. The team had learned that Jean had two daughters—Tobe and Sheila. They located Tobe, who seemed interested in testing but kept postponing the decision. One excuse followed another—including that she'd just had a house fire. When I heard that Tobe was being evasive, I asked CeCe if she thought Tobe could be my birth mother.

It couldn't be ruled out. Tobe's age wasn't quite right—her three daughters were several years older than me. And if they were older, wouldn't they have remembered a younger brother who was abandoned? Still, Tobe's behavior struck me as suspicious. It was one thing to flat-out refuse to test. But to agree to do it, then make excuses—those seemed like the actions of a conflicted person. Carol found a Facebook post that confirmed there'd been a fire in Tobe's house. But the fire had happened more than two years earlier.

"She is never going to test," CeCe predicted.

Instead, the team decided to search for information about Tobe's whereabouts around the time I was abandoned in New Jersey. They also looked for contact numbers for Tobe's three daughters to see if they would test, fully aware they might have already been warned by Tobe. "If she really is Paul's mother," CeCe wrote, "she may get worried and tell the rest of the family that we're crazy." The final test targets were Tobe's sister, Sheila, and her daughter, but they, too, proved elusive.

Still, that I was even able to *suspect* Tobe of being my mother was a kind of milestone for me. We weren't talking about great-great-grandparents anymore. We were talking about someone who might have given me life.

Carol tunneled down one other path—Bertha Rocco's second son, Leonard Rosenthal.

She searched for Leonard's records and came up with a list of associates, including his ex-wife—Barbara Rosenthal. Carol tried the phone number given for Barbara, and to her surprise Barbara picked up.

Carol told her about my story, without giving her my name. Barbara was fascinated. She seemed curious and friendly, but sadly she didn't remember anything about her ex-husband, Leonard, or his brother, Gilbert, that might be helpful. Carol thanked her for her time, and promised to call again.

After Josh Ostroff's test results came back negative, Carol played a hunch and called Barbara again.

"Maybe she'll have remembered something since our last call," Carol told the team. "I have a feeling she wants to tell me more."

—⟋⟍—

Carol reached Barbara, who lived in Florida, on the first try.

"I'm wondering if maybe you remembered anything else," Carol said.

"Well," Barbara said, "I have this old photo album, and I was looking through it."

The photos didn't jog any helpful memories, but the good news was that Barbara was talkative and curious about the case. Carol just had to find a way to tweak information out of her. She gambled and told Barbara my name, and steered her to the *20/20* reports about my case. She hoped Barbara would respond to the fact that this wasn't a typical adoption case. It was an abandonment case, and the abandonment had happened in New Jersey, where Leonard's family had lived. This case could be personal for her.

Barbara was intrigued, but she didn't have anything useful to share. Carol thanked her for her time, and got ready to hang up.

"Oh, you know, there is one thing I didn't tell you," Barbara said.

"What's that?" Carol said, taking her pen and pad back out of her purse.

"Well, it's about the twins."

The mysterious twins—the twins David Rocco had apparently given away. Carol had mentioned them to Barbara earlier in the call.

"What about the twins?" Carol asked.

"Well, they weren't David's twins," Barbara said.

"What?"

"You said they were David's twins and they weren't. They were Gilbert's."

"I'm sorry. What did you say?"

"They were Gilbert and Marie's twins. When Leonard and I were young we'd go and visit them in Atlantic City. One summer they were there, and the next summer, they weren't. One year, the twins were just gone."

Carol held her breath and scribbled down notes as fast as she could. Her hand was trembling.

20

CAROL PUSHED BARBARA for more information. Barbara told her she believed the twins were born in October 1962, or maybe October 1963—one or the other, she was sure of it. The timing didn't quite fit. When a Newark policeman found me in July 1965, he'd estimated my age to be around fourteen months. Had I been born in October 1963, I'd have been twenty-one months old. Maybe Barbara was wrong about the year.

"Oh no, I'm sure it was one of those two years," Barbara said.

Why did she think the twins disappeared?

"Apparently there was something wrong with them," Barbara said, "so they sent them to live with Marie's mother in Ohio."

And you actually saw the twins?

"Oh yes," Barbara said. "We drove all the way up from Miami to see them."

Carol got off the phone with Barbara and immediately called Fred Rosenthal. He hadn't responded to any of her messages, but now she had new information for him. Carol expected she'd have to leave another message, but this time Fred picked up.

"Carol, I only answered to let you know that I don't want you to call me anymore," he said, his voice impatient. "I don't know why you're scamming me, but I don't want you to bother me anymore."

"Wait!" Carol said. "Don't hang up. Do you know your parents had twins?"

"What?" Fred said. "What are you talking about? There were no twins, and don't call me anymore."

Then he hung up.

Next, Carol called CeCe Moore.

"The twins weren't David's," she told her. "They were Gilbert's."

CeCe was stunned. One more person confirming the twins existed was huge. And that they belonged to parents with living relatives who could be tested? That was remarkable. CeCe had a familiar feeling in her gut, a feeling she'd experienced in other cases.

A feeling that said, *This is it.*

But what about the age discrepancy? Barbara said the twins were born in 1962 or 1963. CeCe and Carol looked at records for Gilbert and Marie's daughters, Karen and Linda, and determined the twins had to have been born in 1963. But that would have made me twenty-one months old when I was found. Barbara could have been wrong about the year, but she'd insisted she was certain. CeCe and Carol tried to account somehow for the inconsistency.

Was there any way I could have been seven months older than the authorities said I was?

Then they hit on it—there *was* a way.

The investigators could have been wrong because *they had no idea I might be a twin.*

Everyone on the team was aware that a twin's growth and development is slower than a single child's. A twin can be slightly behind developmentally in his early months and years; the typical milestones can come later. Someone estimating my age could have been off by several months, simply because I looked or acted younger than I was. It was possible.

Still, that wasn't proof of anything. And with Gilbert's son, Fred, refusing to be DNA-tested, how could CeCe establish the twins' identity?

Once again, there was a way.

The Tennessee connection.

CeCe already knew I was connected to the Rocco clan—which made it very plausible that I was the son of Bertha Rocco's son Gilbert.

If CeCe could prove I was also somehow connected to Gilbert's *wife's* family, then I could be one of the missing twins.

But because my connection to the Tennessee group had yet to be identified any closer than distant cousins—and because it definitely wasn't on the Rocco side—the ancestor who connected me to Tennessee *had* to be on my mother's family line.

CeCe immediately built out Marie Rosenthal's family tree. Somewhere in that tree, she hoped, was the elusive person who left rural Tennessee and wound up in New Jersey. The enormous amount of research the team had done on the Tennessee connection—Michelle's relentless triangulations, the Ruth Manis digging, dozens of calls to potential testers—had brought the team here, to a moment of truth. One final Tennessee relative was needed. Just one more.

CeCe knew she was looking for someone from around the area of Byrdstown, in Tennessee's Pickett County, or from neighboring Overton County. That was where the DNA data was pointing. But Byrdstown was about as small as a town could get. The last census listed just 803 residents. What were the odds the person we needed to find hailed from a place that probably had one traffic light?

CeCe found Marie's maiden name—Duncan. She went back another generation and found Marie's father, Cecil Duncan. She started the process of tracing Cecil's journey through time.

—⁓—

There was something else Barbara Rosenthal had told Carol.

She told her she remembered a newspaper article had been written about the twins' birth. By sheer coincidence, they had been born on their sister Linda's birthday—and, she thought, the date of their parents' wedding anniversary, too. A local reporter had found that interesting and wrote up the births for his paper.

The team had to find that article. It might be the only way to prove the twins existed at all.

Carol called Allison, the only team member on the East Coast. Could Allison try to find the article? Allison jumped into her silver Honda Accord and drove three hours up the Eastern Seaboard to Atlantic City. She parked outside the Atlantic City Free Public Library, went inside, and asked an attendant to set her up with microfilmed copies of the city newspapers from October 1963.

Allison sat in a quiet carrel and, inch by inch, scrolled through yards of microfilm. It was a blur of black-and-white headlines and photos and ads. "Formica Laminated Plastic Desks—Easy to Care for and only $19.95." Allison didn't know exactly what she was looking for—a long article? A tiny mention? Something hidden in a list of birth announcements? So she had to go slowly and look at everything. The typeface was excruciatingly small.

Allison loaded a reel of microfilm marked *Atlantic City Press* into the scanner. She scrolled forward to October 1963. She went through a week's worth of newspapers and found nothing. The second and third weeks came up empty, too. She got through the fourth week—all the way to October 30, 1963—before something on page 4 caught her eye.

It was just below a photograph of a barber named Bob Lawless giving a haircut to a lion named Lemo.

A column headline—BY THE SEASHORE.

And beneath that, smaller headlines. DOCTOR'S LECTURE. CAMPAIGN-
ER'S REUNION. NEWS BRIEFS.

SIGNIFICANT DATES.

Allison read the tiny paragraph of text below this last headline.

The 27th day of the month holds significance for the increasing family of
Mr. and Mrs. Gilbert Rosenthal of 201 Seagull Drive, Cardiff. The Rosenthals
became parents of twins, a boy and a girl, Sunday, October 27 in Atlantic
City Hospital. They were born on the birthday of the Rosenthals' oldest
child, Linda, 2.

Allison made several copies of the item, and sent a group text to
CeCe, Carol, and Michelle.

"Got it!"

—\\\\—

Once Carol was sure the twins had been born in 1963, she called Barbara Rosenthal to tell her she'd been right.

Barbara was happy to hear it, and she told Carol she'd found a
book that used to belong to Leonard's mother, Bertha. It was Bertha's
Brag Book, where she kept important photos of her children and
grandchildren. Barbara told Carol she'd looked through the book,
searching for photos of the twins.

She found photos of her own wedding to Leonard, and photos of
the wedding of Leonard's brother, Gilbert, and Marie. She found a
photo of Gilbert's daughter Linda right after she was born, in 1961,
and another photo of Karen, who was born two years later. And she
found photos of their brother, Fred, born in 1965.

But she didn't find any photos of the twins.

Yet something was odd about the brag book, Barbara would later
reveal.

Right around where the photos of the twins should have been, Barbara found that one or two pages had been ripped out.

———∿———

CeCe sat at her desk at home and plugged away at Marie Duncan's tree. The house was quiet; CeCe's young son, Nicky, was playing a game by himself in the next room. CeCe entered the name of Marie's father, Cecil Duncan, on her tree and started searching through historical records that might be connected to him.

The name of a small town in Tennessee flashed on her screen.

CeCe looked at the name of the town and began to cry.

21

I WAS AT WORK when I got a text from CeCe, on a baking hot day in June. "Can you call me?" the text read. "Ten minutes," I wrote back.

I went to the parking lot and got in my car. I turned on the ignition to get the air-conditioning going, but I stayed in my spot. I liked to be somewhere quiet whenever I spoke with CeCe. Whatever update she might have, good or bad, I wanted to be ready to hear it.

I called CeCe, and she told me Michelle Trostler was on the call, too. So were Carol Rolnick and Allison Demski.

"Paul," CeCe said, "what do you think of the name Jack?"

"That's not a bad name," I said. "Strong name."

"Well, that is your name," she said.

It took me a moment to realize what she was saying. This was my name. *My* name. I wasn't Paul. I wasn't Scott. I was Jack. My name was Jack.

"There's something else," CeCe said, before I could even catch my breath. "You have a twin sister, and her name is Jill."

PART THREE

ATLANTIC CITY

22

NO STONE UNTURNED.

That was my rule when the search for my identity and for the real Paul got under way, more than two years before CeCe and the team learned my name. Accept help from wherever it came. Try everything. The answer could lie anywhere. Even, perhaps, with a psychic.

I've always believed in the paranormal, so when a friend suggested I talk to a medium he knew, I agreed. There was no harm to it. Not long after I learned my identity, I made the appointment.

Her name was Bobbi Allison, and she was based on Long Island, but we did our session over the phone. All she knew about me was my first name, Paul. Nothing else. I had no idea what to expect, but I guess some part of me did wonder if I'd learn something valuable. A clue or a tip or a lead. A name. I went into the call fully open to whatever might happen.

"The first thing I see is a battle of three," Bobbi said at the beginning of the call. "You are going through a battle, a very heavy battle, that will last for three years. Or there's three parts to the battle. Either way, you will get through this battle. You will come out of it.

"I'm also seeing three people. Three women. Three sisters. You are connected to this family with three sisters. But I feel like one of them . . . one of the sisters . . . I feel like they are missing. A missing person. Does that make sense to you?"

I told her that it did.

"I also see men. Four men. I see uniforms, like they are in the service, or maybe cops? And they are in a regimented line, side by side. Four of them, in a row, standing there in uniform. And maybe . . . maybe this missing sister is behind them. I can't quite see."

Then Bobbi told me my father was coming through.

"He is making me see tears. Rolling down his face. An apology. Not the best father, not the worst father. He is showing me the cycle of life. From his father to him, and then to you. And he is showing me praying hands. Head down, hands praying. As if he's saying, 'Please forgive me, Son.'"

I didn't comment. I didn't add anything. I just listened.

"Who was adopted?" Bobbi asked. "Who raised someone else's kid? I see abuse, abandonment, drugs, many things, it happened to this one, to that one, a confession, the cycle, no one stops it, it keeps going, until now . . . the cycle stops now. Your father is saying, 'It stops now. That is not you.'

"But, Paul—your identity. You made yourself into this whole new person. But they are showing me a split. Like, one of two. You are one of two. Almost like twins, and they are split, and someone very close to you, same DNA, and you are split up, and they are gone. . . . Paul, are you a twin?"

It felt odd to say so, but I told her that I was.

"Don't think that because you were a boy, you don't remember what happened. You do. All of it. It's still there. But you need to forgive, so you can move on with your journey. It is about forgiveness, but the forgiveness is not to help them. It is to help you. So you can be free, like a butterfly. And you will be free. You will be free.

"Go to the water, Paul. I feel like you need to go to the water. Put your feet in the salt water. Stand by the ocean. The water will be a conduit. It will help you forgive."

23

IT CAME DOWN to Tennessee.

Carol hearing that the twins were Gilbert's was a lightbulb moment for CeCe. A synapse fired and a conclusion formed—*Paul is one of the twins.* No one could ever find a slot for me in anyone's family, not even Gilbert's—his records showed he had only three children. That was the puzzling thing. I should have fit in *somewhere.* But what if my slot had been erased? Could it be a coincidence that one of the families I might have fit into had two children no one could account for?

Still, CeCe had to prove somehow that I was one of the twins.

She did it by tracing the lineage of Gilbert's wife, Marie. Just one generation back, she found Marie's father, Cecil Duncan. She found his birth listing online and saw that he was born in a place called Overton County.

Overton County is in northern Tennessee, just south of Byrdstown, the flyspeck of a place where much of the Tennessee DNA had been pointing.

Cecil Duncan was the Tennessee connection. When he was older he moved to Akron, Ohio, where he met his future wife, Jeannie Noga. Cecil and Jeannie had a daughter, Marie, who eventually moved to New Jersey to marry Gilbert Rosenthal. Cecil was the one who tied it all together—Tennessee and New Jersey, the Duncans and the Roccos, the Rosenthals and me. He was the key puzzle piece.

"When I saw he was born in Overton County," CeCe told me, "I cried."

CeCe didn't stop there. She also traced Cecil's ancestors and learned one of them was from Eastern Europe and one of them was Jewish. That explained my own Eastern European DNA and the maternal Jewish DNA CeCe had seen on my X chromosome. CeCe knew that Lenny Rocco was my cousin, and that Lenny was also a first cousin to Gilbert Rosenthal through his aunt Bertha Rocco, Gilbert's mother. And she knew Gilbert was married to Marie Duncan, whose father traced back to Tennessee, same as me. It all lined up. It all converged. It all pointed to Gilbert and Marie being my parents.

Plus, Gilbert's mysterious twins were born around the very time I was born—and in Atlantic City, just two hours from where I'd been abandoned.

It couldn't be a coincidence. I had to be one of the twins. CeCe would need two more DNA tests to be certain—a close cousin on both Gilbert's and Marie's lines—but she had enough to alert the team and call me with the news.

So it was that I was sitting in my car in a parking lot in Las Vegas, when all at once a fifty-year mystery was solved, and another was created.

—〰—

I was a twin. That was a bombshell. Hearing my birth name—that was just surreal. Jack Rosenthal. Jack. I rolled the name around in my brain, and it made sense to me. I liked it. I'd never felt like a Paul. But Jack—it fit. I know it sounds strange, but I felt like a Jack.

But that remarkable piece of news—something I'd been waiting to hear, really, my whole life—was superseded by what came next. The bombshell. The shocker. I hadn't been born alone. I was one of two. I was a *twin*.

Jack and Jill. Just like the nursery rhyme.

It wasn't anything I could process right away. I can't even recall how I reacted to hearing it, but CeCe tells me I pretty much went silent. I said nothing, because I had nothing to say. How can anyone absorb such a monumental discovery about himself? To think you are biologically one thing all your life, then be told you are another? There was no context or framework for me to assimilate it. It just crash-landed in my life.

The thing is—hearing I was a twin did not trigger anything inside me. No shock of realization, no confirmation of something suppressed. Many people have asked me since if I'd ever *felt* like a twin, and I am sure I didn't. I never had the feeling a part of me was missing. I felt like I was lost myself—like *I* was the one who was missing. But there was never any sense of absence—of a vacancy where someone else should have been. I was aware that many twins have a kind of telepathic connection, and often feel the same feelings thousands of miles apart, and are otherwise bound in ways nontwins can't understand—but I simply didn't have that in my life.

Or at least, not consciously.

I thanked CeCe and the team, inadequately, I'm sure, and called my wife, Michelle. I told her what CeCe had told me.

Michelle fell silent, too. Some of it was shock. Some of it, I'm sure, was relief. But I could tell her feelings were mixed. She loved me, and she was happy for me that I'd learned my identity. But I knew that hearing I had a twin would only make her more anxious. In a way, it was her biggest fear playing out—that no answer would ever be good enough for me. That one mystery would always lead to another. That she was losing me to my endless quest, if she hadn't lost me already.

I don't know if Michelle wanted me to say, "Now I know who I am, this is over." But it never entered my mind that my search was done.

How could it?

—⁓—

When I learned that Gilbert and Marie were my biological parents, I understood exactly what I was hearing—that my birth parents were dead.

I'd prepared myself for that, because I knew that was the fate of many such searches—adoptees hoping to find their birth parents in time to meet them, only to discover they were too late. But my birth parents would not have been impossibly old when I learned who they were. In 2015, Gilbert Rosenthal would have been eighty-two. His wife, Marie, eighty. Roughly the same ages as my adoptive parents, the Fronczaks, who were alive and well.

Yet Gilbert and Marie were both long gone. Gilbert's death certificate revealed he died in September 1995, at the age of sixty-one. Marie died two years later, in 1997, also at sixty-one. I was twenty years too late. Those struck me as fairly young ages to pass away, but when I checked the life expectancy of men and women born around 1935, those ages fit.

What I really wanted to know, though, was how they died. That would be a big piece of my missing medical history. Gilbert's death certificate said he passed away in the King David Care Center in Atlantic City. But on the copy of the certificate we got our hands on, the cause of death was redacted. To get the actual certificate, I had to be Gilbert's legal child—which, in a sense, I was, though I couldn't prove it. You can't walk into a hall of records and show them strands of

DNA. For now, all the certificate told me was that Gilbert's death had been the result of natural causes—no suspicious circumstances. The same was true of Marie.

I also learned Gilbert had been a soldier. He was buried in a veterans' cemetery in Mays Landing, New Jersey. Marie was there, too. Gilbert's occupation was listed as sheriff's officer with the Atlantic City Sheriff's Office. His business: law enforcement.

A man in a uniform, like the psychic had said.

The other instant realization was that my biological parents—the family I'd been searching for for so long—were people who were capable of abandoning a child.

I'd already heard about some dysfunction in the Rocco clan, starting with David Rocco, the boxer or bodybuilder or gangster. Was there some dark streak that ran through the whole line, culminating in the events of July 1965, when I was left on the street? I did not want to demonize my birth parents in the same instant that I'd learned who they were, so I told myself that any action can have extenuating circumstances. Whoever abandoned me left me in a very visible place filled with well-to-do people; it was clear they hoped someone of means would find me and take me in. So was it poverty that led them to do what they did? Did it destroy them to do it? And did it necessarily make them bad people?

I didn't know enough to make any judgments, I told myself. Just wait and find out more. But still—my parents did something unthinkable. I couldn't deny that. They took a two-year-old twin and left him alone on a sidewalk. They wrenched the boy away from his family, his sisters, his twin. And they did the same—or maybe worse—to Jill.

What hard things led them to these dire actions?

And here I was, fifty years later, still alive, carrying their blood. The blood that ran through my daughter, Emma, now.

I needed to know more. I'd found my birth family. Now I had to discover them.

—ɯ—

There was more work to do to prove I was who we thought I was. Everything we knew pointed to me being Jack Rosenthal, one of the missing twins. But to make it a certainty, we needed a conclusive DNA sample—ideally from one of my theoretical full siblings, Fred or Linda Rosenthal. They each potentially shared 50 percent of their DNA with me. If we could get one of them to test, and they matched me, all doubt would be erased.

But Fred was out of the picture. He'd slammed the door on Carol twice. That left the woman who could be my sister, Linda Rosenthal.

The team found an address for Linda in southern New Jersey, west of Atlantic City. But when Carol spoke to Leonard Rosenthal's ex-wife, Barbara—and also to their daughter, Melanie—they'd told her that Linda might be difficult to deal with. The team had decided against approaching her for a DNA sample.

Without one of my siblings to test, CeCe would need a first cousin from both the Duncan and Rosenthal lines. This proved a bit easier. The team lined up Melanie Rosenthal, the daughter of Gilbert's brother, Leonard—theoretically, my full first cousin. They also learned that one of Marie Duncan's brothers was still alive. His name was Frank Duncan, and Carol found him living with his wife in Kentucky.

Carol called his number and reached him at home. Frank sounded skeptical, but he agreed to talk for a while. He told Carol he hadn't been close with his sister, though he did confirm that she'd had twins.

"Do you know what happened to the twins?" Carol asked.

"How about you tell me what this is all about?" Frank asked.

He wasn't keen on taking a DNA test. Next, Allison located

Frank's niece, Melissa Duncan—theoretically, my full first cousin, too. Allison emailed her, and they set up a time to talk. Melissa was sweet and friendly and happy to talk about the family.

"We heard that Marie had twins—can you verify that?" Allison asked.

"Oh, yes, they had twins," Melissa said. "But they didn't raise them—the other side of the family had them. Gilbert's side raised the twins."

That was news. If it was true, it meant that someone on the Rocco side—perhaps even Gilbert's mother, Bertha, whose brag book had been altered—might have been the one who actually abandoned me.

Then Allison told Melissa about me, and how I'd been left on a sidewalk.

"We believe Paul may be one of the twins," she said.

On the other end of the phone, there was quiet. Then Allison heard soft crying.

"He's my family," Melissa said through her tears. "He is part of my family. This puts everything in a whole different light."

Melissa agreed to take a DNA test.

Her test was especially important. Gilbert's niece, Melanie Rosenthal, could match my DNA, but that would only prove I was Gilbert's son. What if Gilbert had an affair? If I matched both Melanie and Melissa, the dreaded non-paternity event could be ruled out.

Both test results came back from FamilyTree DNA around the same time.

Both were close matches with me.

I had two brand-new first cousins. And I had a new family. Now, I knew that for sure.

The final step was searching for my birth certificate.

A friend of mine who lives in New York drove to the New Jersey

Office of Vital Statistics and Registry in Trenton, the state's capital. At window No. 3, he requested a search for the birth certificates of Jack and Jill Rosenthal. About twenty minutes later, the teller summoned him and handed him two sheets of paper. None of us were sure the birth certificates would even exist. But there they were, or at least copies of them, stamped by an official registrar on November 1, 1963. My friend texted me a photo of my birth certificate—not the one New Jersey state officials retroactively drew up for me when the Fronczaks adopted me in 1966, but the one that was filled out the day I was actually born.

That's how I learned my middle name—Thomas.

The certificate confirmed Gilbert and Marie were my parents. Gilbert was twenty-nine when I was born, and Marie was twenty-eight. I came into the world on October 27, 1963, at 10:46 A.M., in Atlantic City Hospital. In the box that offered three choices—single, twin, or triplet—there was a hand-drawn checkmark alongside the middle choice: twin.

Next, I learned that Jill wasn't just my twin—she was also my big sister. She was born fourteen minutes earlier, at 10:32 A.M. Jill's middle name was Lynn.

The birth certificates were a miracle to behold. They were the treasures I'd been searching for—proof of my true identity. Seeing my name scrawled by hand in the slot marked "Child's Name" was the affirmation of something I'd suspected since I was ten years old, and probably longer—that I wasn't Paul Fronczak. I now had an official document that proved it. My identity was indisputable. No more whispers and wonders and questions and suppositions. I was Jack Thomas Rosenthal. Plain and simple.

I don't know if that affirmation should have made me happy—I'm not sure "happiness" was ever the goal. Certainly, finding my birth certificate didn't bring me any kind of joy. Even if it hadn't come with a matching one for my missing twin sister, I don't think I'd have felt elation at solving the riddle that defined my life. There were too many people who'd already been hurt by the search.

The moment wasn't even satisfying, to be honest. It was a milestone that didn't feel like a milestone. If anything, it felt like just another step. Like everything that had come before it, it instantly led to the question, "What's next?" Maybe my brain had become reprogrammed to think that way, just as my wife had feared.

All I can say is that finally knowing who I was—well, it was important. It mattered. How, exactly, I wasn't sure. But the truth is always important. Without the truth, what, really, do you have?

Still, there was no celebration of these astonishing events, at least not on my end. I'd like to think that CeCe and Michelle and Carol and Allison raised a glass of wine, or whatever they preferred, and toasted themselves, heartily. They'd accomplished something I thought might be impossible—reconstructing a life out of utter blackness. They were heroes—*my* heroes. As far as I was concerned, they deserved a parade.

But I also knew that wasn't the kind of people or professionals they were. I had long since learned that, like me, they were *What's next?* people.

—⁂—

I didn't think to call my parents after I learned who I was. I hadn't spoken with my mother or father for more than two years, and I'd accepted that as one of the costs of my search. They couldn't be shaken from their belief that my efforts to learn my true identity meant that I was rejecting them as parents. For a few months early on, I'd hoped they'd soften their stance, but they never did. After that, I stopped hoping.

They never called, and neither did I. Reaching out to my parents now to tell them I was Jack Rosenthal would be, in their eyes, telling them I'd found their replacements. As if I were gloating. Or at least that's how I thought they'd react.

But then my mother called me.

After CeCe and the team cracked the case, George Knapp, the KLAS-TV reporter who broke my story, ran an update describing how I'd learned my identity. Someone at the FBI saw the report and called my parents. That's how they found out. I was home with Michelle and Emma one night when my cell phone rang and I saw my mother's name.

"Hi, it's me," she said, as if we'd last spoken the day before. "It sounds like you're making progress."

Her tone was completely different from our final call two years earlier. There was a softness and openness in her voice I hadn't heard in a long while.

"I'm sorry that we raised you the way we did," my mother went on. "We could have done better. We were going through a hard time."

"Mom, that's not it," I said. "You were amazing parents. You did an amazing job raising me."

"Well, it was a hard time for us. We'd lost the baby, then we got a new house, then we had Dave, and then we got you. It was too much for me. I couldn't handle it all."

I'd never heard my mother share her thoughts and feelings this way. I was touched that she was opening up now. I told her again that my search wasn't about how I was raised. It was about learning the truth. But I didn't go into the specifics of the case. I didn't want to burden her with anything that I wasn't clear about myself. I wanted to enjoy our moment of reconnection. I could tell that my mom had missed talking to me, and I realized I'd missed her, too.

"How's Dad?" I asked.

"He's getting old," my mother said. "He's getting forgetful. But it's nothing."

We talked a little more, and I promised to come see her in Chicago.

"Let's talk again soon," I said. "I love you, Mom."

"I love you, Son," my mother said.

———

The way Melissa Duncan heard it, the twins were handed over to someone on the Rosenthal side. How or why that came to pass, she didn't know. But if that were true, Leonard's ex-wife, Barbara Rosenthal, should have known about it. Could Gilbert Rosenthal have given away his twins without his own brother—who lived nearby in Atlantic City—being aware of it?

Carol called Barbara to ask her about the twins again. What did she know about Gilbert and Marie giving them away?

"All I knew was that one summer the twins were there, and the next summer they were gone," Barbara said. "I asked Marie about them, and she said they were staying with her mother, Jenny."

That contradicted what Melissa had told us—that someone on Gilbert's side of the family had the twins.

But there was more.

"One day I ran into Jenny somewhere," Barbara said, "and she asked me how the twins were doing. Because, you see, Marie had told her the twins were with me."

There it was—the two sides of the family were told different things, and each side believed someone on the other side had the twins. But neither side did.

There had been a cover-up.

"Jenny and I sat down and we compared notes," Barbara went on. "That's when we realized something bad had happened."

Did Barbara try to find out what that something was?

"I didn't. I didn't ask Marie about it. It was just too raw."

Did Barbara think that one or both of the twins may have somehow been harmed?

"I didn't know," she said. "I didn't think about it. Maybe I didn't want to know. But I do know they weren't good to the twins when they had them."

Then Barbara told some stories.

24

ONCE I KNEW for sure I was Jack Rosenthal, I called Barbara myself. There was so much I wanted to ask her. She had known my birth parents, Gilbert and Marie, and she'd been married to my uncle, Leonard. She knew my grandmother Bertha, and my brother and sisters. And she'd seen the twins.

Barbara was friendly and sweet and soft-spoken. She said she was thrilled to talk to me and hear my story, but her voice never rose above its low, slow level. Like someone who is used to not talking all that much. Her first reaction to the news that I was Jack was disbelief.

"I am amazed that one of the twins survived," she said.

That set the framework for all of my future discussions with anyone about the twins. The story of the twins was the story of a struggle to survive.

"We would drive up to visit Gilbert and his mother every year," Barbara told me. "I only remember seeing the twins once or twice. I can't remember what they were like, or which was which. It was so long ago."

I asked her to tell me about the times she saw the twins.

"I didn't notice much about their behavior," she said. "It was only once or twice. But I do remember that I saw little marks on their arms. And I thought those could have been burn marks."

"Like cigarette burns?"

"Yes," Barbara said.

I cringed. Could that have been true? She remembered so little, but that was the kind of gruesome memory that could linger for fifty years.

"I went to see our family doctor," Barbara went on, "and I spoke with him because I was afraid the twins were being abused. And the doctor told me to mind my own business. He said, 'You don't live with them, keep your nose out of it.' He said if I tried to pursue anything, the odds were I was the one who'd get hurt."

I asked Barbara if she thought something really bad had happened to the twins.

"I don't know," she said. "I try to put the whole thing out of my mind."

"What about Jill?" I pressed. "Do you think Jill could still be alive?"

"I would guess probably not," Barbara said.

—⁓—

Barbara put her daughter, Melanie, on the phone so I could ask her questions, too. Melanie was in her forties, and she lived with her mother in Florida. She was a writer. But she had health problems, and she had a world-weary way of speaking. She sounded like someone who had seen her share of hard times. Melanie had been a child when her parents drove her from Florida to New Jersey to visit Gilbert and his family, but she remembered seeing the twins.

"I was five or six years old," she said. "I remember walking in and seeing Linda and Karen and the twins. The twins were sitting in high chairs and they were screaming their heads off. They were being fed oatmeal and it looked like the oatmeal was too hot. They were always screaming."

"Do you remember what they were like as kids?" I asked.

"I don't remember Jill at all. But I do remember Jack. Gorgeous kid. But their personalities? All I ever heard them do was scream."

Melanie described another visit to New Jersey to see my family.

"We walked in and right away I could hear the twins crying," she said. "I walked around trying to see where they were. And I went to this bedroom in the back and I pushed the door open, and it was dark. But the twins were there, and they were in cages."

"Did you say they were in cages?"

"It was like cages. Not made of steel, but made out of wood, like a crate almost. But they were constrained and it was pitch-dark, and they were screaming. I remember Aunt Marie complaining that the twins were always crying."

I scrawled the word *cages* on a notepad. Again, I wondered if that could possibly be true.

"I only saw the twins a couple of times," Melanie said. "The next time we came back, they were gone. I was five years old. My dad said he thought Aunt Marie and Uncle Gilbert killed the kids and buried them. He told me I could never mention the twins to Linda, Karen, or Fred. It was like a warning. He said if I ever mentioned the twins again, it would start a family war. So I never did."

"Did you believe your dad was right about the twins?" I asked.

"Yes, I did."

My mind was reeling. I was learning about a dark family secret—possibly a murderous secret. I tried to summon something, anything, of my life back then, of sitting in a high chair, of screaming, of being kept in a cage, of suffering, of being hurt, but there was nothing. Just an impenetrable wall between me and who I was way back then.

"They thought the twins were retarded," Melanie said. "My dad told me that. My mother said that, too. They were told the twins were retarded, and maybe that's what led to it all."

I asked Melanie what she thought happened, and how I came to still be alive.

"Maybe something bad happened to Jill," she said. "Maybe they panicked after killing Jill, and that's when they got rid of you. If something bad happened to her, it makes sense to abandon the other one."

Then I steered the conversation away from the twins. I wanted to know more, but there was time for that. Melanie was my first cousin, after all, and I didn't just want to interrogate her. I wanted her to know how glad I was to find her—to find my family.

"At first, I thought it was all a scam," Melanie said. "I never thought you could be related to me. But, Paul, let me tell you this. The best thing that ever happened to you in the world was when they left you out in front of that store."

—⁂—

CeCe and the team continued to piece together bits of information about my parents and grandparents. Allison found newspaper articles detailing two sad episodes in my family's history, and both were about my grandmother Bertha. An article in the Philadelphia *Times*, dated March 29, 1932, was headlined COUPLE RECONCILED, COURT ACTION ENDS.

> Following the arrest yesterday of Mrs. Bertha Rosenthal, 21 years old, after she was released from Burlington County Hospital, her husband, Harry Rosenthal, appeared ready to go bail for her. She was charged with trying suicide by swallowing poison.

The story said that the Rosenthals had been estranged, and Bertha had had Harry arrested for nonpayment of child support. On February 12, she went to see Harry to try to work things out. The visit went badly, and Bertha swallowed poison. She was taken to a hospital, where a detective and a prosecutor conferred about what would happen next. The Rosenthals agreed to "begin all over again," and the case was dismissed.

But their fresh start didn't last forever. A *Philadelphia Inquirer* story from 1940 was headlined FAMILY FACES STARVATION UNLESS HUS-BAND RETURNS.

> Come back home, Harry Rosenthal: come back and save your wife and two children from starvation and from eviction from the home that was once yours! That was the message which Bertha Rosenthal, of 1424 South 5th Street, last night asked be sent to her husband, wherever he is. He vanished suddenly four months ago, she said, and unless he returns there will be no roof over her head, nor over the heads of their children, Gilbert, 6, and Leonard, 10.

The Rosenthals owed eighty-seven dollars in back rent. Bertha sold her furniture and pawned her jewelry to buy food, but she couldn't hope to pay what was owed, and a constable served her with eviction papers. Bertha, the paper reported, "was obviously near nervous collapse" when she checked herself in to Mt. Sinai Hospital with one of her sons. The boy was treated for sores on his head and hands caused by malnutrition. "I've thought of everything since my husband disappeared," Bertha told a reporter. "Sometimes I thought of jumping into the river, but I couldn't do that because of the boys."

Bertha said her husband vanished because of a fifteen-hundred-dollar debt. To whom he owed the money, she didn't say. Harry operated a barbershop and "made good money," she said, but after he disappeared she discovered his debt. The next day, the *Inquirer* ran another article about the abandoned family. "If Harry doesn't return by tomorrow," Bertha said, "we will be thrown into the street. I haven't eaten a meal since Saturday morning, and the children are suffering from malnutrition. Gilbert was sent home from school three weeks ago because he was too weak to attend classes." She claimed their house had been unheated for two weeks in the January cold, and the electricity was being shut off in a day. "I gave the constable my last four dollars so we could stay here a few more days," Bertha said. "If my husband would only come home, we'd be alright. If only he'd come home."

The publicity worked, and a day later a Good Samaritan left a bundle of food on Bertha's doorstep. "When I opened the door there was a bag of groceries," Bertha said. "I wish I knew who was so kind and generous." The *Inquirer* ran a large black-and-white photo of Bertha and her two children—my father Gilbert and my uncle Leonard—looking forlornly at a picture of the missing Harry.

It reminded me of the photo of the Fronczaks holding a picture of their missing son.

We never found out what happened to Bertha and her children after that. We know they didn't starve, and we know they went on to live fairly comfortably after Bertha put Harry behind her and married Augie Cipressi, the saltwater taffy maker.

But the takeaway for me was about Harry Rosenthal.

Harry walked out on his family. Not once, but at least twice that we knew of. He left his wife and children with nothing. The exact circumstances were unknown, beyond a shady fifteen-hundred-dollar debt, but what was certain was that Harry left. My grandfather deserted his family.

Was the wandering that defined my life something in my blood? Was I just the latest in a line of men who leave?

—⟋⟍—

That made me wonder about my father Gilbert Rosenthal. Where did he fit into the disturbing story that was taking shape? He stayed married to my mother Marie to the end of his life, but was the act of getting rid of two of his children even worse than walking out? It would seem so. Maybe a tendency to disappear was the least worrisome of my inheritances. Maybe there was a much darker streak I had to be worried about.

Assuming my sister Linda wouldn't be a reliable source of information, as everyone seemed to think, that left two people who had spent a lot of time with Gilbert and knew him as well as anyone still alive—his brother, Leonard, and his son, Fred. I reached out to Fred first, just before the final two DNA tests proved my identity.

All I knew about Fred was that he lived in the middle of the country with his family. I dialed his phone number expecting him not to pick up, but he did. I introduced myself first as Paul Fronczak, then as his brother.

"I am Jack Rosenthal," I said. "I was one of the twins."

Fred was clearly confused. He said he'd never heard about the twins. Never knew they existed. He was born five months before I was abandoned, so there's no way he could have remembered the twins. But to not even have heard of them? That meant his two older sisters, and all his cousins, had heeded the many warnings never to talk about the twins. Which baffled him as much as it baffled me.

"How could a family keep something like this a secret forever?" he asked.

Fred said he'd googled me and found a recent photo. He said we didn't look anything alike. I didn't have a photo of him yet, so I didn't know if that was true, but he insisted. He said there was no resemblance at all. I told him about the tiny newspaper item that mentioned his parents and the birth of the twins, and he asked me to send it to him. He also asked me to let him know once the DNA results were back. He was skeptical, but he wasn't shutting the door.

I quickly emailed him the newspaper item, and he responded right away.

Hey Paul, if this is true, what happened to Jill? This doesn't add up. Giving
birth to three children on October 27th in different years? Highly skeptical. It
doesn't make sense to me.

"I don't have the answers to all of your questions yet," I wrote back,
"but we're working on them." I also urged him to call Barbara and Melanie Rosenthal, who would confirm the existence of Jack and Jill. "The
DNA led us to your family even before we knew about the twins,"
I said.

The next day, Fred sent me another email. He told me he'd been
thinking about the situation day and night. He attached a small color
photo that showed a smiling woman in a housedress sitting in a chair,
with one young girl standing beside her, and another riding a small
rocking horse in front of her. The photo was dated July 1963—three
months before the birth of the twins. In the photo, Fred wrote, his
mother didn't appear to be pregnant at all.

I looked at the photo with something like awe. It was the first time
I'd ever seen my mother's face—the first time I could remember, anyway. It was hard to tell anything because the photo was small and
grainy. But I could tell one thing—I looked like her. The strong jaw—
she had it, too. I got it from her side of the family. This little Polaroid
from fifty years ago was my first real, compelling glimpse into my ancestry. I saw my own face staring back at me from the past.

But my mother was leaning forward with her arms in front of her,
and little Karen and her rocking horse blocked the view even more.
There was no way to tell if my mother was pregnant in the photo
or not.

Just a few hours later, Fred emailed again to say he'd spoken to our
mutual cousin, Melanie Rosenthal. "She confirmed the twins," he
wrote. By then I had the official birth certificates for the twins, and I
emailed them to Fred. He now had all the proof he could want. But

what it all proved, I understood, remained incomprehensible to him—that the parents who raised him had harbored a terrible secret all their lives. "I know this is a lot to take in," I told him. "I'm grateful for your understanding and patience."

Fred wrote back within minutes. "I feel sick inside," he said. "If you are Jack, I am so sorry that this happened to you. And I want to know what happened to Jill."

That started a friendly email correspondence between us. It felt good to be able to share some of my feelings with someone who'd experienced the same kind of shock I'd felt—who'd had the underpinnings of his self-knowledge rocked and rattled. But more than that, it felt great to be able to communicate with my brother. My brother! Yes, we were strangers, essentially, but we were also full siblings. In some ways, we *had* to be alike. Just those few early emails with Fred made me hopeful about having a relationship with him. In a way, it was already a more emotionally honest relationship than the one I had with my adoptive brother, Dave.

In another email, Fred asked me how I was dealing with the whole situation. He said he felt like someone had dropped a ton of bricks on him, and he couldn't even imagine how I must have felt.

"When I first found out I wasn't Paul, I felt like you do now," I answered. "Every day is a struggle, but every day brings me closer to the truth."

"They say the truth hurts," Fred wrote back, "but this is beyond hurt."

—⟋⟍—

I called Melanie Rosenthal back to ask about her father. He'd grown up with my father and, presumably, visited the twins when both he and Gilbert lived in Atlantic City. If anyone could tell me what kind of person my father was, Leonard could—he knew him longer and better than anyone still alive.

But Melanie, I discovered, wasn't eager to talk about Leonard. She said she hadn't seen him or spoken to him in years, and she wanted to keep it that way.

"It's not a daughter and daddy thing," she said. "It's about a person who is evil."

The story she reluctantly told was frightening. She painted a picture of a man who was violent and sadistic. "Leonard loved to be cruel," she said. "He was born with the evil in him. I grew up in a house of horrors."

Melanie said she couldn't go into specific stories about her childhood. "It takes me to a place where I don't want to be," she said. "Certain things, I just can't repeat." But she described an atmosphere of sheer terror, where she and her two stepsiblings lived in fear of their unpredictable father. "Physically, mentally, emotionally, he was abusive," she said. "He abused me, and he abused my brother and sister right in front of me. The more he could hurt you, the better. And no one could stop him."

It was a litany of savagery. She described her father throwing the family puppy against a wall and killing it. She said pets came and went with alarming speed in her household, and only later did she realize what was happening to them. She said Leonard punished her with a strap and punched his stepdaughter in the face and shattered her nose. She said that when she was five she searched her house up and down for adoption papers, because she was desperate to believe Leonard wasn't her real father.

"I was actually the only kid he could get along with for more than five seconds," Melanie said. "He hated everyone, he just hated me a little less."

Melanie also described a recurring dream she could not shake. "I am young again, and I am living in the same place where we grew up," she said. "My mother and my sisters are there, too. And Leonard is there, but he's not doing anything. He's just there and we can't get rid of him. And just him being there fills me with terror. Because I don't know what he's going to do."

After a while, Barbara came on the phone to talk about her ex-husband. From her tone, I could tell she'd accepted his barbarism as part of her unlucky lot in life. There was no anger or bitterness in her voice, like there was in Melanie's—just the same flat tone I'd heard before. I understood now she'd probably had the life sucked out of her, and maybe she hadn't gotten it back yet.

Barbara told the story of how she and Leonard met. When she was young, she went to a bowling alley with a girlfriend, and they sat at the bar. Leonard was in the seat next to her. Barbara's girlfriend complained about her roommate, who was being a problem, and after a few minutes Leonard chimed in.

"Why don't you just kill her already?" he asked Barbara's girlfriend.

Barbara didn't find that charming. But Leonard was a fast talker, and he had opinions and he was confident. "He was interesting to listen to," Barbara said. He asked for her number and she gave it to him. They went on a date to a movie, and afterward it rained. "We came up on this big puddle, and Leonard picked me up and carried me across it," she said. "That was it. That was the beginning of my downfall."

Leonard, she and Melanie explained, was a master manipulator. "Everything out of his mouth is a fabrication," Melanie said, "but he will make you believe it's true." Leonard joined the Army in 1946, but was shot during basic training and discharged. "He shot himself in the foot to get out," Melanie said. "He told everyone it just went off. And they believed him." After that, Leonard never held a job that anyone knew of.

Melanie escaped him first, when she was seventeen. "He stalked me for weeks afterwards," she said. "He would camp outside my apartment twenty-four hours a day. Everywhere I went I would see his old green Pinto. He got me fired from a job once by threatening my boss. You didn't even have to do anything for him to hate you, but if he got one less meatball than everyone else in a restaurant, he would go off."

Barbara worked up the nerve to leave Leonard, too, but he found her and convinced her to come back. She spent the next five years afraid for her life. "I was weak," she said. "But I knew it was a mistake to come back. One night he was yelling and yelling at me and I lay on the sofa and I felt myself trembling and my lips shaking and I said to myself, 'If I stay with him, I'm going to die.' I just knew it in my bones that I'd be dead."

Barbara worked as an assistant in a law firm at the time, and a lawyer there helped her draw up divorce papers. Two local sheriffs served the papers for her, and escorted Leonard out of the house. "He wasn't allowed to come back in and he didn't," Barbara said. "But he stalked me and followed me for years. It was very hard for me to have a new life. It took me ten years after leaving him before I felt like a human being again."

—◊—

I didn't learn much about my father in that call. Barbara and Melanie did say that Gilbert wasn't like Leonard, which was nice to hear,

240 PAUL JOSEPH FRONCZAK *and* ALEX TRESNIOWSKI

but that wasn't saying very much. Melanie said that my father was the manager of a housing project in New Jersey, and gave Leonard a place to stay there. She also said Gilbert suffered an injury in the war, and came back with pain and stiffness that eventually left him hunched over. And they confirmed that my sister Linda was a difficult person. "She ran that family," Melanie said. "They were all afraid of her. 'Get me this for dinner, Daddy,' and he would run off and get it. Everyone cowered around her. A very angry person."

It was a devastating portrait of my family. A portrait that suggested madness and crippling dysfunction and perhaps, in its extremes, evil. The existence of someone like Leonard Rosenthal—if he really was as bad as his ex-wife and daughter described him—was chilling to consider. I shared roughly a quarter of my DNA with this man. Was he a genetic aberration in my family? Or was he a collection of inherited traits—Harry Rosenthal's callous disregard, David Rocco's violent temper—distilled into one abhorrent person? I knew I wasn't evil or sadistic—but what did I have inside me that was also inside him?

"I got it in me, too," Melanie told me. "I have to fight to keep all that evilness away from me. I believe I have the ability to do all the things he did. I really believe that. Only I never would, not in a million years. But I can feel it. I can feel the evil coming."

I asked Melanie if she knew where I could find Leonard. I told her I wanted to talk to him face-to-face. I needed to see him, and I needed to know who Leonard really was. If he actually was that evil, then it wasn't far-fetched to believe he might have had something to do with the disappearance of the twins. He was there with them. He had access. What did he see, and what did he know, and what did he do? I needed to find out those things from Leonard.

Both Barbara and Melanie were quick to say they had no idea

where he was—and that was by design. All they knew was that he'd lived in a succession of fleabag motels in southern New Jersey. Once in a while they'd get a call from him—they'd see a 609 area code, which they knew was in the Atlantic City area—but they never answered it. They made it very clear they wanted nothing to do with Leonard, and nothing to do with helping me find him.

Finally, I asked them if they knew for certain whether Leonard was still alive.

"Sure he is," Melanie says. "He's out there somewhere. The only reason he's still alive is because God don't want him."

I thanked them for being so honest with me, and I apologized for making them relive such horrible memories. I also told them I intended to find Leonard, one way or another.

Melanie had one last warning.

"Be careful," she said. "Leonard doesn't worship the devil. The devil worships him."

25

EVERYTHING THAT WAS happening with my birth family overshadowed the reason I'd started my search in the first place—finding the real Paul Fronczak.

The FBI was still on the case, but they never provided me with updates. I wasn't directly connected to the kidnapping, nor was I related to the real Paul. To the FBI, I was the same as anyone else who might be interested in the case. And protocol prohibited them from commenting on an open investigation to anyone outside the case.

After Sam Miller, our most promising lead, turned out not to be Paul, things slowed down. Middle-aged men with murky adoption histories continued to contact ABC because they believed they resembled the composite photo of the real Paul, but I'd stopped letting myself get my hopes up. I had learned that *lots* of people in this country have complicated identity issues.

Three men in particular closely fit the profile of the real Paul. Joe Lang had been adopted at age eight under circumstances he called suspicious. "Nothing adds up," he told *20/20*. "Nothing is normal. Everything is different all the time." Another man, Cody Hall, from Colorado, never knew his birth parents and was told he'd been found and raised by his current family. His wife thought his baby photos looked exactly like the hospital photo of Baby Paul. A Californian named David Fisher lived a troubled life because of his uncertainty about his identity, and contacted ABC after his daughter told him he was a dead ringer for the age-progressed real Paul. "If I had no mustache," he said to 20/20, "it would be me."

But DNA tests ruled out all three men.

—ɷɷ—

I booked a trip to Chicago to see my parents Dora and Chester in late 2015, but two weeks before the flight I got a call from my mother.

"Your father's not doing great," she said. "Can you come right away? I'd like you to come before something bad happens."

Her voice was heavy with sadness. We'd spoken a few times since our reconnecting call, and she'd talked about how she felt her family slipping away. My brother Dave lived in Colorado and came for visits about once a month. I hadn't been around in two years. And now my father was slipping away, too. He'd been taking a bath when a vein in his leg burst and sprayed blood everywhere. He screamed for my mother, and she called for an ambulance. Eventually, my father was diagnosed with skin cancer. But in the course of his many doctor visits, he was diagnosed with something else, too.

My father was suffering from the onset of dementia.

I wasn't prepared for that. I knew what it meant. It was possible that, in the two years since I'd last seen him, the father I knew had been lost.

"Come now," my mother told me. "I don't want the next time I see you to be at a funeral."

I rescheduled my flight and went to Chicago the next day.

My parents insisted on picking me up at the airport. I tried to talk them out of it. They were in their eighties, and I didn't want them attempting to maneuver around Midway Airport, but they wouldn't hear otherwise. They showed up at passenger pickup in their big silver Buick, my mother driving, and I jumped in the backseat.

"It's so great to see you guys," I said, as I felt my eyes well up.

"We missed you so much," my mother said.

My dad turned around in the passenger seat and looked at me. When we'd spoken on the phone in recent days, he'd forgotten my name and called me Mark and Frank.

"Hey, pal," he said this time.

"Hi, Dad," I said, putting my hand on his shoulder.

My mother asked about my flight. I told her it was the worst experience I'd ever had on a plane. I'd endured six minutes of terrifying turbulence, the plane seeming to drop out of the sky, plummeting hundreds of feet, bags flying, passengers weeping, the flight crew failing to mask their fear. A chilling silence, except for sobs and quiet prayers. I honestly thought we were going down. I believed I'd never see Emma again. A thought entered my head—*Really? This is how it ends?*

But we straightened out, and we laughed the giddy laughter of people who'd brushed against their own mortality.

I tried not to see any symbolism in the flight.

My parents still lived in the home where I was raised. They set me up with a bedroom on the second floor—my brother Dave's old room. The bigger bedroom. I saw that they'd preserved the room exactly as Dave had left it. Same bed, same posters on the wall. My old bedroom, the smaller room, had been converted to a sewing room.

That first night, the three of us sat in the basement rec room, my father and I sharing a few beers, all of us keeping the conversation light. Just catching up on little things. My father looked okay to me—frailer, weaker, yes, but not as bad as I'd imagined. A little distant at times, but engaged at others. We spent a couple of hours in the basement, and they were the warmest moments we'd had as a family in many, many years.

The next day I drove my parents to a local Best Buy. The pretense of my trip was to help my folks get a new computer and download Skype, so they could call us and see Emma whenever they wanted. We picked up a Dell desktop computer and a webcam, and back at home I set it all up. My mother seemed genuinely pleased.

On Sunday morning, the three of us sat at the kitchen table and had breakfast. Coffee, fruit, eggs, bacon. And we talked. Freely and casually. I think we were all enjoying our new, easy rapport. Suddenly, my mother reached into a drawer and pulled out a photo album. She placed the album in front of me on the table.

"What's this?" I asked.

"Take a look," she said.

I glanced at my father, and he smiled at me knowingly. Then I opened the photo album. I was shocked. These were the photos of me when I'd been in the care of Claire and Fred Eckert in Watchung, New Jersey, after I'd been abandoned. Photos of me as a young boy. Me getting my first haircut. Playing a tiny plastic guitar. Frolicking by the backyard pool. Sitting with Fred Eckert, smiling up at him. An astonishing array of sweet and happy moments. Pages and pages of Polaroid snapshots held down by unsmudged plastic sheets. It was a view into a part of my childhood I couldn't have imagined.

A part that was loving and joyful.

"They told me they didn't take pictures of the other children like this," my mother explained. "They really loved you. You were the special one."

"You've had this my whole life?" I asked her, incredulous.

"You know, we kind of forgot about it."

I didn't see how it was possible to forget about something so important, but I let it go. My mother also gave me the letters Claire Eckert had sent her, describing my likes and dislikes, my routine and personality. The letters were filled with expressions of love and concern. "He gives Eskimo kisses by rubbing noses," Claire wrote. "He will say he is tired and he likes you to hold him and sing 'Rock-a-Bye Baby.'" She said I liked flowers and I called them "flows." She said I liked pretty things and I'd point to them and say, "Pret."

"I will be hoping all is well," Claire finished the letter. "Please give my love to Scott."

I looked over at my mother, and she was crying. I was crying, too. We were crying for all the years that she'd felt she had to bury these letters. For all of the time we'd lost. I didn't want to spoil the moment by going too deep into our issues. But I also wanted answers, and there had never been a better time, a more open time, than this.

"What were you thinking when you brought me back home from New Jersey?" I finally asked, hardly believing that we were talking this way.

My mother wiped her eyes and let out a sigh.

"I had to worry if you were really my son," she said. "I had to ask myself, 'Is this really him?'"

It was the first time she'd ever expressed that sentiment to me.

"Could we have just said, 'That's not him,' and then be judged for not taking you?" my mother said. "Or could we just take you and save a child?"

She hadn't been sure. Not at all. In fact, she may have even known, deep down, that I wasn't her son. But she'd been put in an impossible situation. She was asked to look at me in a cold conference room and determine, within minutes, if I was her son. With people watching. With policemen and lawyers and reporters waiting for her decision. After having held me for just a few hours two years before. The pressure had to have been enormous. Maybe she felt there was no way she could say no.

"In my heart," my mother said, "I was hoping it was you."

Around then, my father got up from the table and walked out of the room. I could tell he didn't want to discuss these long-ago issues, or maybe he couldn't recall them. But that was okay. I hadn't expected him to. I was happy for the chance to talk about them with my mother. We sat and talked for the next ninety minutes. I asked her about the day her baby was kidnapped.

"I felt so terrible for handing him over," my mother said through tears. "I have felt guilty about that since it happened."

"Mom, it was a nurse," I said. "You were in a hospital. A nurse asks for your baby, you hand him over. How could you have said no to her?"

"Even so," my mother said. "I should have known. I shouldn't have just handed him over."

It struck me that my mother had shouldered two oppressive burdens—the guilt of possibly having picked the wrong boy when she brought me home, and the guilt of placing her real son in the hands of a kidnapper. Either one of those burdens would have been crippling. But both of them? Two monumental, unfathomable, life-altering actions, each with its own set of catastrophic results? My mother was in her early twenties when all of that happened. Those two decisions— the giving of one boy, the taking of another—were staggeringly consequential in ways someone so young couldn't possibly have known. And now I could see those two events had filled her life with regret.

My doubts about who I was had led to decades of restlessness for me.

Hers had led to a life of quiet suffering and guilt.

I felt I'd been given a better understanding of what my mother went through fifty years earlier. After burying these events and emotions for so long, it was incredibly cathartic to be able to pull them out into the light. I got to ask all the questions I'd wanted to ask for so long. It was as if my mother and I saw each other as flawed and fragile human beings, and not as unfortunate adversaries, for the first time. Our conversation wasn't about blame. It wasn't about anger. It was about accepting what had happened, and forgiving.

I also felt like my mother was given a better understanding of why I did the things I did. Why I went against her wishes and sent in her DNA test and wrenched open something she had carefully packed away.

"I was just so different, Mom," I said. "I look at Emma now and she is completely like me and Michelle. But I wasn't that way with you and Dad. And Dave was. How could you ignore that? How could I?"

Later that day, a few hours before I was set to fly back to Las Vegas, I went down to the basement to shoot some pool with my father. When he was younger, my father had been a pool shark, hustling games in Chicago pool halls. And he was still pretty good. He'd taught me how to play, and I was pretty good, too. I won the first game, and the second one.

Then I noticed my father stand up straight and look away. His face scrunched up.

"What am I doing?" he asked.

"What do you mean?"

My father just looked at me. I could see the confusion in his eyes.

"We're playing pool, Dad," I said.

He was lost. He had no idea how he'd just spent the last half hour. It broke my heart. He'd always been the big, tough guy. The strong and silent guy. Now he looked small and frail. I noticed for the first time that I was taller than him.

I pulled my father back into the present, and we shot six more games. I missed a shot here and there, and I let him win them all.

When we finished, I put my cue back in the rack. Then my father did something strange. He came up to me, and he hugged me. Not a quick half hug, either. A real hug.

"I love you, Son," he said.

"I love you, too, Dad."

At first I hugged my father back tentatively. But as he held on, I let go and fell into the hug. I just released. And I felt a flood of deep, deep relief. I gripped him a little tighter.

A memory flashed in my mind. It was me when I was in high school, bringing a girl back home before my father returned from work. Me seeing my father pull into the driveway and hustling the girl out the back door. My father coming into the living room and seeing the girl's winter gloves on the sofa. I'd always thought my father hadn't really noticed the gloves. But now, I realized he had. He saw them, and he gave me a little smile. Then he pretended he hadn't.

My parents insisted on driving me back to the airport. When we got there, my mother handed me an envelope. Inside, there was a greeting card, and inside the card was three hundred dollars in cash.

"We are so glad you came to see us," my mother wrote in the card. "We hope you can do it again really soon."

I was going to tell my parents I didn't need the money and hand it back to them, but I didn't. I just folded the twenty-dollar bills and put them in my pocket. I knew what my mother's thinking was. For two years, they hadn't sent me cards or gifts on my birthday. Now, they were making up for it.

I hugged and kissed my mother, and I told her I loved her. I turned to my father, and we slipped easily into another hug. We were old pros at it now. And it felt pretty good.

I told my parents I still wanted to find their real son.

"If not for you," I said, "then for me."

My mother shrugged.

"Well, I hope he had a good life," she said. "That's all we need to know."

My parents got back in the silver Buick and waved to me as I disappeared into the terminal. My flight back to Las Vegas was smooth.

—⟶⟶—

I didn't talk to my brother Dave about learning my identity. We hadn't spoken since he refused to take a DNA test to help me find the real Paul. That was nearly two years earlier. I didn't imagine he'd changed his mind since then.

But I did continue to trade emails with the brother I'd just found—Fred Rosenthal. We were drawing up plans to meet in person—he wasn't crazy about flying, so I said I would travel to meet him—and in the meantime we tried to help each other with the complicated emotions of our new relationship.

"Do you blame me for any of this?" Fred asked in one email.

"I don't blame you for anything," I responded. "I'm just happy to know who I am and my real birthday."

I asked Fred to send me a photo of him. He was hesitant, but he did it. When I got it, I can't say I saw myself in him. He was right—we didn't look all that alike. But maybe it was just the angle or lighting in the photo.

Fred also sent me a phone number for our sister Linda, the one who lived in a trailer outside Atlantic City. He said he'd called her and told her about me. He didn't say anything about her being difficult or unreliable. He just said I should call her.

I asked Fred how my mother and father died. He told me that in 1995 Gilbert died of pneumonia while in the hospital with another illness, most likely cancer, though Fred wasn't sure. My mother, Marie, died of cancer in 1997. Thirteen years later, my older sister Karen died of a stroke. She was only forty-seven.

"We were a very dysfunctional family," Fred wrote. "Five people living separate lives." He said the family went on vacations, and he and his father went to Philadelphia Phillies and Sixers games, but no outing was ever enjoyable. They were all strained. "We never sat around the dinner table laughing and talking and having fun," he said.

Fred said Gilbert was the family's sole provider, and gave his children all the material things they could want—everything except love. Gilbert had a mean side, and could be verbally abusive, while Marie was docile and did what she was told. Fred said he felt sad for how his mother had been treated by her husband.

Fred told me about my siblings. Linda was the oldest, and hadn't been very nice to him or Karen growing up. He gave an example that made me smile: One time Fred snuck a girlfriend into his bedroom through the window as Karen stood lookout in the hallway. But Linda ratted him out to his parents. Sneaking a girl into his bedroom—he sounded like my brother for sure.

Fred told me he had a happy life now. He had a wonderful wife of more than twenty years and awesome children. He said they all hang out and talk and laugh and really enjoy each other's company. Everything he wished he'd had in his own childhood. Fred explained that he had essentially deleted his past from his memory, until the moment I called him. "I hope that I can be someone you can be happy to have found and to call a brother," he wrote.

I told him I was more than happy to have found him, and that to me he already felt like a brother.

—〰—

The psychic had told me to go to the water, and finally I went.

It was time for me to meet my new family. Beyond Linda and Fred, my closest new relative was Melanie Rosenthal, my first cousin, down in Florida. But Melanie was having health problems and couldn't meet with me anytime soon. My next closest relation was Lenny Rocco, the doo-wop singer, first cousin once removed. I called Lenny and we made plans to meet in Philadelphia, near where he lived. He sounded excited. He was bringing his girlfriend, Barbara, and his daughter, Lenai. He'd also invited my second cousin Aimee Gourley, who'd played such a big part in cracking my case.

In late 2015, I touched down at JFK Airport in New York City and drove two and a half hours down I-95 toward Philadelphia. We were meeting in a family-owned, old-world Italian restaurant called Paganini in Doylestown, a Pennsylvania borough twenty-seven miles north of Philadelphia. I was the last one to arrive. The hostess directed me to a flight of stairs that led to a semiprivate room below the main floor. At the top of the stairs, I looked down and saw a long table crowded with people. I stood there for a moment, soaking it in.

That was my family down there.

Our first few moments together were awkward. I said hello and they said hello, and then I just stood there, next to the table where they were all seated. Some of them were pinned against a wall and couldn't get up. Some looked like they weren't sure who I was. I didn't know if I should just wave at everybody or try to shake hands or maybe go for the big group hug. Instead I just stood there and said, "How's everyone doing?" in the best New Jersey accent I could muster.

The first hug I got was from Lenny. He had on a black short-sleeve shirt unbuttoned to the top of his chest, and he wore a gold chain with two small gold boxing gloves attached. He was a thick-bodied guy, but also fit and muscled. When he hugged me, I could feel it. I also felt an instant familiarity with him. I studied his face, and he studied mine. Nothing was identical, but everything was similar.

"You both have the same smile," Barbara said.

"Well, he's my cuz," Lenny said, flashing his bright white teeth. Barbara was right. We did have the same smile.

The dinner was amazing. Lenny's spirit shone through. When the waitress read out the specials and mentioned rosemary chicken, Lenny raised an eyebrow and joked, "I'll take Rosemary." Barbara elbowed him gently. The rest of the meal was just as loose, and Lenny and Aimee were charming and open. There was no pretense, and not even that much fussing over me. It was like I was a member of the family they just hadn't seen in a while. Just *Come over, pull up a chair, let's catch up.* I felt more comfortable than I'd expected. I laughed more than I thought I might.

Lenny and I compared notes about ourselves. We already knew that we both loved music, but now we learned that we both loved motorcycles. Lenny mentioned his favorite bike had been a Harley Sportster.

"I have a Sportster now!" I said excitedly.

Lenny told me he was surprised when he first saw me walk down the stairs. "I was expecting an olive guy," he said. "Your father Gilbert was olive, like me. But you have a light complexion, like your mother. So you didn't register right away. But now I can see how you talk and how you move, and you're definitely Gilbert's kid."

Lenny told me I sounded like my father, too. "The same kind of voice, maybe an octave lower," he said. "And you walk like him."

"My daughter says I walk like I'm important," I said.

"Yep," Lenny said, "Gilbert did that, too."

I learned that Lenny and my father had been very close when they were younger. They were first cousins and they hung out together on the mean streets of Philadelphia, where they both grew up. Lenny told the story of how they used to sell eggs in tough neighborhoods when they were in their twenties. "We'd go down to the docks early in the morning and buy a couple of cases of eggs for cheap," he said. "Then we'd take the station wagon and go into these bad neighborhoods and undercut the store price. I'd yell out the window, 'Egg Men! Egg Men are here!' We sold out every time."

Until the day the men on the docks sold them a crate of rotten eggs.

"We sold those out, too, but the next day everyone got sick and they wanted their money back. Gil and I got out of there and never went back."

My father, Lenny explained, was a smooth operator. "If somebody challenged us I'd get all worked up and want to fight them," he said. "But your father would say, 'You got a point,' and then he'd get over on them. He'd never get into a fight, but he never let anyone push him around. He knew exactly how to work people."

In an instant, I realized that was exactly what I'd been doing my whole life—working people. Charming them, getting hired for jobs, getting what I needed. I blended in with everyone, fought with no one. "I never knew where that came from," I said.

"It's a Rocco thing," Lenny said. "We're good at working people."

I told Lenny I thought he was a great singer. His voice, he said, had a range of four octaves, right up there with the top singers. When he was young, he didn't plan on being a crooner. He was an acrobat and a tumbler and eventually a boxer. "Some guy told me I belonged in a ring, so they threw me in there and I knocked the guy out. Four guys in a row, I knocked out. So I became a pro. But I had this little vocal group on the side."

One night he sang in a show in a Philadelphia club, and afterward a man approached him and asked if he wanted to record an original song. Lenny said the man introduced himself as Ahmet Ertegun, the cofounder of Atlantic Records. "You have a great voice," Ahmet told him, "and I just bought you. Come and record with me."

Lenny went into an Atlantic studio and auditioned by singing "Misty." Ahmet offered him his choice of original songs in the Atlantic catalog. Lenny picked one and recorded it. An engineer turned to him and said, "Looks like you're the next superstar, kid."

But a few days later, Lenny learned Ahmet had given the same song to another singer, who turned it into a hit. "Had to do it," Ahmet said. "He's a big star. Don't worry, we'll give you another one." But Lenny didn't want to hear it. He felt betrayed.

"I walked out and I went back on the road with my band," he told me. "I felt like I didn't need anyone's help. Screw him."

Then Lenny got a different look in his eyes.

"Idiot me," he said. "Idiot me. I had a big head back then, you know? How dumb can someone be. I had my chance, and I blew it."

Lenny recorded a couple of hit singles, but never made a dime from them. He taught himself to cook and opened two successful Italian restaurants in New Smyrna Beach, Florida, but gave them up because the hours were killing him. He got married twice and moved dozens of times—just like me.

"I never wanted to sit in the same spot for too long," he said, "like a spider caught in a web."

I understood what he was saying better than he knew.

I asked Lenny about my father's brother, Leonard. I wanted to know if he was as bad as his daughter and ex-wife made him out to be.

"He was a gorilla," Lenny said. "Your father wasn't like that. Your father was a nice guy. But Leonard—he looked different. He had this rough, scaly skin, and he was crazy. Always that way, always weird. A vacancy upstairs. You couldn't ever sit down and talk to him. At the end, Gilbert stopped talking to him altogether."

In fact, Lenny said, when he heard from Carol Rolnick that one of the mysterious twins was still alive, he remembered they weren't his uncle David's twins, as he'd originally told Carol. But he still didn't think they were Gilbert's children.

"I thought they were Leonard's," he said. "What happened with the twins, I couldn't imagine Gilbert ever doing something like that. But with Leonard, I could. Leonard was the kind of guy who could abandon his twins in a heartbeat."

—⁓—

We stayed at the restaurant for three hours, talking and trading stories. Every once in a while I could sense Lenny looking at me, as if he couldn't quite believe I existed. "It's sinking in," he kept saying. "I can sense it. You and I are family."

When we got up to leave, Lenny pulled me aside.

"I can feel the emptiness in you, Paul," he said. "You're grasping for something. I can see that. And I want to help you if I can."

I told him he'd already helped me more than he could imagine.

"There's a streak," Lenny went on. "It runs through our family. It's a mean streak. An edge. Maybe it's destructive. Maybe it's self-destructive. But it's there. Through all of us. I have it, too. My bass player told me if he had my talent, he'd be rich. 'But you're a defeatist, Len,' he told me. 'You bring defeat on yourself.' That's the streak, Paul. The streak that runs through our family."

26

LENNY ROCCO HAD TWO SISTERS, Joy and Sandy, and the day after our dinner I drove out to see them. They didn't come to the dinner because they weren't speaking to Lenny. There was a feud over a business deal gone wrong, or something like that. I didn't sense any real animosity toward his sisters when Lenny talked about them; it was more like weariness. As if they didn't need a reason anymore not to get along.

I met the sisters in Joy's beautiful home in Richboro, a township in Bucks County, Pennsylvania, near the state border with New Jersey. They were my first cousins, too. Joy and Sandy greeted me with happy smiles and pulled me inside. They looked alike—pretty faces, big blond hair—and they were warm and inviting in the same way. The house was bustling; someone making spaghetti sauce in the kitchen, children running around, a mammoth flat-screen TV playing a football game. I lost track of everyone I was meeting. Some were relatives, some weren't. It didn't seem to matter.

We sat in the living room on a big sectional sofa, circling an over-size ottoman. The sisters had laid out some black-and-white photos on the ottoman for me to look at. They were the keepers of the Rocco family's photographs, I learned, as well as of a good portion of the family's oral history. But before we went in that direction, we talked for a bit about their brother Lenny.

"He has trouble making any real attachments," Sandy said. "When he was young he got five girls pregnant at the same time, and he walked away from all of them."

One of them, I figured out, was Alan Fisch's mother.

That story made me think of something Lenny had told me the night before. "When the girls like you, it makes you keep moving," he said. "You just want to keep hearing girls tell you you're good-looking. You end up living for that."

Lenny and I shared the wandering gene. Two spiders always fleeing their webs.

Joy and Sandy showed me an old picture of my grandmother Bertha Rocco. I'd seen her in the photo that accompanied the hard-luck stories in *The Philadelphia Inquirer*, and I knew she was short and squat. "We used to say she was four by four," Joy said, laughing. "Four feet wide by four feet tall. She was tiny, but she was also big. This big body balanced on two tiny feet. We were always told she wore a size four shoe."

Bertha, I learned, was the key figure in the Rocco family history. The matriarch. The driving force. Large than life. A woman of remarkable appetites. Joy and Sandy told the story of how Bertha would send them to the store to buy pounds of ham and salami and cheese when they were little. They'd bring it back and watch as Bertha created an enormous sandwich, piled three inches high.

"We all expected she would cut it up and give us each a piece," Sandy said. "But she just raised it to her mouth and took a giant bite and went on to eat the whole thing. Right in front of us!"

That mirrored a story Lenny had told me the night before, about Bertha coming over to his house for dinner when he was young, and devouring a monstrous plate of spaghetti. "My mother would kid her and say, 'Did you eat enough, dear?'" Lenny recalled. "And Bert would get in a huff and say, 'I'm gonna run around the block and sit down again and eat another bowl, is that okay with you?'"

Joy and Sandy also spoke of the Rocco family's history of toughness. It traced back at least to my great-grandfather John Rocco, the boxer who fought under the name Thomas Murphy. Joy showed me an old sepia portrait of John; his wife, Sarah; and three of their children. It was taken in a photographer's studio, against a velvet curtain backdrop. John Rocco, young and handsome, wore a dark pin-striped suit and bow tie, his black hair slicked back. His face was wide and square-jawed, his expression neutral. Yet even though he was seated, with his family standing behind him, he conveyed a kind of power and strength—a solidness. His hands rested on his thighs, curled into fists. It wasn't hard to imagine him pummeling someone in a boxing ring— not hard at all.

The family toughness worked its way down to John's son David— the bad seed. The character you didn't want to mess with. Joy and Sandy explained that David was the strong-arm boss of a Mack truck union—the kind of man who would settle a score with neighbors by defecating on their lawn. He had a maniacal laugh and a lightning-quick temper. I heard different versions of the story, but apparently David went to prison for killing a man in a fight—then may have killed another man in prison. It was his own mother, Bertha, they told me, who initially turned David in to the police.

"Why'd you do that to your own son?" someone asked her.

"Because he was a no-good son-of-a-bitch," she replied.

David's wife, Shirley, too, could be a brawler. Joy and Sandy remembered her getting into a bloody fistfight with their mother on a sidewalk after arguing over whose baby was more beautiful.

Then there was David's nephew Leonard Rosenthal. The sisters agreed he was an intimidating character. They remembered not liking him when they were little girls, and putting mounds of pepper in his soup while he wasn't looking, just to see what would happen. They watched in awe as Leonard ate all the soup and never flinched.

Finally, I asked Joy and Sandy about the twins.

Sandy remembered her mother answering the phone one day, and hearing Bertha yell through the receiver: "It's twins! Jack and Jill!" I was relieved to hear my birth had been a source of happiness for someone. Sandy also remembered her mother sitting her and her sister down two years later.

"The twins died," her mother told them, "but, you know . . ."

Then their mother trailed off.

I asked Sandy what she thought that meant—her mother saying "but you know" and trailing off. "It was like an insinuation," Sandy said. "Like there was more to the story."

But like everyone else, they were told never to mention the twins to anyone, and all they heard over the years were fragments of stories with one common theme.

"Jill was dropped," Sandy said. "That's all we heard—Jill was dropped. But how does that explain what happened to the twins?"

—⁓—

I went through dozens of photos with Joy and Sandy. Photos of my father Gilbert as a boy, posing alongside Leonard and their mother, Bertha. In the photos, Leonard looked enormous next to my father— taller, wider, stronger. Photos of Gilbert and Leonard with Joy and Sandy, standing stiffly and forcing smiles. Photos of aunts and uncles and cousins and long-gone ancestors—photos of everyone, except of me or my parents.

"We have no pictures of Gilbert and Marie," Joy said. "There's a lot of him when he was young, but then they just stopped."

It was as if my father lived the last forty years of his life in self-imposed secrecy. I wondered if the photos had stopped after the twins disappeared. Could that have been the dividing line between anything that was light and good and worth celebrating in my father's life, and the darkness that followed?

Both Joy and Sandy remembered seeing a photo of the twins when they were younger. They remembered because the names Jack and Jill were written across the bottom of the photo. They'd dug through three huge bins of photos but hadn't found it, and they apologized for not looking through two or three other bins they said were buried beneath mounds of boxes in various closets. I said that, if it was okay with them, I'd like to try to find those bins.

We set out on a massive search of Joy's large house, focusing on a closet in her laundry room. Bags and boxes came out, clearing a path to a large plastic bin on the floor. Finally, we yanked it out and dragged it to the living room. It was loaded with photos, but not the photo we were looking for. The photo of Jack and Jill.

I didn't want to stop looking for it, but I knew I shouldn't be tearing up Joy's house in a frantic bid to find it. It's just that, without even really knowing it, I was longing to see what my twin sister looked like. I was longing to see us side by side, before whatever happened happened. Did she look like me? Would we be smiling? Would our arms be around each other? All I had to prove that Jill existed was a tiny newspaper item and a copy of a birth certificate. A photo would have helped me see her as more than just the missing piece of my family puzzle.

But it wasn't to be. We didn't find the photo. Joy and Sandy promised they'd keep looking. It had to be somewhere, they said. All things have to be somewhere.

—〰—

The next morning, I left Pennsylvania and took the Atlantic City Expressway to Mays Landing, New Jersey, about nineteen miles west of Atlantic City. I was getting closer to the water. Mays Landing was the home of the Atlantic County Veterans Cemetery—the place where my birth parents, Gilbert and Marie Rosenthal, were buried.

The cemetery was inside Estell Manor Park, a seventeen-acre park bordering the Great Egg Harbor River. I drove through acres of barren trees until I reached the end of a dirt road that was blocked by a wooden fence. My GPS had led me there, but I was lost. I called the main office of the cemetery and asked for directions. "Everyone misses the turn," a cheerful woman told me, before explaining where I could find the entrance.

Ten minutes later I was there. It was a bright, sunny day. I parked and walked over to a sign that told me the cemetery had been built on the site of the old Estellville Glass Factory. Nearby, a glassed-in bulletin board showed a map of all the burial plots, but I couldn't quite make sense of it. I looked around, and all I saw were flatlands. No headstones. There was a statue of a soldier and a tall flagpole flying the American flag. But everything else was just grass.

Another movie scene flashed in my mind. The final shoot-out from *The Good, the Bad and the Ugly*. I was Tuco, the Mexican bandit, running frantically through a sprawling cemetery, searching for a grave without a name.

Fortunately, I knew the numbers of the plots I was looking for, so I just started walking around. It took me about twenty minutes to find them. I found Gilbert's first, and then I saw Marie's right next to his. The graves were about two feet apart, marked by bronze plaques laid an inch into the ground. The plaques were covered with crumbling leaves. I knelt over my father's plaque and brushed the leaves away.

GILBERT R. ROSENTHAL, PVT US ARMY, KOREA, his plaque read. I hadn't found my father's military records yet, so that was how I learned he'd fought in Korea. Beneath his rank, there was a Jewish star and the years of his birth and death. Below that, the inscription BELOVED HUS-BAND AND FATHER. My mother's plaque was simpler: just her name, her birth and death dates, and a matching inscription: BELOVED WIFE AND MOTHER.

I found myself in another moment when I felt I should have been emotional, but wasn't. I got down on one knee and lingered over my mother's grave, trying to feel whatever I was feeling—to let whatever was inside come out. But there wasn't much there. I hadn't known these people. I couldn't remember them. As much as I wished they had been, they were not "beloved" to me. I did feel sad, but part of that was because of where I was. The late afternoon sun cast a dazzling golden light that washed over all the grave sites, and that alone filled me with melancholy. The contrast between the living and the dead, the beauti-ful and the buried. The slow passage of time that had consumed them, my parents, ending, I hoped, whatever guilt and suffering they had carried. The sadness of what was lost. I felt all that, and if I'd tried a little harder, I am sure I could have cried.

But I didn't. Instead, I leaned a little closer to my mother's plaque and said something that surprised me to hear.

"Where's Jill?" I said. "What happened to Jill?"

—◇—

I had one final place to go before my trip was over—Atlantic City.

The expressway took me there in twenty minutes. On the drive in, the scattered casinos appeared as hazy blocks on the horizon. Beyond them was the ocean, which had its own strong pull. I felt like I was driving into a place of myth—a place larger than its limits. A place where anything could happen.

I'd never been to Atlantic City—well, not since being born there—but I'd read up on it. A little strip of a city, on an island off the southern coast of New Jersey, a final narrow jut of land before the vast Atlantic. The World's Playground, site of the country's first boardwalk, home of the Miss America pageant, basis for the game of Monopoly, birthplace of saltwater taffy—so named, the legend goes, after a storm flooded a taffy store and soaked everything in ocean water.

But the flip side to Atlantic City's glamour is a history of lawlessness. Shiny Prohibition-era hotels—the Chalfonte-Haddon Hall, the Marlborough-Blenheim, the Traymore, the Claridge—gave way to the garish casinos of the 1970s, but the lifeblood of the city—kickbacks, payoffs, extortions, corruption—never stopped churning. The racketeer Enoch "Nucky" Johnson, immortalized in *Boardwalk Empire,* paved the way for Nicodemo Scarfo, the heartless gangster who cut his teeth in Atlantic City before taking over the murderous Philadelphia–South Jersey mob.

A place, it seemed to me, where the past was constantly paved over but never truly suppressed. A place as likely as any to be home to ghosts.

And it was here where my family lived, here where I was born.

CeCe and the team had helped me find the records that showed me where my parents had lived. In 1960, the year Gilbert and Marie were married, they moved in with his mother in her large but narrow, white-shingled home at 107 North Georgia Avenue, in the neighborhood known as Ducktown, Atlantic City's equivalent to Little Italy—just up the street, in fact, from where Nicky Scarfo had owned a home.

In September 1963—one month before the twins were born—my parents bought a home at 201 Seagull Drive, a few miles inland from the boardwalk. We found records that showed they sold that house less than two years later, in January 1965—only a month after their last child, Fred, was born. Fred's birth certificate already listed the family's new address as 278 North Mississippi Avenue—site of Pitney Village, the state's first public housing community, and the place where Gilbert went to work as a security officer. But there was no evidence my family lived at that address in 1965 or even 1966—housing authority records listed the house as vacant both years. My father was first listed as the home's occupant a year later, in 1967. Whether they lived there in 1965—the year the twins disappeared and I was abandoned—or elsewhere, perhaps in Bertha's home up the block, I didn't know.

I drove into Atlantic City wanting to see the streets where my parents had walked. The house on Seagull Drive was first, but I couldn't find it. The street numbers had changed. I had a small picture of the house, which I compared to the homes I could see, and I think I figured out which one it was, but I couldn't be sure. Down the street, I saw an elderly woman fussing with something on her front lawn. I walked over and tried not to frighten her as I approached. I told her I was looking for my family's old home, and I asked if she'd lived in the neighborhood for long.

"Sixty years," she said, without stopping her pruning or looking at me.

I asked if she happened to remember the Rosenthals, who lived at 125.

"No, I don't," she said. That was the end of our conversation.

I wasn't that interested in 201 Seagull Drive anyway. I knew that my parents had moved out five months before I was abandoned. If something had happened to Jill that led my parents to get rid of me, my thinking was it likely happened not too long before I was left on the street. I couldn't imagine Jill being given away or hurt or even killed, and my parents waiting five months before deciding what to do with me. I imagined that whatever happened, happened fast. First Jill, then me. Over and done with. Which meant that whatever happened likely happened where my parents lived after selling their home on Seagull Drive. If they didn't move into their new home until 1967, my guess was that they went back to live with Bertha at 107 North Georgia Avenue.

In Ducktown, in Atlantic City.

That was my next stop. I drove down the expressway, past Baltic Avenue and into the city, turned right, and traveled a few blocks toward Bally's Casino. Two blocks from the casino was North Georgia Avenue. The neighborhood had seen better days. A quarter of Atlantic City's residents live below the poverty line. These streets reflected that reality. It was a bright, sunny afternoon, but the area was all but empty. All the activity was two blocks away, between the casinos and the boardwalk. Just a few hundred yards inland, the town felt nearly deserted.

I looked at the numbers of the houses and found 105 North Georgia Avenue. The next house, which was several lots over, was numbered 113. The house where Bertha Rocco had lived was gone. All that remained was an empty lot, hemmed in by a chain-link fence.

I parked my car and took a walk into the lot. The house next door, 105, seemed like it had been there a hundred years, so I could imagine what Bertha's house might have looked like. It would have been two stories high and fairly deep, but narrow—maybe thirty feet across. There would have been a front porch and a back porch, and a small backyard. It would have been a fine and lovely home. Our records showed Bertha bought it in 1948 and sold it in 1967, twice flipping the ownership from her to her son Leonard and back. That was nearly twenty years of living in this slot. Children raised, a million meals cooked—a family come and gone. More than likely I'd lived in this spot, too, if only for a few months.

Now, there was only trash and rocks and scrub. Broken bottles, old wrappers, the tiny red arm of a Spider-Man figurine. The ground crunched as I walked. I stayed for a while in the back of the lot, where the yard would have been. It would have been perfectly visible from the back decks of the neighbors on either side. The houses on the block were built literally side by side, with a few inches, at best, between them. The backyards might have even been shared rather than separated by fences. It would not have been a very private place back there at all.

But still, I couldn't help but wonder. If something bad had happened to Jill—something really bad—could she have wound up here, in the backyard?

—⟋⟍⟍—

Just one block away, I searched for the spot that used to be 278 North Mississippi Avenue, the home listed on Fred Rosenthal's birth certificate. I already knew it was no longer there. The historic Pitney Village had been demolished in the 1990s by the Casino Reinvestment Development Authority—razed to make way for a giant parking lot. There was no trace of what used to be there, no way to pinpoint where my parents had lived without the help of a surveyor. It was all concrete now, the past neatly buried.

My final stop in Atlantic City was the hospital where I was born. It used to be called Atlantic County Hospital, but now it was known as AtlantiCare Regional Medical Center. It was between the Caesars and Resorts casinos. I had a thought to go in and look for the room where I came into the world. But when I called the main office, they told me the maternity ward had long since been moved. For all I knew the spot where I was born was a cafeteria now. I saw no reason to go inside, so I snapped a photo with my phone and drove away.

I left Atlantic City and headed back to my hotel. I had another night and another half day on the East Coast before flying back to Las Vegas. I was tired, and I wanted to eat dinner and call Michelle and Emma and go to sleep.

But all along I knew there was another stop I had to make before I flew home. I just wasn't sure if I would make it. I had a feeling I'd put it off until the very end of my stay, and decide at the last minute if I would go. But no—that was nonsense. Driving out of Atlantic City, I realized I had a choice. Of course I had to go there.

So I went.

On the way, I stopped in a store and picked up a fake orchid to bring as a gift. I thought of what I might say when I saw her, but I decided against any kind of speech and figured I'd just say what I felt. A traffic circle spun me around and into the trailer park where she lived. A nameless dirt road brought me to her home.

The place where my sister Linda Rosenthal lived.

I hesitated before walking up to her door. All I'd heard was that she might be a difficult person. I tried not to think any bad or scary thoughts, but I did anyway. Who knew what was waiting for me on the other side of the door? I pushed the bad thoughts aside and told myself I was being ridiculous. Then I slowly made my way to the trailer door.

There was a car out front, and my guess was that Linda was home. I knocked on the side of the screen door, lightly at first, then more firmly. I knocked several times, but no one answered or even moved inside the trailer. Seagulls squawked overhead. A yellow school bus drove by. I held my ground and knocked again. But I moved slightly off center to the door. The image of a shotgun appeared in my mind.

I was there for a solid five minutes before I decided to knock one last time. I also leaned toward the trailer and hollered inside.

"Hello? Is anyone there? This is Paul. Paul Fronczak."

Still nothing, still silence.

Then, I imagined I heard something. A shuffling across a floor. But I hadn't imagined it. It was real. Someone was moving inside the trailer. The door creaked open, and I took a half step back. Through the screen door I saw my sister Linda.

"Hi," I said. "I'm Paul. Your brother."

"I know who you are," Linda said. "Come inside."

—∽—

The trailer was dark and stuffy. At least one cat lived there, probably more, judging from the smell. I sat on the sofa, which was covered with a blanket. Linda sat in a chair across from me. An old, unplugged computer monitor was on a table against the wall. A fuzzy, white, midsize dog ambled into the living room, looked me over, growled a bit, and walked away.

For a moment, Linda and I just looked at each other. That had become a ritual for me—examining the faces of newly discovered relatives to see which features we shared. At first glance, Linda and I didn't look much alike. Her face was roundish, while mine was long and edged. I didn't think we had the same eyes or lips or anything. But as we started talking, I saw more and more of myself in her. A softness around the eyes. A little half smile that I recognized as my own. Even Linda's chin—more prominent than I'd realized. We *did* look similar. But Linda had led a hard life. Much harder than mine, from what I'd heard. Whatever dark circumstances had caused me to be abandoned on a sidewalk were the very circumstances Linda had had to endure her whole childhood. We looked different because we'd been raised differently. Linda hadn't gotten away.

She told me she'd watched the 20/20 specials about my case. She knew my story. I asked her how it felt to have her long-lost brother suddenly sitting across from her. She smiled and let out a laugh, but didn't answer other than that.

Then I asked her what it'd been like living with my family. The Rosenthals. What had I missed? Linda's expression changed.

"It was tough," she said. "Our father was not a nice person. Nobody liked him. No one went to his funeral. When he died, my mother was happy he was gone."

I was taken aback. No one went to his funeral? Could that be true? I asked her where the family lived in the years after Fred was born. She told me she remembered going to live with her grandmother Bertha in her home on North Georgia Avenue. "We used to call it the white house," she said. "We liked living there."

My hunch had been correct. After my parents sold their house on Seagull Drive, and before they moved into Pitney Village, they'd lived with Bertha again. Almost certainly I had lived there, and so, most likely, had Jill.

I asked Linda if she remembered the twins, or if she knew what happened to them.

"I don't remember them at all," she said.

Linda would have been three or four years old when the twins disappeared. It was possible she had no memory of them. But that didn't seem likely to me. Still, I didn't want to push too hard. I was happy to have found her, and to be sitting with her, and I didn't want to blow it by being too inquisitive. There would be time for that later. Now, I just wanted to get to know my sister a little bit.

Just a few minutes into our talk, the door of the trailer swung open. A small teenage girl walked in. Her long dark hair covered most of her face, and she was listening to music through earbuds. At first she didn't even notice me sitting on the sofa. When she saw me, she froze.

"This is your uncle Paul," Linda said.

I waved at her and said hi. I think she said hi back, but I couldn't be sure. Then she sat in a chair at the table in the back of the trailer, hunched over a book, and put her earbuds back in. Linda said something to her, and she pulled off the buds and said, "What?" Then she disappeared again into her book and her music. Linda and I continued our talk with the niece I'd met for the very first time sitting in total seclusion a few feet away.

Linda told me she and our brother, Fred, didn't get along. They texted every now and then, but they hadn't seen each other in years. Fred had never even met Linda's daughter, who was sixteen. With everything she told me, my heart broke a little more. The deep dysfunction that Fred had described in his email to me—the lack of any closeness or affection in the family—was, by Linda's telling, an understatement. The family, if it could even be called that, was hanging on by the thinnest of seams. There were ruptures and wounds and grudges everywhere. The streak that Lenny had warned me of—disruptive, destructive, inescapable—had laid waste to these people. The ones who hadn't died seemed to be fighting just to survive.

I wanted to get up from the sofa and pull Linda into my arms for a hug. But I didn't. I didn't dare. She was so broken. Beaten down by life. There was anger and hurt and bitterness in her, but none of it came out as venom. Instead, there was resignation. A weariness. This was her lot. This was her family. What could she hope to do about it?

We talked for about a half hour. I didn't want to stay too long, because I didn't want to keep asking questions that led to painful answers. I wanted our first meeting to end on a lighter note. I told Linda I had to go, but I asked if I could take her and her daughter to lunch the following day.

Linda smiled. She straightened in her chair.

"I'd like that," she said.

She walked me out of the trailer and onto the deck, and there we finally hugged. She seemed genuinely happy to have met me, and happy to have the chance to see me again. She gave me her phone number, and I told her I'd call her in the morning to set up a time, then come by and pick up her.

"We'll go anywhere you want," I said. "We'll pick a really nice place."

I left feeling more hopeful than I had in a while. Everything I'd heard about my family was horrible, and the damage was worse than I'd thought. But maybe, just maybe, we could move beyond all that, those of us who were left, and salvage whatever connection was still there. Linda and I. Fred and I. Lenny and Joy and Sandy. Maybe together we could forge something new, something healthy. Not a family, perhaps, but something. Something that might help us all heal.

I drove back to my hotel and called Michelle and told her about Linda. I also texted a photo I took of Linda and me to CeCe. I wanted her to know I'd connected with my sister, and that all her hard work was paying off. I googled "best restaurants Atlantic City" to find a place where I could take Linda and my niece to lunch.

A bit later that evening, I checked my emails on my phone. I saw there was an email from Fred. He hadn't written in a while, and my last two emails to him had gone unanswered. So I was glad to see his name pop up. I guessed he'd spoken to Linda and was writing to share his thoughts about our meeting.

But that's not why he wrote.

Hi Paul, I have to be honest with you. I am not interested in meeting you nor establishing a relationship. I'm not convinced that we are related, but even if we were, I would feel the same. So please do not try to make contact with me, I wish to be left alone. Thank you.

I called the number Linda gave me, but no one answered. I tried her again the next morning, but she didn't pick up. Around noon I drove to her trailer and knocked on her screen door again. Several knocks.

This time, the door never opened.

27

I CALLED LINDA A few more times after I got back to Las Vegas, but she didn't answer. Something had happened after our meeting that caused her to shut me out, and I struggled to understand what it was. Clearly she had spoken with Fred. His email couldn't have been coincidental. Maybe I'd asked too many questions about the twins, and that spooked one or both of them. And together, they decided to keep their stories buried. Or maybe Fred called the shots and had warned Linda not to talk to me again.

What was Fred afraid of? He'd told me he was a private man and didn't want to end up on a *20/20* special. I understood that, and all I wanted was the chance to meet him—to see if we could get along and possibly help each other. But after I knocked on Linda's door out of the blue, he might have figured I'd do the same to him one day—just show up. And so, perhaps, he shut the whole thing down.

I didn't answer Fred's email. The truth is, I was angry. Hurt and angry. If he didn't want anything to do with me, fine—I didn't want anything to do with him. I probably should have shown more compassion for him and what he was going through; after all, I knew what it was like to get shocking news about yourself and your family. But all I felt was anger. I'd found my family after all this time, and now they were doing to me what my parents had done fifty years earlier—they were casting me out. And that rejection hurt.

—⁓—

At home, the situation with Michelle hadn't improved. As she'd feared, the discovery of my identity had only led to more questions, more searching, more time away from my family. We still had our fights, but mostly we were settling into a chilly distance from each other. I could see the frustration in Michelle's face whenever we talked.

"If you gave your family half the energy that you're giving this case, we'd be fine," she said.

I could also tell Michelle was starting to believe she really didn't know me. We'd been together for ten years, but ten years with someone doesn't guarantee you get to see who they are. What upset her was the ease with which I walked away from attachments. For instance, she knew how much I loved playing my Rickenbacker bass guitar; she'd see me pick it up and play it around the house all the time. But then I abruptly stopped playing, and sold the Rickenbacker. Just like that, it was gone—something that had been a part of my life, a symbol of my passion. Michelle just couldn't understand it.

"Why would you sell a guitar you love so much?" she asked.

"I wasn't playing it anymore," I said.

For a while Michelle and I took up shooting at a gun range. She could tell I loved it, and she was happy to see me get together with her father to go to the range and shoot. But then, abruptly, I dropped that, too. I just stopped doing it and I sold the gun I'd only recently bought. Nothing sticks. Nothing lasts.

She also didn't understand how I could not talk to my parents for two years. The conflict that drove us apart—that was one thing. But that I could go so long without trying to reach out and mend fences—that baffled her. I didn't even seem all that bothered by not seeing them. What was it about me that allowed me to walk away from people so easily? she wondered. And if it was that easy for me to do, wasn't she right to be scared that I would walk away from her, too?

Then there was the question of genetics. Michelle felt deep anger toward the people who had abandoned me. But she also knew those people were *my* people. They were my blood. She would hear the bits of information about the Roccos and Leonard Rosenthal, and it dawned on her, as it dawned on me, that some of the men in my family were hard, dangerous men. Something twisted and broken ran through the line—and maybe that something was what allowed me to walk away from jobs and people so easily. Not that I was evil, or even that I did what I did intentionally—just that I had an ability to separate my emotions from my actions. Maybe that was how the Rocco streak affected me.

On top of all that, Michelle could see that our daughter, Emma Faith, was turning out to be a lot like me. Michelle was the rules follower, the regimented one. I was the improviser, the one who was okay with paying bills late. And Emma was more like me in that regard. She was all over the place, trying new things, jumping from branch to branch, her curiosity insatiable—a blur of energy that was often unfocused. Michelle couldn't help but worry about which of my traits Emma had inherited, and what kind of person that would make her. I was worried about the same thing.

"Why don't you quit your job, Daddy?" Emma said to me one day. "So you can spend more time with me?"

"What would I do for work if I quit?" I asked her.

She thought about it for a moment, but only for a moment.

"I don't know, we'll think of something," she said.

Which was exactly how I'd viewed every job I ever had—if it didn't work out, I'd think of something and be just fine.

But that had been the whole point of my search—to learn the

truth about myself, so I could better understand why I acted the way I did, and change it if I needed to. So I could set a better example for Emma. I never thought it would take three years to learn the truth, and I guess that was naïve. I also never considered what I would do once I learned it, as if just learning it would somehow fix whatever was wrong with me. But now that I knew my true identity, and was discovering more and more about my family, it was obvious the process was just beginning. I was only at the very start of the disruptive phase—the phase where everything gets blown apart. Whatever healing might happen—if healing was even possible—was still a long way off.

If I'm being honest, I have to admit I never sat down and took stock of the emotional repercussions of being Jack Rosenthal. The complexity of the search gave me an excuse to get lost in names and addresses and DNA results, rather than take a hard look at what was going on inside my head. I'd known I'd been abandoned since I was ten and found those newspaper articles, and that presented its own set of psychological problems, which, sadly, I'd never dealt with. But now to learn I had a twin sister, and that she was missing—and possibly dead—took things to another level. I began to notice that people who knew about my case felt really bad for me. It was there in the Facebook messages—outpourings of empathy and compassion. It was there in my arguments with Michelle—an underlying sadness at what I'd had to go through. Whether or not I realized it myself, I was a seriously damaged man, or at least that's how the world was starting to see me.

I'd never been in therapy, other than the few sessions of marriage counseling I went to with Michelle. My parents, the Fronczaks, weren't the type of people to sit around and hash out their problems, much less share them with a stranger. I didn't learn to be self-analytical, and I never saw the need. But now, I was beginning to see the need.

Still, I didn't want to start any kind of counseling while I was searching for answers about Jill, and about the real Paul. It wasn't time to unpack everything yet. But I did ask a friend to talk to two psychologists he knew, to get a general idea of the issues someone like me might be facing. The psychologists specialized in childhood trauma. It was a kind of back-door way to maybe get an answer to what, clinically speaking, might be wrong with me.

What my friend reported back was sobering. My guess had been that I had attachment disorder, which is common among adoptees. People who have attachment disorder can behave in ways that reflect their early relationship with their parents. For instance, someone who felt an insecure attachment to her mother or father might hold on too tightly to loved ones in adulthood. Someone whose parents were unpredictable might grow up acting as if he doesn't care about attachments. Chaotic parenting styles can make people commitment-phobic.

But my case wasn't just about parenting styles.

It was far more likely, the psychologists told my friend, that someone like me was suffering from post-traumatic stress disorder.

Suffering trauma as a child—even if we can't remember it—can dictate how we act as adults. One psychologist told the story of a patient who felt the strong urge to drink alcohol at the same time every day, and didn't understand why. Therapy helped him realize he was drinking at the very hour his father used to beat him when he got home from work. These "anniversary reactions" are the imprinted reminders of suppressed trauma.

"The body remembers," the psychologist said.

There was another term that came up—*burnt child*. It referred to a syndrome that was often diagnosed through Rorschach testing. A burnt child was someone who attempted to contain and bury the pain he was feeling—who showed an inability to access emotions. That brutal term has now been replaced by the slightly less disturbing *toxic stress.*

Someone like me, the psychologist said, "could be frozen. Numb. Not capable of remembering things in the same way most people are. Not able to verbalize it or deal with it, other than by burying it. He may have an adaptive talent—he can be functional. But that is not optimal. There is getting over something, and there is pushing it under. Optimal development is not about pushing things under."

Those suffering from PTSD could also be resistant to treatment, I learned. My friend related the story of an PTSD experiment that separated the test subjects into two groups—one that would receive therapy right away, and another that would follow in a few weeks. Normally, in a medical experiment, people clamor to get into the first group. They want to get their treatment right away. But not PTSD patients. "They were begging to be put on the wait list," one psychologist said. "They wanted to wait. Even after they'd realized they had serious problems and agreed to be part of the study, they wanted to wait. They wanted to avoid treatment as long as possible."

Why? Why would they do that?

"Because they could imagine the torrent of pain once the floodgate was open."

My friend told the psychologists about my discovery that I was a twin, and about how my sister was missing and maybe dead. Neither psychologist wanted to diagnose someone they weren't treating, but they offered opinions about the special circumstances of my case.

"He doesn't know what is frozen inside the bottom of the glacier," one said. "If his twin suddenly disappeared, and the next day there was an empty space where she used to be, that is something he will have carried his whole life, even if he didn't realize it. An empty space. A tremendous sadness about his sister."

What if the twin didn't just disappear? What if she'd been murdered?

"Then down at the bottom of the glacier, what he could possibly discover is that he was there when it happened. He may have seen it all."

—⁂—

After Fred and Linda shut me out, I turned my attention to Leonard Rosenthal.

He had emerged as the most intimidating of the dysfunctional Roccos. He was elusive; no one knew where he was or what he was up to. It's possible he was on the run from something or someone.

And he'd been there. He'd been there when the twins were alive. Property records showed he lived with his mother, Bertha, at 107 North Georgia Avenue in Atlantic City, at the time my parents likely moved there, five months before I was abandoned. I'd heard harsh things about both Gilbert and Marie, but nothing that suggested they could be capable of killing a child. One theory was that Gilbert's crippling arthritis may have caused him to accidentally drop my twin sister, resulting in her death, and that was certainly possible. But could you kill a two-year-old child just by dropping her?

And my mother? By all accounts she was under tremendous stress, after giving birth to five children within four years. Was it possible that she snapped and hurt one of the twins? Yes, it was possible. But I wasn't leaning that way.

With a family that was riddled with violent, broken men, I couldn't bring myself to pin the most heinous act of all on my mother.

But Leonard? What I'd heard about him suggested he might be different. He apparently had it in him to bring harm. And he had been right there when the twins disappeared. He was an old man now, in his mid-eighties, and fifty years removed from whatever happened. But still, I felt I needed to find him and talk to him. I needed to look him in the eye and ask him point-blank: *What happened to Jill?*

His ex-wife, Barbara, and his daughter, Melanie, insisted they didn't know where he was, and I believed them. They'd been trying to rid themselves of him for a long time, and even talking about him brought him too close for comfort. As if they could invoke the turmoil he had brought to their lives simply by saying his name.

I ran a basic records search for Leonard Rosenthal, but all I found were some old addresses in Florida. I knew he'd lived there with Barbara and Melanie, but the only bit of information they'd given me was that he was back in South Jersey, occasionally calling them from a 609 area code. The last known addresses for Leonard in New Jersey weren't current. For the last ten years, he'd barely left a trace.

I needed help. A friend connected me with a private investigator based in Maryland. His name was Nino Perrotta, and he'd done investigative work as a special agent for the Secret Service and the Department of Homeland Security. I called Nino and told him my story, and he agreed to help. He said every case was personal for him, and he said he'd been touched by what I'd gone through. I told him that by all accounts Leonard was a slippery, elusive character.

"Don't worry," Nino said, "we'll find him."

—⁓—

I'd soon learn that Nino was a special breed of investigator—intuitive, charismatic, relentless. His parents had emigrated from Benevento in southern Italy in 1965 and opened Perrotta Salumeria, an Italian delicatessen in Mount Vernon, New York. Starting at a young age, both Nino and his younger brother, Anthony, helped out at the deli, stocking cans, cleaning shelves, mopping floors, and, eventually, making fresh mozzarella and manning the register. Nino's dream, however, was to get into law enforcement. It was a dream born of a family tragedy.

Nino told me the story of his grandfather, who sold vegetables strapped to a donkey in Italy. One day at the market, someone's coat was stolen, and police arrested Nino's grandfather. He hadn't done it, but the shame of the arrest was too much of a stain on the family name for him to bear. Just hours before the real thief was found, Nino's grandfather slit his throat in prison. He left behind a young wife he hadn't known was pregnant.

"It was *la bruta fortuna*," Nino said. "A sad, unlucky situation. He couldn't tolerate being unjustly accused of a crime. And my grandmother never remarried."

Ever since hearing the story when he was young, Nino has been driven by an impossible goal. "All I want to do is go back in time and solve the case before my grandfather kills himself," he says. "I want to save him by solving the case. But I can't. I can never save him. And it haunts me."

Nino majored in political science at Fordham University before becoming one of the first civilian investigators hired by New York City Mayor David Dinkins to root out police corruption in the 1980s. From there he went to work in the Bronx district attorney's office and learned the nuts and bolts of organized crime cases. He moved on to the investigative arm of the Secret Service, then was recruited by the Department of Homeland Security two years after 9/11. A few years ago, he started a side business as a private investigator.

Nino began the hunt for Leonard with a more sophisticated data search than the one I'd performed. A police contact provided information that Leonard had been on the radar of law enforcement for some unknown crime as recently as a year ago. Another data search listed a hotel in south New Jersey as one of Leonard's most recent residences.

Nino called the hotel and asked for Leonard's room. He was told there was no Leonard Rosenthal there.

Nino told the hotel clerk he was a relative who needed to find Leonard. The clerk told him he wasn't allowed to give out information about current or previous guests. Nino kept pushing. He assumed a role—the role of an elderly, frightened relative who had to find Leonard and find him soon. He pleaded for the clerk's help. Nino's thinking was that Leonard was lonely and likely talked to anyone who would listen, especially a captive audience like a hotel clerk. If Leonard had been there, maybe he'd told the clerk where he was going next. But the clerk didn't budge. He had no information. Nino kept digging. The conversation went on for ten minutes.

Finally, the clerk told Nino that Leonard had indeed been there, but left a few months ago.

It was a sighting. Leonard was in South Jersey. But where? Nino took a step back and imagined Leonard's life. He was old. He was probably in bad health. He didn't have much money and he'd recently stayed in a hotel that cost sixty dollars a night. Almost certainly he didn't own a car. So where could he go? Where would his next stop be?

He would go somewhere close. Somewhere he could get to by taxicab. A short, cheap cab ride. Nino sat down and began calling all the inexpensive hotels and nursing homes within ten miles of Leonard's last sighting.

—〜〜—

Five days after I hired Nino, I got an email from him.

"LEONARD FOUND!" read the subject line.

I'd been searching for Leonard on and off for months. Nino found him in less than a week.

Nino told me how he tracked him down. The first twenty or so phone calls he made led nowhere. Eventually he called a hotel in Hammonton, New Jersey, thirty miles from Atlantic City but just down the road from where Leonard was last seen. It was called the Red Carpet Inn, and rooms there rented for forty-three dollars a night. Nino slipped into another role—an elderly woman who needed help finding a friend.

The clerk at the Red Carpet was an Indian woman who spoke very broken English. Nino had to slowly spell Leonard's first and last names to get her to check if he was there.

"No, ma'am," the clerk finally said. "Not here."

Nino pretended he didn't understand.

"No, no, I'm calling to *confirm* that Leonard Rosenthal is there," he said.

"No, ma'am, not here."

"I'm so sorry to bother you. But I am *confirming* that Leonard is there."

They went back and forth for several minutes. Recalling the moment later, Nino told me what he was thinking. "I was thinking that this hotel clerk believed she was dealing with a half-dead little lamb," he said. "But actually I was a wolf about to suck all her blood."

"Okay," the clerk finally said, "he's here."

She put Nino through to Leonard's room. A gruff voice answered. Quickly, Nino switched roles—this time, an elderly woman who had the wrong number.

"Hello? Oh, I'm so sorry, who is this?"

"This is Leonard."

"Oh my goodness, I'm so sorry, I'm confused. Oh, and you sound like such a sweet person."

"You do, too, honey."

"Are you a Jewish boy? What's your name again?"

"Leonard Rosenthal. And what's yours, dear?"

"I'm Mary, and I'm so sorry. I don't know why they transferred me to you."

A few minutes later, Leonard invited "Mary" out for a cup of coffee. Mary politely declined.

—ww—

Nino urged me to act on the information as soon as possible. There was no telling how long Leonard would stay where he was. He was a leaver, after all, and he could leave at any moment. Unfortunately, I couldn't fly back to New Jersey right away. I'd started a new job as a blood drive coordinator at a blood bank, and I couldn't miss any of my training. I scheduled a trip for three weeks out, and I prayed that Leonard would stay put.

And then I was back in New Jersey, barreling down the Garden State Parkway toward the southern part of the state. The Red Carpet Inn was just a short ride from Atlantic City, on a street called White Horse Pike. Once again, I felt like I ought to show up with something—God knows why—so I stopped in a diner and picked up a fresh peach pie. I pulled into the asphalt parking lot and found a spot toward the back, away from the front desk. I needed a few minutes to get ready. There were about twenty ground-floor units, bordering three sides of the parking lot. Besides mine, there were only three cars in the whole lot.

I thought about what I might say. I had to be careful; if Leonard was on the run, I could easily spook him by bringing up the twins. I had to come in under the guise of wanting to meet my long-lost uncle. Nothing heavy, just a hello. I found that I was nervous, so I took several deep breaths. Then I headed to the front desk, the peach pie in my hands.

This time, a TV show flashed in my head—*The Sopranos.* I was Tony the mob boss, having to confront the impulsive and ruthless Richie Aprile. Because, after all, it couldn't be me here, in a dingy motel, trying to find a man whom God didn't want.

Yet here I was.

There was an elderly Indian gentleman standing behind the front desk. I told him I was looking for my uncle Leonard Rosenthal. He didn't seem to understand. His English was broken, too. I pulled out my pen and wrote Leonard's name in big block letters on a hotel pamphlet. The clerk studied it and hit some keys on the front desk computer. Several minutes went by.

"No, sir," he finally said.

"There's no Leonard Rosenthal here?"

"No, sir."

"I was told he was here. I'm his nephew. I need to talk to him. What room is he in?"

"No, sir, he's not here."

I remembered Nino's story, and I kept pushing. It was important that I see him, I said. I knew he was there. I'd been told he was there. All I needed was his room number. But the clerk held his ground. I asked to speak to his manager. He said he was the only one there. I reached into my pocket and pulled out a hundred dollars in twenties. I laid them on the counter but didn't say anything about them. I followed the clerk's eyes to make sure he saw them.

"Please," I said. "What room is Leonard in?"

"No, sir," the clerk said.

It was no use. If Leonard was there, the clerk was putting up a brilliant front. Finally, I asked if he could call someone else I could talk to. A manager, another employee, anyone I could plead my case to. He got out a bulky cell phone and dialed a number. Someone answered, and the clerk said a few words in an Indian language. Then he handed the phone to me.

"I'm looking for Leonard Rosenthal," I said. "I'm his nephew. I know he's here."

"He's not there," the man said in clear English. "He was there, but he checked out two weeks ago."

"Are you sure?"

"I'm not supposed to tell you anything about our guests. But yes, I'm sure. He was there and then he checked out. I have no idea where he went."

I went back to my rental car and threw the pie in the backseat. Later, I left it in the lobby of my hotel for someone else to enjoy. I called Nino and told him I'd let Leonard get away. I told him I felt like I'd let him down. Nino told me not to worry. He said he'd found Leonard once and he'd find him again. But I was afraid Leonard had figured out someone was on his trail. He'd left the Red Carpet Inn within a few days of Nino tracking him there. The chances were he was long gone, maybe even back in Florida.

For the first time, I had the feeling I was in over my head.

—✲—

While I was in New Jersey, I did one last thing. I called a company that performs ground-penetrating radar sweeps of properties in South Jersey. I told them I believed some family heirlooms might be buried in an empty lot where my family used to live. Luckily, they didn't ask me if I was the owner of the lot. Normally, a staffer explained, they searched for things like water lines and gas pipes, but their radar unit would pick up any major disturbances in the soil.

"How far back?" I asked him. "Could you detect a disturbance that happened fifty years ago?"

"It's possible," the staffer said.

"What about . . . dog bones?" I asked. "I think my old dog might be buried there."

"That's possible, too," he said. "But we usually tell people not to expect too much. It's not like we're going to give you a photo of what's under there. All we can tell you is where there's a contrast in conductivity between two materials. Basically, areas of interest."

"Good enough," I said, and I gave him the address: 107 North Georgia Avenue, in Atlantic City.

28

I FOUND A PARKING SPOT across the street from the site of Bertha's house. Down the block, a police cruiser was parked in front of a Con Ed crew making repairs on a streetlamp. But there were no officers in sight, and the street I was on was empty. It was the middle of the afternoon, bright and sunny, and no one was around. I waited in my car for the radar guy to arrive.

He pulled up right on time, and lowered something that looked like a giant, clunky lawn mower out of his truck. It was an SIR-3000 ground-penetrating radar-processing unit with a four hundred-megahertz antenna. It worked by sending pulses of energy into the ground and recording the time required for the signal to return and its strength. The pulses could reach as far down as ten feet.

The technician, Billy, was an easygoing young man with a minor league baseball cap on. We shook hands, and I led him to the rear of the empty lot. I was worried there was too much trash in the yard, but Billy told me that was no problem. The radar could even work through concrete. I asked him about pipes and gas lines and things like that, and he said there was a separate device mounted on the SIR-3000 that detected electromagnetic fields and identified live power lines and metallic pipes. The radar wouldn't be fooled by those common things. It would only detect other anomalies in the soil.

I narrowed the search area to roughly twenty square feet—what would have been the backyard. Billy turned on the SIR-3000 and slowly rolled it over the dirt and grass in a tight grid pattern. The machine was absolutely silent. Data was instantly uploaded to a monitor mounted on top of the handles. A pattern of waves would show any significant disturbances in the soil. It took Billy about forty minutes to cover the whole backyard.

He stopped five different times and painted big Xs on the ground with white spray paint. These were the areas of interest—locations where you could bring in an excavation crew and dig. Billy showed me the readout on the monitor, and I could see a disruption in the waves. But that's all it was—a pattern of waves. No shapes or outlines or anything. All Billy could tell me was that something was likely there.

"I don't know what kind of heirlooms you're looking for, but these are probably not going to be metal boxes," Billy said.

I rolled the dice and told Billy what I was really searching for. I hadn't earlier because I feared he might call the police or turn down the job. But now that he'd finished, I wanted his opinion about what might or might not be under the ground. I hoped he wouldn't get spooked and pack up and leave.

Instead, Billy got kind of excited. He was intrigued. He had me tell him more about my story. I said that it was a long shot to find anything there, because I wasn't even sure if my parents had lived in the house when I was abandoned, but I had to try to find out. I pointed to the largest X Billy had painted on the ground, near where the back of the house would have been.

"Could that disturbance be a grave site?" I asked.

He looked at the wave patterns again.

"It would be consistent with that, yeah," he said.

—⁓—

CeCe and the team had never stopped working on building my family tree. I'd been focused mainly on the Rocco side, probably because that's where all the colorful stories were coming from. But Allison found an obituary for my mother that listed two brothers, John and Frank. One of them, Frank Cecil Duncan, was still alive, and Allison found an address for him in Tennessee. Carol got his phone number and called him.

"He's going to be a tough nut to crack," she reported back. "He remembers that his sister had twins, but he says he was never close to her and doesn't know what became of them. He says he 'doesn't want to get involved' and said 'definitely not' when I suggested he take a DNA test. I'm not holding my breath."

The team eventually persuaded Frank's niece Melissa Duncan to test, and it was her test, along with Melanie Rosenthal's, that confirmed I was Jack. Carol later got a call from Frank's wife, Jan, who, unlike her husband, was curious about my case. "She wants to help," Carol told the team. "She talked about what a STRANGE family the Duncans were."

Jan Duncan also found an old Polaroid photo of Marie and mailed it to Carol. Not much later, Carol shared it with me.

It was surreal. It showed my mother standing on a merry-go-round, holding on to a little girl—one of my sisters, Karen or Linda—on one of the carousel horses. They were probably on the boardwalk in Atlantic City. My mother is looking over her shoulder, as if someone hollered her name so they could take the shot. She is wearing a white headband, and she is smiling. It looks like a happy moment. The kind of moment anyone's family could have.

But that's not what stood out to me. In the photo, my mother is clearly pregnant. She is wearing a loose-fitting top that drapes over her belly. At the bottom of the photo is a date: "August 63." My mother is six months pregnant.

And she is pregnant with the twins.

In a way, this was the photo I'd been so desperate to find. Me and my twin and my mother, all in one place. And to see that my mother was smiling—that was wonderful. Maybe she'd only smiled for the photo. Maybe by then she was already feeling the stress so many people told us about. But I chose not to see it that way. This could be the only photo I ever found of my mother with the twins. I wanted to think it had captured a joyful moment.

—◊◊◊—

Way back in April 2013, I'd gotten an email from a reporter named Josh Levin. He sent me a copy of a lengthy article he was posting to the online magazine *Slate*. "I thought you might be interested in this," he wrote. "Please let me know your thoughts."

The article was called "The Welfare Queen," and it was about an infamous Chicago con woman who'd been singled out by then Governor Ronald Reagan for her treachery in 1976. "She used eighty names, thirty addresses, fifteen telephone numbers to collect food stamps, Social Security, veterans' benefits for four nonexistent deceased veteran husbands," Reagan said in a campaign rally speech. "Her tax-free cash income alone has been running $150,000 a year."

Levin's article was divided into twelve parts. The part that concerned me was number 7.

It was called "Who Stole the Fronczak Baby?"

Levin described how Linda Taylor had been arrested twice in the 1960s for "absconding with children," though neither arrest led to a conviction. Levin tracked down Taylor's grown son Johnnie, who said his mother often brought mysterious children into the house. She saw them as commodities to be acquired and sold, he said, most likely for welfare fraud. According to Levin, Johnnie recalled "a white baby named Tiger who showed up out of nowhere and then left just as mysteriously. I asked him if he knew where these kids came from or who they belonged to. 'You know they wasn't hers,' Johnnie said."

What's more, Levin wrote that law enforcement officials once got a tip about Taylor from her ex-husband that "she appeared one day in the mid-1960s with a newborn baby, although she had not been pregnant." Taylor's explanation to police was that she hadn't realized she was pregnant until the morning she gave birth. Johnnie also told Levin that she often claimed to work in a hospital, and even owned a nurse's outfit.

Finally, Levin quoted Jack Sherwin, the retired Chicago police detective who chased after Taylor for years. Sherwin told Levin he remembered seeing the composite sketch of the phony nurse who kidnapped Paul Fronczak. "I looked at it for a second," Sherwin said, "and I knew it was her"—Linda Taylor.

Could Taylor have been the kidnapper? Could the mysterious baby named Tiger she bought home have been the real Paul Fronczak?

I wasn't quite sure what to make of the theory. For one thing, Linda Taylor appeared to be African-American in several of the photos accompanying the article, while the sketch of Baby Paul's kidnapper clearly showed she was white. Then again, a 1940 census document listed Linda Taylor and her whole family as W—white. Levin noted that Taylor could pass for several different ethnicities to suit her needs. I also knew that police had looked into the possibility that Baby Paul's abduction was part of a much larger child-kidnapping ring in Chicago. It wasn't too far-fetched to think that Linda Taylor, or someone she was in cahoots with, had been part of that ring and had stolen Paul.

But proving any of this would be next to impossible. Taylor herself was dead, and the baby known as Tiger was missing. I tried to contact

Taylor's son Johnnie myself, to ask him about his mother, but every number I found for him had been disconnected.

One year later, I got an email from someone named Maritta Brady. She was a college student from Texas who'd learned about my case from watching *20/20*.

"I truly hope I am not a bother to you," Maritta wrote, "but my father's family is in a very similar predicament as the Paul Fronczak case, and I feel as though these cases might be related." She explained that back in the 1960s and '70s, her father's mother brought several different children home, even though she was never pregnant. One of those children showed up in 1964, not long after Baby Paul was kidnapped. That alone was enough to make me take note. But what Maritta revealed next was startling.

"It is unknown where she acquired that child," she wrote, "but when he was growing up, he was always called Tiger."

—◊◊◊—

Another mysterious child named Tiger, just like in the Linda Taylor case? That didn't sound like a common name to me, nor did it strike me as a coincidence. Still, what was the connection between Taylor and Maritta's grandmother? Maritta sent me two photos of them for me to compare. They looked like they could be sisters.

I wrote back to Maritta and asked her to tell me more about her father's family.

It was a strange and complicated story. Maritta's grandmother's name was Peggy, or at least that was one of her many aliases. Peggy told Maritta's father, Kenneth, that she had adopted him. She said he was handed over to her in a parking lot when he was five days old, which was why she had no birth certificate for him. But Kenneth long believed that his brother, the boy named Tiger, *was* Peggy's natural son—until an aunt told him that wasn't true. His aunt "informed me that he was not really her biological child and his true origins were unknown," Kenneth wrote to me. "She stated that he couldn't have been her child because she hadn't even been pregnant at the time."

His mother, Kenneth said, "moved a lot and never stayed in one place too long. She claimed to be a registered nurse. And she had connections to Illinois, where she was born. My mother made it her life's work to come up with a lot of different children somehow."

I followed up with Maritta and asked her a question I dreaded the answer to—was the boy her father knew as Tiger still alive?

"That's where the story gets very sad and even more confusing," Maritta wrote. "Tiger was killed under very mysterious circumstances when he was fifteen years old."

Maritta sent me more information about Tiger, including about how he died. A couple of articles stated that Tiger had killed himself. A Colorado state trooper and a police officer pulled up to Tiger's car, which was on the side of the road with a flat tire. Tiger and another teenager who was with him couldn't produce ID. The officers told them they needed to be questioned further, and Tiger—according to the officers—went back to the car, pulled out a .22-caliber pistol, briefly aimed it at the police officer, then shot himself.

"[Tiger] started getting into the car in the front seat on the left side of the car," one of the two officers wrote in his witness statement. "He crawled across the front seat to the right side of the car and reached down under the seat. All of a sudden [the other officer] pulled his gun. I got my gun and got down behind the front door of the patrol car. [Tiger] was waving his gun around his head and pointed it at his head. I heard a gunshot and I saw him fall in the floor board of the car." Tiger was put in an ambulance and died on the way to the hospital.

The teenager who was with Tiger, a kid named Joe, confirmed this account. "We were headed for Cody, Wyoming," Joe—who, like Tiger, had run away from home—wrote in his witness statement. "Then we had a blowout and we started to fix it and then the patrolman pulled up and we talked with them for about 5 minutes, and then since we didn't have I.D. they said for us to go down to the P.D. with them. Tiger said he wanted to get his cigarettes but instead of getting his smokes he got a twenty-two pistol and aimed it at one of the patrolmen and then Tiger put the gun to his head and said that he would shoot, and then he did."

Maritta told me she didn't believe the witness statements. She didn't believe Tiger had killed himself. Her father told her that when he saw Tiger's body at the morgue, there were two bullet holes in his head, side by side, not just one. She also tracked down the boy who'd been with Tiger when he died, and he refused to discuss it, making her even more suspicious. She wasn't sure how Tiger's death tied in to the mystery of where he came from, but she believed the two events were connected.

Around the time she contacted me, Maritta also called the FBI. The top agent on my case, Lora Richardson, agreed to look into Tiger's story and eventually told Maritta this was their best lead yet in the Fronczak case.

"My dad remembers all these kids coming and going," Maritta told me. "And Peggy had a nurse's uniform and told everyone she was a nurse. My father is determined to find out if Tiger was the real Paul."

The FBI investigation, Maritta told me, was moving slowly. She said one of her aunts had a trunk full of Tiger's things—including items that could be canvassed for DNA. But the aunt told the FBI she didn't have the trunk. The next step was petitioning the county where Tiger was buried to exhume his remains and obtain a DNA sample.

"But we're hitting a brick wall," Maritta said in an email. "The judge has been very rude and unhelpful." She was optimistic the FBI would be able to exhume Tiger's body. But it hadn't happened yet.

In the meantime, Maritta had vowed not to give up on finding out who Tiger was and where he came from. She even switched her college major from art to criminology. She visits Tiger's grave in an Amarillo, Texas, cemetery, to tidy it up and leave some flowers. "I heard his favorite holiday was the Fourth of July," Maritta said. "So on July 4th I went to his grave and left him some fireworks and a little pinwheel that turns in the wind."

I compared some photos of Tiger that Maritta sent me to photos of my brother Dave when they were around the same age. Certainly Tiger looked a lot more like Dave than I did, but I couldn't be sure if they were similar enough to be brothers. They could have been. You couldn't rule it out from the photos. Tiger even looked like my mother Dora.

But what did that mean? A lot of people resemble a lot of people— that's what I was learning as one possible real Paul after another got ruled out. You could drive yourself crazy comparing the slant of someone's eyes or the shape of their chin or the way they smiled in a desperate bid to link those features to someone else's. I definitely looked like Marie Duncan Rosenthal in the two photos I'd seen of her, but that was never enough proof of anything. The real proof was the DNA. The stuff that's in our blood and bones.

So until an excavation crew says a prayer and takes Tiger's body from the ground, it's hard to feel hopeful. And until that happens, the real Paul remains missing, and Maritta's doomed uncle Tiger remains another tragic case—a child haunted by his uncertain past, who died rootless and restless, his questions unanswered, along the side of a road.

One of the relatives located by CeCe—someone who knew my parents and was probably a good source of information—didn't want to talk to us about the family. This person didn't want to be mentioned in any account of my case, and if they were, they didn't want their name or any identifying details used. They knew things and they had stories to tell—that much they shared—but they made it clear they weren't all that keen on doing it.

I will call this relative X.

It took a few months, but I finally persuaded X to meet me. I went to X's house, and we talked.

"You look like your mother," X said when I walked in.

X didn't grow up in Atlantic City but did spend time with my father Gilbert when they were both young. "We had fun together," X said. "When we were kids our parents used to let us walk on the boardwalk alone with ten cents to buy a soda from the fountain machine. Then we'd play in the sand and the water. Gilbert wasn't a wild kid. He was nice."

X was there when Gilbert married Marie in a synagogue in Atlantic City, and X visited with the couple in their apartment not too much later. "I stayed for a weekend and they bent over backwards to make it special. They insisted I sleep in their bed. I said no but they insisted. They seemed like a very happy couple. I was happy for them."

X remembers hearing about the twins when they were born but never got a chance to meet them. By then, X and Gilbert had drifted apart, busy with their own families. One day, X heard from a relative that the twins were gone. "I was told that someone dropped one of the twins. Something bad happened to the twins, and one of them was dropped—that's what I heard. I assumed it meant that the twins were put away somewhere. That's what people did in those days, if something bad happened to a child. I asked Gilbert's mother about the twins once or twice. I asked her what happened to them."

Bertha's response, X said, was "We don't discuss that."

That secretiveness, that reticence, came to define the family—or, as X saw it, to destroy it. Grudges, fractures, lies, secrets—nothing was confronted, so everything got worse. Rifts deepened. Memories darkened. "It was just this big, terrible tangle," X said. "It was all these stories going back and forth, and all these people who were angry with each other, and it just wasn't pleasant. It wasn't a pleasant family. Something was off.

"This family—if something good happened, they had to make it wrong. If someone was good, they had to say bad things about them. After a while, I didn't want to live like that. I didn't want to be part of a family where no one liked each other."

—⁂—

I was putting together a portrait of my family on my father's side, and it wasn't very pretty. What X told me was the same as what Lenny Rocco told me—that there was something wrong with the family, some self-destructive streak no one quite understood. The more this picture of dysfunction took shape, the easier it got to believe that something terrible had happened to my twin. Maybe, as X heard it, she'd been accidentally dropped. If that were true, then the crime wasn't her injury. The crime was how the family handled it—by getting rid of me.

As much as I didn't want to, I had to accept that someone in my family had been capable of bringing harm to the twins. And after a few months of learning about my family, I did accept it. I could hardly deny it. If my uncle Leonard could be violent, what was his brother, Gilbert, capable of? By everyone's account—with the exception of my sister Linda—Gilbert was nothing like Leonard. There was no evidence he ever hurt anyone. But then why did X break off all contact with him? And why did no one attend his funeral, as Linda remembered? My father had dark secrets of his own—chief among them, abandoning me on a sidewalk.

Was harming Jill, either intentionally or on purpose, one of those secrets?

I was becoming more convinced that the "Jill was dropped" story was a cover-up. The bad things that happened to the men in my family did not happen by accident. The horrors in Leonard Rosenthal's life, it seemed to me from what I'd heard, were the result of his own actions. Maybe the same was true of his brother. Maybe my father brought whatever tragedy triggered my abandonment on himself.

The question was—would I ever learn what that tragedy was? I came to believe that my best hope, possibly my only hope, was finding and talking to my father's brother, Leonard.

—⁂—

In the meantime, I got the chance to speak to another important relative—my mother's brother, Frank Duncan.

Frank had been skeptical at first, and he'd pushed Carol away when she called him. But he came around. Carol sent me his number, and one night I gave him a call.

He turned out to be a sweet and likable man. He told me about his father, Cecil Duncan—my grandfather—and how Cecil had moved from Tennessee to Akron, Ohio, and met his future wife, Jenny Noga, there. "My father used to be a barber, but he got into a bad car accident and had one of his arms torn off," Frank said. "They sewed it back on, but he couldn't use it. Eventually he went to work making tires for Firestone."

Frank was one of Cecil and Jeannie's four children, along with his brothers, Jim and John, and his sister—my mother—Marie. But Frank was the only one of the four left alive. The other three died young. "Jim passed away at fifty-three from stomach cancer," Frank said. "John passed away at sixty, from what? I'm not sure. And Marie, she died at sixty from cancer, too." Their father, Cecil, didn't even make it to sixty, passing away at fifty-eight.

I said it was sad that so many people in the family died so relatively young.

"Well, the hardness of their lives may have had something to do with it," he said. "My father and my brothers and my sister, they all drank."

This was the first I'd heard of my mother being a drinker.

"My father was an alcoholic who mistreated everyone," Frank went on. "He was verbally abusive, and he hit my mother and the kids. I am the last survivor of the family, and I left early, when I was eighteen. I grabbed my girlfriend and took off."

So there was trouble on my mother's side of the family, too. The Duncans had their own ghosts and demons. For instance, Frank told me the strange story of his brother Jim. One day Jim left his car and his house in Akron behind and disappeared. He was presumed dead for the next eight years, but actually he was living in California. He faked his death, apparently, to flee his wife and take up with another woman. Then his father died, and the death was reported in a newspaper. Somehow Jim saw the article, and decided to attend his father's funeral back in Akron.

"So he just showed up after eight years!" Frank said. "People were shocked! It was like seeing a dead person come back to life."

The story made sense to me in the context of my two families. Someone disappearing and reappearing, I knew as well as anyone, wasn't all that strange in this crowd.

Before speaking with Frank, I'd attributed almost all of the dysfunction in my family to my father's side. But that's because I hadn't heard about my mother's side yet. According to Frank, my mother had been an odd person, too. "Growing up, she was the oldest one and she always kept to herself," he said. "Like when it was time for supper, she would come out and take a plateful of food and take it back to her room to eat with the door closed. She stayed in her room all the time and I never saw her. A very private person."

In fact, Frank could only summon a single happy memory of him and Marie.

"One summer when I was fifteen I had a rowboat, and Marie came out on Portage Lake with me in the rowboat," he said. "That was nice. But that's all I can remember."

The two were never close as adults, even though Frank and his first wife lived nearby in Atlantic City for a while—including the year the twins were born. I asked him if he ever met the twins.

"I can't even remember if I did," he said. "I knew about them, but the memory is very vague. I do remember when my sister got pregnant, because we were staying with her then. But she gave us the impression that we were invading her privacy, so we left."

Frank was still living in New Jersey in 1965, the year the twins disappeared. I asked him if he knew anything about what happened to them.

"I don't know," he said. "But I do know that Gilbert walked out around that time."

I asked him to repeat what he'd said—my father walked out? On his family?

"Yes, Gilbert left, for about six months, I think. It was right after they lost their house."

"They lost their house?"

Frank was talking about the house at 201 Seagull Drive—the house I'd believed my parents sold in 1965, one month before my brother Fred was born. But the property records stated only that ownership of the property changed hands in January 1965, from the Rosenthals to another family. I assumed that meant they'd sold the house, but according to Frank they hadn't.

"They lost it because Marie wasn't making the house payments," he said. "She didn't pay the mortgage or the utilities or anything. I don't know where the money went instead. But like I said, my sister drank quite a bit. She was under a lot of pressure because of the children, and she drank a lot of wine."

I put all the pieces together and imagined a scenario. My mother already had two young girls at home when she got pregnant with the twins. Jill and I made it four children in her first three years of marriage. Then my parents lost their house.

According to Frank, that was when my father ran out on his family. He stayed away for about six months, which would have put his return sometime in the late summer of 1965.

Right after I was found on a sidewalk in Newark.

Could that have been what happened? The problem drinking, the ruined finances, the lost home, the pressure of raising twins who were constantly crying, *and* the shock of her husband leaving—this is what my mother was facing at the start of 1965. Was it possible she saw only one way out of her terrible predicament? Only one way to convince my father Gilbert to come back?

Did she see her only hope for salvation to be removing the twins?

"I don't know if Marie was capable of such a thing," Frank said. "I can't say. But whenever I did talk to Marie, all she did was complain. She'd say, 'Every year I get pregnant and have another baby, and I really don't like it.' That's why she drank so much. But was she capable of harming those twins?"

Frank took a long pause.

"Yeah, I guess she was."

—⁂—

Just one day after I spoke with Frank Duncan, I got an unexpected call from Nino Perrotta, the detective. He'd vowed to stay on Leonard's tail, but I hadn't heard from him in several days, and I assumed we'd lost Leonard forever. I blamed myself for losing him.

But we hadn't.

"I got him," Nino said. "I got the slippery sucker."

I couldn't believe it. Leonard was still in New Jersey. But he wasn't in a fleabag hotel or a nursing home.

He was in a hospital.

"What hospital?" I asked Nino, though I already knew the answer.

Leonard was in the same hospital where I was born.

Four hours later, I was on a red-eye, heading back to Atlantic City.

29

I WAS IN A CHUCK E. CHEESE when Nino called. I'd just picked up Emma from school and we were having lunch. Emma settled on corn dogs, mozzarella sticks, and frozen yogurt, and I went with the same. I told her she'd made a good choice. I asked her how school was going, and she told me it was fun. Everything was fun for her. She said she liked all her friends. Emma liked everyone. Then she told me about a girl in her class who'd shared a story that day—the story of how she'd been abandoned as a baby.

"Who would do something like that to a baby?" Emma asked.

She'd just given me the perfect setup. Michelle and I hadn't told her about my history; Emma was just six, and we felt she was too young. She was aware that something was going on with me, because she'd see me on TV and point and say, "There you are, Daddy." But we didn't tell her the hard facts about what happened, and she never asked. Had she asked, we would have sat her down and explained the situation as best we could.

But now, I had an opening. I looked at my daughter, my smart, kind, loving, innocent, sweet, sweet daughter, and all of a sudden I wanted her to know the truth.

"Emma, I was abandoned, too," I said.

"What?"

"When I was little. My real parents were having problems and they left me somewhere so someone else could find me and take care of me."

I could almost see the gears turning in her head.

"So Grandma and Grandpa Fronchie adopted you?"

"That's right."

Emma thought it over. I'm sure she had more questions, but she didn't ask them. She just went back to eating her fro yo, and so did I.

—∞—

About ten minutes later, Nino called. I told him I'd call him back in a few minutes, to get all the details. The confluence of those two events—me telling Emma, Nino finding Leonard—was strange. Almost as if being honest with my daughter had tipped a balance somewhere, and dislodged the elusive Leonard. But I didn't want to even think about my daughter and Leonard together in any context. They were absolute opposites—angel and devil. They weren't even part of the same species, the same universe. They couldn't be.

And yet, they were. They were blood.

I drove Emma home and called Nino back. In the days since we'd last spoken, Nino hadn't stopped searching for Leonard. He ran Leonard's name through more databases. He reached out to a contact in the telephone business. Every day he called ten or fifteen new hotels, expanding his radius. One background search coughed up a new name—a friend who'd apparently known Leonard for a long time. A running buddy. But finding this new lead was difficult. Like Leonard, this person left only a nearly invisible footprint. The hardest people to find were the ones who kept moving on the fringes on society. Pick up, pack up, go.

Nino was hitting a wall. He found himself thinking about Leonard all day long—when he woke up, while he was driving, during dinner. Leonard had wormed into his brain, just as he had into mine. Did Leonard figure out he was being tailed? Was he that clever, that stealthy? Why could we get only fleeting glimpses of his moving shadow? In Nino's experience, people who were so perfectly elusive usually had good reason to be. Mobsters. People on the run from the mob. CIA. One of the stories I'd heard about Leonard was that he often bragged about having worked for the CIA. I shared that with Nino, and he didn't discount it as fantasy. At eighty-six, Leonard was proving a worthy adversary. Anything was possible.

Nino's training and years of sleuthing gave his investigations a structure. There were steps to follow. So when he hit a wall, he knew what to do. "Go back to step one," he said. "If you're stuck, that's what you do. Start over, bear down." For Nino, step one was calling Leonard's ex-wife, Barbara Rosenthal.

I'd given Nino her number but warned him she would probably shut him down. Nino tried anyway, and called her early on in his first search for Leonard. They got along nicely, as Nino seemed to with every source he called, but Barbara didn't give up anything. Her fear of Leonard was clear. Her nightmare was doing anything that might draw Leonard back into her life. Still, Nino suspected she was holding back.

Then Nino found Leonard without her help, but I let him slip away. So now Nino tried Barbara again. He was his charming self, and they had a friendly conversation—but still, nothing. Barbara hadn't heard from Leonard. She didn't know anything about what hotels he was checking in and out of. She wished she could help, but she couldn't. Nino got ready to end the call.

"You know, there is one thing," Barbara finally said. "Two days ago, I got a call from someone at a hospital."

"A hospital? What hospital, dear?"

"I don't know. They just said they needed my daughter to sign something."

"What did they need her to sign?"

"Something about permission for a surgery."

This was it. It had to be Leonard. He was too old or too crazy to consent to his own surgery. His daughter, Melanie, was his next of kin. Nino asked if whoever called had left a number. Barbara said they had.

"Dear, do you think you can give me that number?"

—m—

Barbara didn't give up the number. But it didn't matter. Nino called the biggest hospital in the Atlantic City area, and asked if a patient named Leonard Rosenthal had recently been admitted. The answer was yes— there was an L. Rosenthal in the trauma unit.

The name of the hospital was AtlantiCare Regional Medical Center, formerly Atlantic County Hospital.

The place where, a half century before, I was born.

I dropped Emma back home. She had an event at school the next day, and we were both supposed to go. I told her I'd have to miss it. But there was another event the day after—Lunch with Daddy. I promised Emma I'd be back for that. Then I called the airport and booked a red-eye—leaving Las Vegas at 11:39 P.M., touching down at JFK Airport at 7:30 A.M. I would be in Atlantic City by noon.

Michelle didn't try to talk me out of going. She knew how much I wanted to find Leonard. But she was worried. She'd been worried all along about Leonard. We both knew he might be a bad person. It was possible that he was the worst of a bad bunch. We knew his ex-wife and daughter were still shell-shocked and shattered years after he'd gone. "You don't want to find him," Melanie Rosenthal told me more than once. "Once you find him, he will attach himself to you. He will live to ruin your life. You have no idea. It's Pandora's box."

I didn't take her warnings lightly. I didn't ever want to expose Michelle and Emma to such an evil force. But I had to find him, and I had to see him. I had to. My gut told me he knew what happened to Jill.

I owed it to Jill to track him down and get that answer.

—⁓—

I had a room number for Leonard in the hospital's trauma wing—31-17. I didn't tell anyone there I was coming, because I didn't want them to tell Leonard, and risk him running away. When I touched down, I called the hospital to confirm Leonard was still there, then I rented a car and took the familiar drive down the Garden State Parkway.

I didn't really have a plan—not much of a plan, anyway. I would say I was Leonard's nephew, which was true, and that I'd heard he was sick. If they asked me for some kind of proof I was his nephew, I'd be in trouble. I had no documentation that linked me in any way to the Rosenthals. All I had were newspaper clippings and a birth certificate that proved Jack Rosenthal was Leonard's nephew. But I couldn't prove that I was Jack. If things got sticky, I planned to say his ex-wife and daughter had asked me to come, to make it sound like I knew Leonard's family. Nino told me to be confident. Just walk in like you belong.

I parked in the hospital's cavernous indoor lot and made my way to the reception desk. I was more nervous than I'd expected to be, and I forced myself to take deep breaths. I told the receptionist I was there to see my uncle, and he gave me a name tag and pointed me to the elevators. It felt good to get by the first hurdle.

I rode up to the third floor of the trauma wing. The door to pass through to the rooms was locked; I needed to get buzzed in. I pressed a button and a voice asked me who I was there to see. As calmly as I could, I gave them Leonard's name and said I was his nephew. Several seconds passed with no response. I pictured a security guard coming out and asking me to leave. Finally, the buzzer sounded, and I pushed open the door and walked through.

Now I was at the third-floor front desk. Another scene from *The Godfather* ran through my head—the scene where Michael walks through a hospital looking for his bullet-ridden father. I walked up to the front desk and told the nurse there who I was looking for. She didn't ask me who I was. She just pointed down a long hallway and gave me Leonard's room number. Up until that moment, some part of me wasn't even sure that Leonard was actually there. But apparently he was. And all I had to do was walk down the long hallway to see him.

Could it really be this easy? Walking toward Leonard's room, I thought about the day the real Paul Fronczak was kidnapped. That had been easy, too. A woman in a nurse's outfit simply walked into the hospital, took Paul out of my mother's arms, and walked out. Fifty years later, here I was, creeping toward Leonard's room and trying not to stand out. Stalking my prey in the dreary halls of a hospital. The moment had a spooky kind of familiarity. It was as if everything I did in pursuit of my real family was a distorted reflection of some terrible action that had played out long ago. As if the past wasn't really over and done with.

I followed the descending room numbers to the very end of the hallway. It was the middle of a weekday, and the floor was busy but not overly so. The nurses were scurrying, but not in an urgent way. An elderly patient held tight to a nurse as he walked slowly down the hallway. Just past the nurses' desk, there was a large room set aside from the others. It was marked NEURO ICU 31-17. The door was open, though a curtain partially obscured the hospital bed in the back. But there was a big window, and the room was very bright, and I could see into it clearly. From ten or so feet away, I tilted my head slightly so I could peer in without being seen.

There was a blue hospital chair in the middle of the room, next to the bed.

And in that chair was Leonard Rosenthal.

I realized I'd been holding my breath. I let it out and stayed where I was, ten feet outside the room. Leonard's head was leaning back against the top of the chair, and his eyes were closed. I had the chance to look him over, and I did.

I'd been expecting the devil himself.

But what I found was an old man.

He was wearing a white hospital gown. Both of his forearms were purple—bruised deeply and completely by attempts to connect IVs. He had a tube sticking out of each arm, and another out of his neck. He was thick in the middle, and he was bald. He didn't look feeble, not at all; in fact, he looked like an old bear. Weathered, wounded, fading, but still a bear. From the hallway I could see the bright digital readouts on a monitor behind him. Leonard's blood pressure was 185 over 76.

I took a deep breath and I walked into his room.

He was there alone. It was a private room. When I walked in, he opened his eyes. His features were harsh, and his eyes were narrow slits. His brow furrowed as he looked at me, confused but not alarmed.

"Hi, Leonard," I said. "Do you know who I am?"

"No, I don't," he said in a thin voice. "As long as you're not Hillary Clinton."

I got a good look at Leonard's face for the first time. They'd told me he had terrible skin, but it didn't look that bad to me. His complexion was pale and he looked unhealthy, but his dark eyes were alive. His eyes told me he was still there, still kicking. He looked at me like he was trying to place me, but without any real concern for who I was. Like it wouldn't really matter if I was a doctor or a lawyer or a relative. What Leonard needed was someone to talk to. Leonard liked to talk. He liked to tell stories. He was good at telling stories. And I was someone new he could pull into his world of tales.

"I'm Jack Rosenthal," I told him. "I'm Gilbert's son."

Leonard looked at me even harder now.

"Fred?" he said. "You're Fred?"

"Not Fred. I'm Jack. I'm one of the twins."

Leonard looked away from me and tried to put the pieces together. He was old. He might have been senile. He was probably hopped up on hospital drugs. But the word *twins* cut through all that. I saw recognition in his eyes.

"You're one of the twins," he repeated. "Oh my God, you're my family."

A young nurse walked in and said hello. I explained I was Leonard's nephew Jack.

"Oh, how nice," the nurse said. "What a nice surprise. Your uncle is quite a character. He's been telling us a million stories."

When the nurse walked in, Leonard's face changed. It hardened. He looked at the nurse, then looked at me, then whispered, "She's trying to kill me." Then he followed her around the room with his eyes, watching, seething. There was genuine anger there, maybe even loathing. It was an unsettling look. Maybe I'd been conditioned to think of Leonard as an intimidating character, and that's why I saw hatred in his face. But I think anyone would have found his expression chilling. The word that came to mind was *malice*.

I backed off asking Leonard about the twins. It looked like I wasn't going to get kicked out, so I had some time. And Leonard was clearly okay with talking to me; he'd already enlisted me as a coconspirator against the nursing staff. "They want to pump me full of drugs so they can use my corpse," he said in an urgent whisper. "They're trying to turn me into a junkie. I tried to get up but they wouldn't let me. I see them putting white powder in my vials. I haven't had any food or water in eight days."

I realized that Leonard was probably not in his right mind, and my heart sank. I already knew he was a magnificent liar—"everything out of his mouth is a fabrication," Melanie had told me. But now he might have been addled by all the medication he was on. How could I believe anything he said? And would he even remember events that happened fifty years ago?

I pulled up a small chair and sat five feet across from Leonard. I asked him about various family members, trying to gauge his state of mind.

"You were Karen's brother?" Leonard said after I mentioned her. "That is so sad. She was so nice. What a tragedy that she died so young."

I told him I'd heard that no one attended his brother Gilbert's funeral.

"They never even told me he died. I would have paid for the funeral myself. He was a good man, my brother."

I asked Leonard how he ended up in the hospital.

"Blood in my stool," he said. "My stomach hurts. I was just eating something and the next thing, I was here."

A doctor later filled me in. Leonard's bleeding might have been caused by complications from a previous aneurysm surgery, or from cell erosion in his large intestine. If it was the latter, Leonard would need a risky surgery to remove parts of his large intestine. The doctors deemed Leonard unfit to make decisions about his own care and called around for a family member. This was another indication that Leonard had likely lost touch with reality.

"He told me he hasn't drunk or eaten anything in eight days," I said.

"Oh, well, that part is true," the doctor said. "We may give him some broth today."

A trauma patient who loses six pints of blood is almost always bound for surgery. Leonard had lost nine pints. But the doctors said his vital signs were stable, and they were no longer sure surgery would be needed. They'd have to wait and see. Instantly, I knew there'd be no surgery. Leonard was a survivor. He had the devil on his side.

When the doctor left I asked Leonard about his relationship with my father. "It's so sad," he said. "He was my brother. But he stopped talking to me. I don't know why. I wrote him letters, but he never answered. I wrote one final letter and Marie got it and she wrote back pretending to be Gilbert. She said, 'I don't ever want to see you again.'"

I asked him about his father, Harry Rosenthal, who left the family when Leonard was young. Did he remember him?

"Of course," he said. "My father had a barbershop and he made good money. It was right around the corner from our home in South Philly. But he ran a card game in the back. My mother used to send me there to get him and bring him back from his gambling. That's why he left. He owed the mob money."

I asked him if my mother had a drinking problem.

"Yeah, Marie drank," he said. "She had a nervous breakdown. She never wanted to get married to Gilbert. She only got married because she got pregnant."

Leonard couldn't hold his thoughts for too long. He'd drift away and start talking about Mercedes McCambridge, a 1950s actress he knew from his days in Florida. He talked about Donald Trump, whom he'd been friends with and knew to be a braggart. "I never held a job," Leonard said. "I was always the brains." He mentioned a famous Atlantic City restaurant and claimed it was his idea. "It used to be a newspaper place and I told the guy to start selling sandwiches. Now look."

A different nurse came in and asked Leonard questions about how he felt.

"What is this, an inquisition?" he spat out, the contemptuous look back on his face. "I'm trying to have a private conversation with my nephew."

Then Leonard told her to turn off the monitor behind him because it was too loud.

"If you don't shut that machine off I'm gonna shoot it. If I can steal a gun."

We'd been talking for an hour now. It was time to ask about the twins.

"What happened to the twins?" I asked him. "Why did they give me away?"

"It's so sad," he said. "I'm heartbroken that our family fell apart. I would have raised the twins myself."

"But what happened? Why did they give me away?"

"I don't know."

"But you were there. You were there when it happened."

"Sometimes you're too close to the pie to smell it," he said. He was saying that whatever had happened to the twins happened right under his nose, but he didn't notice it happening. I kept pushing.

"Did something bad happen to Jill? Is that why they had to abandon me?"

"This was my family, and we fell apart. It breaks my heart."

"But what happened? What made it fall apart?"

"You're asking me to remember things, but that was a long time ago, and I'm doped up. They're turning me into a junkie."

"Just try to think," I said. "You saw the twins. You would visit the twins. They were always crying, remember? Why did Jill all of a sudden disappear?"

"I don't know," Leonard said, shaking his head. "It's so sad. Family is the most important thing."

It looked like he was genuinely scanning his brain to try to come up with something. Or it all could have been an act. I didn't know. The sadness—it looked real. His body slumped and he looked like he might cry. But he was a manipulator. He could work people. We all could. That's what we were good at.

Suddenly Leonard squinted tightly.

"Now that you are asking, you're taking me back," he said. "There is one story I remember."

—⟋⟍—

"We went to visit Marie and Gilbert in their home," Leonard said. "Me, Mom, Dad, Marie's mom, all of us, we were there. We just showed up. But she wasn't expecting us, and she got mad. We surprised her and she was angry."

Leonard said someone asked where the twins were.

"They're upstairs," Marie said. "Sleeping."

Someone else said they wanted to see the twins, and could they come down?

"I'll bring them down," Marie said.

"She went upstairs, and she came back out with the twins in her hands," Leonard said. "One in each hand. She was holding them by the . . . by the wrist. Each one by the wrist. Like you'd hold a chicken by the neck. Just dangling. The boy didn't have any clothes on.

"Then she started coming down the stairs holding the kids. Like chickens by the neck. And when she got to about the fourth step . . . she dropped them.

"She dropped them and she said, 'Here are the twins.'"

—◊—

My hands were shaking. I was taking notes, and I was trying to sketch the image he was describing—my mother holding the twins like two chickens by the neck—but my hands were shaking.

"The boy got up and ran over to me," Leonard said. "I don't know why, but he ran to me. And he hugged me and he held on to me, you know? Like . . . like you'd hold on to someone if you were scared. He just held on and wouldn't let me go."

"What about the girl?" I asked.

"I don't know," Leonard said, shaking his head.

Then he drifted away. A nurse came in, and Leonard seethed again.

"If that's not an Italian ice you're bringing, I'm gonna shoot myself."

I stayed another hour. Leonard was lucid sometimes, sometimes not. I asked him if he was surprised he was still around, since so many others in the family had died young.

"God has always been there for me," he said. "I'm a good guy, and I have a good heart."

Finally, I got up to leave. Leonard motioned me over and asked me to get something out of his pants, which were folded and in a drawer. It was a phone number scribbled on a piece of paper, and Leonard was convinced the nurses were going to take it and use it to get into his apartment and steal the money he had stashed there.

"I want you to get it before they do," he said. "I want to give you fifty thousand dollars. You're my family. And family is all we have. Family is the most important thing."

I told Leonard I had to go, but that I would call him to see how he was doing. Just before I left, I asked him something point-blank, like a detective might.

"Where is Jill?" I asked. "Where. Is. Jill?"

"I have no idea," he said.

I gave him a pat on his shoulder. A nurse had come by and strapped inflated cushions to his lower legs. The cushions and the tubes and the wires pinned him to his chair. He was an old man, and he wasn't well. But he wasn't dying, either. Just before I left he said something to me.

"I found the secret to a long life," he said, with something like a smile. "Never let anything bother you. And stay away from bad people."

—⁂—

A few weeks later, I flew back to Atlantic City to look for my sister Jill.

My working assumption was simple: if something bad did happen to Jill, as Leonard suggested, it most likely happened while my parents were staying with his mother Bertha in her house at 107 N. Georgia Avenue, in the first half of 1965. And if what happened to her was fatal, there was a chance she'd been buried in the backyard of that house. A radar sweep confirmed a disturbance in the soil right where the backyard began. It was time to find out what had caused that disturbance.

Bertha's house was long gone, but I looked up the property records and found the name of the current owner of the empty lot. At first he didn't answer my calls, and when I finally reached him and told him my story, he was highly skeptical. He was sure he was being scammed. This was Atlantic City, after all. Sucker's playground. Hustler's paradise. A place where the past was never truly buried, but never welcome, either. I got the feeling the owner just wanted me to go away.

But I kept at him. I needed his permission. I could have gone to the local police and let them open a missing person investigation, and they would have forced their way onto the property, but I didn't want to do that—not yet, anyway. I was on the outside of the FBI investigation into the Fronczak kidnapping case, and I didn't want to risk getting shut out of the search for my own twin sister. I wanted to look for her myself. I needed to be the one who found her. I had to be the one to dig the hole.

It took a lot of calls and a lot of persuading—and some good-faith cash to cover his expenses—but the owner finally relented. We arranged a day and a time to meet at the empty lot on N. Georgia Avenue. The night before, I flew into Newark, New Jersey, and got some good sleep before setting out for Atlantic City in the morning. On the way down I stopped at a Home Depot and bought three fiberglass Ames shovels for $16 each. It was a hot and brightly sunny day, so I picked up some bottles of water and Gatorade, too.

I'd arranged for a couple of local workers to meet me at the lot and help me dig, but they never showed up. Luckily, there was a construction crew working on a big project just down the street. It looked like the crew was on a break, so I approached two men and asked if they had any time for another job. It's nothing too complicated, I said. Just digging a hole.

"Well, that's what we do," one worker, a twenty-seven-year-old mason and general contractor named Shane, said. "We dig holes. We dig lots of holes."

Shane said he had a free hour and agreed to help.

The radar sweep had identified four possible areas of interest in the lot, but three of them were small and out in the open. The fourth area was bigger—some six feet across and four feet wide—and close to where the back of the house would have been. That would have been the most private spot to dig a hole without the neighbors wondering what you were doing. And, unlike the other areas of interest, there was no chance that something metal had caused this disturbance. I reached into my pocket and unfolded a printout of the radar sweep of the spot, which showed the radar wave patterns all the way down to thirteen feet below the surface. At almost exactly six feet deep, there was a clear disruption in the patterns. I showed the printout to Shane and said, "That's what we're trying to get to."

He didn't ask what we were looking for, and I didn't tell him.

The lot was thick with garbage and weeds. The big white X that the radar technician had spray-painted on the ground to mark our spot weeks earlier was gone now, washed away by rain and pushed apart by weeds. But I had a photo of the spot, and we figured out exactly where it was. Shane had his own weathered and wood-handled shovel, and he got straight to it. He was big and muscled, and he jammed the steel tip of the shovel into the dirt and forced it all the way down with his boot. I got my new fiberglass shovel and started digging, too. The soil was fairly soft and came up easily, but within a minute we were both sweating hard under the afternoon sun. Seagulls flew overhead, their shadows streaking across the hole that was just starting to form.

I hadn't thought about what I was digging for, and I guess that was on purpose. I just thought of the dig as a job I had to do. I'd find what I'd find, and I'd deal with it then. But as I started plowing into the earth, I couldn't help but think about Jill. I tried to picture what she would have looked like at two and a half years old. She would have looked like me, at least a little bit. And also like my mother—a soft, pretty face. She might have been blond with curly hair, a perfect cherub of a child. Small and slender, maybe even fragile, like a tiny bird. I pictured her as a beautiful girl, but the picture was vague. I couldn't focus hard enough to bring up any features. She had been the person closest to me in the entire world—the person who entered it with me. My other half. My other self. The bond between us unbreakable.

But it *had* been broken. So thoroughly broken that I went through life not knowing she even existed. And now she was a stranger to me. I didn't know her; I couldn't even picture her. But maybe I could change that by finding her. Maybe that's why I'd been drawn here—to this city, this block, this lot, this very spot. Maybe I'd been pulled there by some strange magnetic force. Maybe the bond hadn't been broken after all.

When Shane and I had cleared about two feet of dirt, I abruptly told him what we were looking for. For some reason, I wanted him to know. I told him my whole story, starting with the kidnapping. Shane stopped digging and leaned on his shovel and wiped his forehead as he listened. He said "wow" a couple of times, then he didn't say anything at all. When I finished my story, he finally spoke.

"I have a young daughter," he said. "She's four."

We drank some water and got back to digging.

—◊◊◊—

When the hole was about three feet deep, Shane jumped in and did the hard work by himself. There wasn't room anymore for two shovels.

Steadily, Shane brought up heaps of soil and muscled them over the lip of the hole and onto the growing pile beside us. Coincidentally, Shane was 6'2", almost exactly the length we had to dig down. We knew that when his head was level with the rim, we'd be there.

From time to time, people stopped on the sidewalk at the entrance to the lot some thirty feet away to watch what we were doing. It was obvious we were digging a hole, and also obvious we weren't part of a construction crew, and that made them curious. They'd linger for a while before shuffling away. One woman, though, walked right up to us.

"What y'all digging for?" she asked.

"I lost a contact lens," I said.

Eventually, she wandered away.

The dirt changed color. For the first two feet, it was dark brown. Then it was a lighter brown. At three feet, it became a sandy gray. At four feet, it was damp and heavy. Atlantic City is on an island and the ocean is never too far from the surface. Though the dirt went down several more feet, saltwater began to bubble up and puddle at five feet deep.

The shovelfuls of dirt unearthed several objects. Early on we found shards of dinner plates, jagged pieces with different patterns, the color faded but still there. We found a number of small bottles, remarkably all unbroken. One looked like a beer bottle, but the others had odd shapes. They might have held medicine or liquor, I couldn't tell. One bottle still had a cork in it, as well as about two inches of liquid inside.

Shane's shovel hit on something solid with a clang. He reached down and pulled up a length of what looked like a metal pipe, about a foot long. He handed it to me. It was caked in dirt and solid and heavy. I didn't know what it was.

"That's an old cast-iron window counterweight," Shane said.

We found a small, red-handled paint chipper, and an unopened clamshell, and an intact conch shell about the size of a softball. I made a row of all our discoveries along the edge of the neighbor's backyard porch. We came across lots of broken bits of clamshells, their whiteness easy to spot in the dirt. Each time we found one, I held my breath a bit. Each time, I wondered if it would be what we came to find. Shane would turn the fragment over in his hand and declare it a shell and pass it up to me. I added the shell bits to my display of artifacts.

Within an hour, Shane had dug a hole that was nearly six feet deep and four feet across, and we hadn't come across anything of interest yet. At one point something hard stopped his shovel, but it turned out to be a tree root. It belonged to a tree in the neighbor's backyard and over the years it had forced its way across this yard and into the hole we'd just dug. It came through at about five feet deep, and I imagined it had pushed the soil beneath it downward as it spread. That could have caused the disruption in the radar waves. The tree root could be the disturbance.

I felt myself becoming disillusioned. The energy I felt just an hour earlier was draining away. We weren't finding anything out of the ordinary in the hole, and we were just about done digging. Shane took a break and stood in the pit, breathing heavily. He asked me if I wanted him to keep going. He said he was happy to dig as long as I wanted him to. I could see this wasn't just a job for him anymore. It had become a kind of mission.

"Let's clear another two feet this way," I said.

With Shane digging below and me shoveling at the surface, we began making the hole two feet longer. We were on the very outer edges of the radar disturbance now. It hardly seemed likely that we would find anything in this extra two feet if we hadn't already found it in the center of the area. But neither of us wanted to give up just yet. So we kept digging.

I was breaking up dirt with the tip of my shovel when Shane stopped digging beneath me. He took off his gloves and reached to pick something up. He was six feet down and the ocean water was collecting. Shane held the object for a while before handing it to me. It was the size of a baseball and fairly light and caked a dark drown. It was also hollow. Filled with dirt, but hollow. I cleared away some of the dirt and the object took shape.

It was a bone.

The bone was intact on one end, ending in what would have been a joint. I couldn't tell what bone it might have been, or if it was even human. It seemed a bit big to be a child's bone. But it was unmistakably a bone. Shane and I fell silent. I felt a gravity—a significance—that I hadn't felt before. Was this actually happening? Had we found what we came to find?

Shane kept going. A few minutes later he stopped and gently pulled up another object. It was smaller than the first one, only four inches long and a half-inch thick, but it was also well-defined at one end. Almost certainly it was another bone, and this time it actually looked like something skeletal. A femur, maybe.

More fragments came up, including two tiny pieces that looked like vertebrae to me. Within just a few minutes, we'd collected ten objects that very much looked like pieces of bone. Together, they didn't appear to form anything, or even part of anything. It wasn't like a skeleton was assembling before our eyes. The fragments were random and different. There was no single object that struck us as conclusive—a skull of a certain shape and size, for instance. These were just scattered fragments. But what did we know about bones? What did we know of what happens to bones after being buried for fifty years? All we knew is that we went looking for bones, and we found them. We would need an expert to tell us whose bones they might be.

"I've dug a lot of holes," Shane said, "and this is the first time I found anything like that."

It was late afternoon now. Shane had to go. We filled the hole back up and marked it with bricks. I carefully put the bone fragments in a plastic bag. I paid Shane for his time, twice as much as I'd originally planned to, and shook his hand. His white T-shirt was soaked through with sweat.

"Thank you," I told him. "I couldn't have done this alone."

"I'm sorry about what you had to go through," he said. "I hope you find out what happened to your sister."

I took his number and said I'd let him know what I learned about the bones. I almost told him to go home and hug his daughter tight, but I could tell he was the kind of father who did that all the time already.

Then I got in my rented Jeep and raced back up the Garden State Parkway to Newark for my evening flight to Las Vegas. I took one little detour. In downtown Newark, I drove to the corner of Broad Street and Cedar Street—the spot where the old department store McCrory's had once stood.

The spot where I'd been abandoned a half century before.

I parked at the corner, put on my hazards, and got out. McCrory's was long gone, but the building that had housed it was still there. I could tell by the three-story-long sign affixed to the corner of the four-story building. Fifty years earlier, the eight letters that spelled

MCCRORY'S had run downward in single file from the top, heralding the fine shopping inside. But now those letters were gone, replaced by four scripted and connected letters that ran upward.

The letters spelled NIKE. It was a Nike store now. I stood near the double-doored entrance, a few feet to the right. The spot where I guessed I'd been left in my stroller. I stood there for about five minutes, trying to imagine myself back then. Alone. Terrified. Missing my sister. But once again I felt no connection to the spot. Too much had changed. The past had been cleanly erased and replaced by something sleek and modern. That is how time works. Time buries the past.

But sometimes, the past refuses to stay buried.

—∿—

The next day, I googled "forensic anthropologist," made some calls, and found someone who could tell me if the bones were human or animal. His name was Adam Watson, and he was the cultural resources manager in the archaeology department of the American Museum of Natural History in New York City. His specialty was archaeozoology, or the study of faunal remains, which are the objects left behind when an animal dies. I sent Dr. Watson some photos of the bone fragments, and he called in a colleague, Gisselle Garcia, to look them over. Within an hour, they had their assessment.

"We are 90 percent certain they are all animal bones," Dr. Watson said.

In that instant, I didn't know if that was good news or bad news.

Dr. Watson explained that the largest bone fragment was likely the distal humerus of a cow, while the piece that looked like a femur had likely been part of a young pig. The two fragments that resembled vertebrae were actually a pig's calcaneus, or heel bones. Most of the fragments showed evidence of roasting or cooking. What we'd found were soup bones.

But that wasn't even the worst news. Dr. Watson told me that the bones of a two-year-old child are not fully formed and extremely fragile, and probably would not survive the kind of weathering that fifty years of exposed burial would inflict on them.

Most likely, a child's bones would have crumbled to dust.

30

THERE WAS A STORY I heard about my family that stood out—not because it was sad or gruesome, but because it wasn't.

I heard it from the relative I call X. It went all the way back to before I was born. It was set in Atlantic City in the 1940s, a time of beach bunnies by the water, Tommy Dorsey and Frank Sinatra playing the Steel Pier, the smell of roasted peanuts blanketing the boardwalk. X was young, and so was my father Gilbert—eight or nine years old. It was a holiday, maybe the Fourth of July.

My grandmother Bertha was hosting a gathering in her big white house on North Georgia Avenue. She sent X and my father to buy some bread at the Italian bakery a few doors down. X and Gilbert ran through an alley between two houses to the bakery out back, the sweet aroma luring them on. Outside, old Italian women were sitting and knitting a sweater—one knitted an arm, another knitted the other arm, another the torso. Back at home, Bertha was cooking one of her famous Italian meals—after all, she'd once run her own restaurant on Massachusetts Avenue, and she knew how to cook for a crowd. Everyone was there—aunts and uncles, nieces and nephews, children and old folks. The radio was playing, and "The Star-Spangled Banner" came on. Bertha made everyone stand up and sing along, hands to their hearts.

"It was such a fun day," X remembered. "It was like the American Dream."

In so many ways, my family did embody the American Dream. My great-grandparents came over from Italy, crossing through Ellis Island. They settled in Philadelphia, the cradle of democracy. They played stickball in the streets, started their own businesses, had big families. I am sure they had important plans for the children.

But somewhere along the line, their sweet American Dream turned bad.

—◦◦◦—

I don't know where the fracture was that turned my family into what it became. Maybe it was more than one fracture; maybe it was several. Harry Rosenthal's gambling debt. Cecil Duncan losing an arm. Lenny's uncle David killing a man. Maybe it happened long, long ago, way before my great-grandfather John Rocco, somewhere far back in time. Maybe there was never a fracture at all. Maybe families fall apart for no reason, unable to hold together any longer, too brittle for the pressures of life. Like bones in the dirt.

Even before I met Leonard Rosenthal, I realized that the portrait of my family I was putting together would always be incomplete. There was just too much I could never know. Different people had different stories, many of them contradictory. Was Gilbert a sweet, gentle man? Or was he mean and friendless? Did he walk out on his family? Or was he driven away? What about my sister Linda—was she a victim or an aggressor? Even Leonard, so feared and loathed—is he a monster or is he something else? X told me that because Leonard's skin was so bad, he was mocked and shunned as a child. Did the unluckiness of life twist his mind and damage his soul?

I could never know these things. The stories, the viewpoints were all different. Or maybe it had been silly to think these people had to be one thing or another. Of course it was more complicated than that. All of us have many facets; all of us are vulnerable to different forces. Can't any one of us, in a terrible moment of lost control, do something that wipes away a lifetime of goodness? Can't we all fathom some monstrous act that we're capable of, if everything around us happens to go horribly wrong?

Maybe my mistake was making my search about learning my identity. What if such a thing isn't really knowable? Look at one dictionary definition of *identity*—"the fact of being who or what a person or thing is." What does that even mean? To assume I could discover myself simply by finding the people who made up my family—in hindsight, I suppose that was naïve. Through the miraculous efforts of so many smart and unheralded heroes, I did find my family. But I did not discover myself.

What did I learn, in the end? I did learn something about my medical history—which, after all, was why I started the search in the first place. I learned my family has a history of aneurysms and cancer. I learned there was a history of alcoholism. I learned an inordinate number of people in my family had died too young. And I learned, once and for all, that I am not an alien.

But pretty much everything else is going to be guesswork. The story Leonard told me about my mother, holding the twins like chickens and dropping them down the stairs—that story fit with other stories I was told. It was plausible. But was it true? I was told not to trust anything Leonard said. In fact, I was told *everything* out of his mouth was guaranteed to be a lie. But I heard him tell the story. I sat next to him as he summoned the memory. If it was all a fabrication, then Leonard was a master storyteller. More than that, he was a master *actor*. Or maybe it was all part of a mad fever dream, induced by medication. The thing is, there was no way for me to know if what he told me was true. And I may never know.

But if I can't answer the question *What happened?*, I ought to be able to answer the logical next question—*What do you* think *happened?*

For a long time, I agreed with the prevailing theory that CeCe and the team came up with—something bad happened to Jill, the family covered it up, and in a final, desperate act of compassion, my mother dressed me in nice clothes and left me where I would be found. Nothing I learned knocked that theory down.

For a while, I wanted to believe that my parents abandoned *both* Jill and me—and that Jill was still out there somewhere, adopted anonymously while I got snagged in the scandalous story of a kidnapping. But would my parents have abandoned two children without some terrible precipitating event? Maybe my father walking out *was* that event, and it forced my mother to do something drastic to get her husband back. But I found it hard to believe that my mother could have left both of her twins somewhere, each of us in a separate lonely place, each of us crying for the other, and then just turned and walked away and gone back to her life.

It was easier to believe that one tragic event led to another—that Jill's death, inadvertent or not, led to my abandonment. You can't explain away one missing twin. But you *can* make it look like both of them were living somewhere else, and that's just what my parents did. If you ask me now what I think happened, that is what I'll say. One tragedy led to another.

But then I'll quickly add that I'm not sure.

Toward the end of our talk, I asked X what I should do next in my search. X had a very strong opinion about that.

"Paul, you know enough," X said. "You know enough. How much more do you want to know? What else can you find out? People will tell you things that aren't true, or they will tell you things they think are true, but aren't. You know enough. This was your family. They were strange and they turned good things into bad."

Still—I can't help thinking there is more I need to know.

—⚒—

I made plans to drive across the desert and finally meet up with my dream team of genealogists—CeCe, Michelle, Carol, and Allison. We got together in Michelle's lovely house in Southern California, and Michelle showed me the wall of stickies in her upstairs office. Then we sat around a fire pit in her pretty backyard.

We talked about the ups and downs of the case, the incredible twists, the times when things looked hopeless, the moments of sheer euphoria. I realized, for the first time, how much my case meant to these four remarkable women. I knew they were caught up in it, and I knew they had devoted hundreds of unpaid hours to solving it. But I could finally see in their faces how much it meant to them personally, not just professionally, to be able to crack a case like mine.

"The four of us became like sisters," Michelle said, tearing up. "We went through this thing together and we will always be bonded because of it."

They did what they did because they wanted to *help* me. The DNA work, the theorizing, the sleuthing, the puzzle solving—they loved that stuff, clearly, and they were *great* at it. But the big prize for them is connecting people to their families. Their work is never abstract or academic. It is always about people and their hopes and fears and dreams. I was touched by their humanity. I was humbled by it.

I gave each of them a thin necklace with a sterling silver tree attached. It was called a Tree of Life necklace, but what made it appropriate was that it looked like a family tree, with branches curling outward and upward. They all put the necklaces on right away, and wore them the rest of the day. I wanted to somehow convey to them how deeply grateful I was for what they had done, but I don't think I did. It's the kind of thing I'm not very good at. But I hope they know. They did the impossible—they rolled back time. They reached into my past and changed my future. They took a black hole and they flooded it with light. I will never be able to repay them for that.

I also booked another trip to the East Coast, to see my cousin Lenny Rocco.

When we first met, and shared our mutual love of music, we'd promised to meet up again soon and play together. Lenny gave me a couple of songs to practice on my bass guitar back home, and I was ready when I showed up at his house outside Philadelphia. He led me to a big garage behind his two-story home, which he'd turned into a work-space-slash-stage. Lenny was a woodworker, and half the garage was packed with a table saw and a sawhorse and a wood-graining machine. He also had a pool table, and four microphones set up in front of two amplifiers. A poster on the back wall advertised THE LENNY ROCCO TRIO: DOO-WOP, ACAPELLA, COMEDY.

Lenny handed me an old bass guitar that weighed about thirty pounds.

"This my old Fender," he said. "I used to play that forty years ago."

Lenny's girlfriend, Barbara, and a friend named Jocelyn were his backup singers. He took the mike in between the two, and I sat on a stool to their left. The barnlike doors were flung open to a large grassy field beyond. The late afternoon light was golden, and there was a pleasant breeze.

We ripped straight through five songs. We opened with "Under the Boardwalk," then moved into "Up on the Roof," Lenny's signature number. We closed with "Will You Still Love Me Tomorrow." Lenny didn't just sing. He put on a show. He flirted with his backup singers and played to an imaginary crowd. And he hit the high notes—all of them. We fell into an easy groove. It was a sweet, sweet moment.

"Paul, you're better than I thought," Lenny told me between songs.

"You sing pretty good, too," I said.

I'd never been able to share my love of music with anyone in my family.

Now I had.

—⟋⟍—

The psychic had told me to go to the water and forgive. The forgiveness wasn't for them, she said. The forgiveness was for me.

The question, then, is this—have I been able to forgive my birth parents for what they did to me?

The answer, so far, is no. It's far too fresh and raw. I don't really understand what they did, or why they did it, so I can't bring myself to accept it. It is a heavy, heavy thing—to leave your two-year-old child in the street and never look back. It is an act with enormous consequences for everyone. An act that most people could never conceive of doing. And yet they did it—they abandoned me. They discarded me. What they did goes against the very laws of nature. They cast their own child out into the hostile world.

No, that would not be an easy thing to forgive. Maybe someday, but not yet. The psychic also told me to put my feet in the salt water, but I never made it all the way to the ocean. The closest I got was the boardwalk. Maybe one day I'll go back and actually walk into the Atlantic. And maybe I'll even scream at the top of my lungs, releasing all the anger I feel. Whether or not that will help me forgive, who's to say.

On the other hand, I was able to reconnect with my adoptive

parents. In fact, I feel closer to them now than I ever have before. That was one of the great blessings that came out of my search. It was painful along the way—we didn't talk or see each other for two years. And in that time, my father started slipping away from me. But now I can talk to my mother and father more freely, and joke with them, and even hug them and tell them I love them. There's a warmth there that was missing for a long time, or maybe wasn't ever there before.

"I still want to find your real son," I told my mother.

"*You're* our son," she said.

My brother Dave is another story. I still don't know exactly why he decided not to help me and shut me out. I assume it was because he felt I was hurting our parents. But we never got the chance to talk it over. One day not too long ago, I was Skyping with my mother when I saw Dave walk behind her across the kitchen.

"Is that Dave?" I said. "Tell him I love him."

My brother heard what I said but just kept walking, until he was gone.

I haven't called him in a while, but someday soon I will. I'm not mad at him, or maybe I am. My mother told me recently she wished we could have all embarked on my search together, as a family. I told her that's all I ever wanted. But while I understood why they shut me out, it was harder for me to see why Dave did it. I know we never got along well. He has probably always thought of me as cocky and condescending. But in a moment when I really, truly needed his help, he wasn't there for me. And that stung. It still stings.

Then again, how much of our feud is his fault, and how much is mine? And does it matter? I have seen how members of my birth family just drift away from each other. Frank Duncan and his sister, Marie. My father Gilbert and X. Lenny Rocco and his sisters, Joy and Sandy.

A perceived insult, a missed signal, anything, really—and then they just stop talking. And they don't talk again and they let the years pass, until it all gets erased in the end.

I don't want that to be the story of Dave and me. I love him and I know he loves me. We are brothers. That will never change.

As for my other brother, Fred, I have honored his wish. I haven't reached out to him and I've stayed out of his life. Some might say that I shouldn't give up so easily—that I should fight for the relationship, for both our sakes. But that's not how I feel. Part of me is still angry. It hurt to be rejected. It was my family casting me out all over again. A guy can begin to take that personally.

But another part of it is that I don't feel like anything is final. Maybe Fred just needs more time to come to terms with what he's learned. Maybe I came on too strong. Maybe we will both get to a place where we can help each other—which, I believe, is what we both want. That may never happen. But I am optimistic.

My sister Linda—I think she is at that place already. I may have misread her, but I truly think she was happy to see me. Happy to have me in her life. I saw it in her face, when she smiled. I like to think that Linda still has that fake orchid I gave her, up on a shelf somewhere. And I hope that, when she looks at it, she thinks about me. I have tried to call her a few times, but she never picks up. One day soon, I will go back to Atlantic City and knock on her door again.

And this time, I hope, the door will open again.

—⁂—

One of the hardest, coldest facts I had to confront about my family was the legacy left to me by my father and grandfather. I went into my search looking for reasons why I was such a drifter. Why I could walk away from people so easily. And maybe I found that answer, in the genes of Harry and Gilbert Rosenthal. Harry walked out on his family and never came back. Gilbert walked out, too, at the worst possible time, though he eventually returned. But they both left. That was the sad truth. I don't know if they felt bad about what they did, though I imagine they must have—particularly Gilbert. But what if they didn't? What if leaving was easy for them, as it had been for me?

Not long ago, Michelle and I separated. I moved into a house nearby, and we set up a schedule to take care of Emma. Nothing about that process has been easy. Michelle's worst fear—that trying to find a family I didn't know would destroy the family I had—was slowly realized right before our eyes. We had our differences long before I even knew I wasn't Paul Fronczak. But my mission to learn my identity took a harsh toll on our relationship. I was pulled in another direction. Michelle has said that, after ten years of marriage, she doesn't really know me. She doesn't know who I am inside. All I can say is I don't really know who I am, either.

"You are searching for something and you don't know what it is," Michelle said once. "But you just won't stop looking."

I wish I could say she had it all wrong. But I can't.

Whatever the future brings for us, one thing is certain—we both love Emma more than words can say. I'm aware that I went through some rough times—some known to me, some not—when I was around the age that Emma is now. And I never want her to have to go through anything even remotely like that. I don't want her to ever feel uncertain about where she belongs, or who's on her team. I started the search so that I could become a better man and a better father to Emma. If I fail to live up to that goal, then that will be the real tragedy of my story.

—m—

The first step is learning the truth. I believed that before the search, and I believe it now. "Not everything that is faced can be changed," the writer James Baldwin said, "but nothing can be changed until it is faced." It took me a long time to face my doubts about my identity—more than forty years. And it took me three hard years of searching to find my identity. But now that I know—now that I have a name, at least—I can move on to the next step of the journey.

Whatever that is.

Almost surely, I will have to sit down with someone and talk it through. A therapist, I mean. I'm not crazy about the idea, but I know it's something I need to do. I need to stop seeing my life in terms of movie flashbacks—stop slipping into different characters who aren't me whenever the going gets tough.

I need to stop being a stand-in.

And I need to confront just how broken I might be. What if, because I am unable to tell the full story of my abandonment, I communicate it to others the only way I can—by making them feel some of the pain I surely felt as a child? What if the only language I have to convey what I went through is abandonment itself—if I walk out on others as a way of showing them the true horror of my ordeal? A horror I can't comprehend myself, but still feel the need to express? If that's the case, or anything like that, then I've got an awful lot of work to do.

I used to think I needed to do it in order to unlock any suppressed memories—to find new clues that could lead to the truth about Jill. And that very well may happen once I start the process. But I don't want to fool myself into thinking I'm going to therapy so I can crack the mystery of my twin. It has to be about me. If I was serious when I

said I wanted to learn why I act the way I do, so I can change my behavior, then this is what I have to do—I have to do the dirty work that
leads to change. I'm sure it won't be easy. I know it will be painful. I
hope I don't take the easy way out and run away from it. But it's up to
me now. The next step in the journey is whatever I make it.

"The last chapter in his story hasn't been written yet," one of the
psychologists told my friend when they discussed my case. "He can
add more twists to it. He can take the story in another direction. He
can be the author of what comes next."

But rising above trauma, the psychologists well know, can be the
challenge of a lifetime. What happens to us in our first two or three
years on earth—even if we can't remember it—can leave a nearly in-
delible imprint on our souls. And the worse the trauma, the more
hopeless overcoming it may seem.

"For some people," one psychologist said, "the only hope they can
find for salvation is in the spiritual. Not medicine or psychology, but a
spiritual path. That's the only way they can find something strong
enough to hold all the pain. Something that gives them the strength
they need to crawl their way back to the surface."

I had literally dug into the earth looking for my twin sister, Jill.
Now I had to start digging into my mind and my soul in order to find
myself.

—⁂—

I am fifty-two years old. I know that now, for sure. My daughter is still
young, and she's going to need me for a long time. She is worth the effort. I am worth the effort. Whatever path is going to lead me to where
I need to be, I will take it. The alternative is too frightening to consider.

But that doesn't mean I will ever stop looking for Jill. And I won't
stop looking for the real Paul, either. Nino Perrotta, the investigator

who found Leonard not once but twice, said he wants to help me figure out what happened to both Jill and Paul. With him by my side, my chances are greatly improved. Recently, I also got a call from Bernie Carey—the former FBI special agent who stayed in the Fronczaks' home for three weeks after Baby Paul was kidnapped. He's retired and living with his wife in Florida now, but he's never forgotten the case and he's still as sharp as they come. He called me with a suggestion—a good suggestion. I asked him if he wanted to help me find the real Paul. Bernie said he would love to. So he's on the team now, too.

There is something else I want to do.

Since my search started, I've received hundreds and hundreds of messages and emails from people going through the same struggle— the struggle to learn who they are and where they came from. They've been incredibly supportive, and they've made me feel as if any victories I achieve are their victories, too. Like we're all in this together—the disinherited ones. A lot of them, I can see, are afraid. Afraid to begin searching for the truth because of what they might find out—or what they'll never learn. I understand that. I was there. I'm still afraid now.

But here is what I've learned—anything is better than living with a lie.

A lot of people choose to live that way, and I nearly did. It's possible to do it, and sometimes it's not even that hard. You just accept that authenticity will not be part of your life. That most of what you do and say will basically be pretending. I was pretty good at doing that. I imagine a lot of people are. It's not that we want to live that way. It's that living that way is how we make it through life.

But there is another way, and it starts with learning the truth. Every case is different, and I would never offer a blanket encouragement to others to do what I did. There is a cost to learning the truth, and it can be very high. I have lost things I can never get back, and I have hurt people I never wanted to hurt. From the outside looking in, the cost may strike some people as simply too great to bear.

But not knowing who you are—how can anyone truly live with that? If your life is based on a lie, you can ignore the lie, or you can hide it or deny it. But you can't do those things forever. Not if you want to live a genuine life. Not if you want to finally stop pretending.

I understand some people will never learn the truth of who they are. That could easily have happened to me. I was extremely lucky, in that my case went public and I had several incredible genealogists helping me nearly around the clock. Most people won't have access to those kinds of resources.

And even if they do, some people won't be able to learn the truth, because it's gone forever. The document they needed, the only person they could test, the simple clue that cracks the case—those things may not exist anymore. I am not saying those people are doomed. I'm saying that trying to find your roots, and your family, and your place in the world, is a worthwhile thing. The search itself changes us. Our quest for identity matters.

To that end, I will try to help as many people in similar predicaments as I can. It might just be encouragement. It might be advice. I hope it can be inspiration. I hope that what I went through will resonate with other people searching for their identities.

And what I will tell them is that, after a long and difficult search, I finally know my real name.

But I will also say that, like everyone else, I will keep searching until I learn who I am.

Epilogue

Las Vegas, Nevada
October 27, 2015

BACK IN APRIL, I celebrated the first of my two birthdays. Michelle bought me a shirt, and Emma gave me a handmade card. She drew a big house, and a big yard, and the three of us were together in the yard, with her on a big swing between us. It was the sweetest card I ever got.

Six months later, I had my second birthday of the year.

My first *real* birthday.

After I was abandoned, and given to the Eckerts to care for, Claire Eckert came up with a birth date for me—April 15. It was basically a guess. Then when I was handed over to the Fronczaks, I was given the real Paul's actual birthday, April 26. And for the next fifty years I celebrated my birthday on April 26. But then I found my real birth certificate, which of course listed my real date of birth—October 27. So that became my new birthday.

Legally speaking, my situation is a mess. The process of changing over all my official documents to reflect my true identity—Jack Rosenthal—will be complicated and time-consuming. Legally, I am still Paul Joseph Fronczak. I guess the first step is deciding what I want to call myself. Do I drop Paul Fronczak altogether? Or combine the two names? Jack Fronczak? Actually, I don't mind that last choice at all. I never felt like a Paul, but I do feel like a Jack. Maybe I don't need a new last name.

But will having parts of two different names be subconsciously harmful? Or what if I called myself Paul Jack? Or Jack Paul?

You see? It's a mess.

I will sort all of that out eventually. There's a whole lot of sorting in my future.

For now, I'm happy to know my actual birthday. Michelle and Emma threw a little party for me, with more presents and a big cake. I'm not sure Emma understood why I was having a second birthday, but that was okay—any excuse for cake. She jumped into my lap, and she and Michelle sang "Happy Birthday."

Then the cake came out. It had vanilla frosting and a handful of lit candles, but not fifty-two of them. A handful was enough. I told Emma to close her eyes and make a wish and help me blow out the candles. She closed her eyes tight, thought for a second, then opened them and huffed and puffed. Most of the candles went out.

Then I closed my eyes, and I made a wish, too.

I wished for Emma to know only peace and love and safety, and I wished the same for Jill, wherever she is, and for the real Paul, too, and I wished it for everyone who wakes up one day and finds that they are lost.

Acknowledgments

THANK YOU FROM the bottom of my heart to my beautiful daughter, Emma Faith—you are the reason I set out on this journey, so I could be a better father to you. I love you forever. Thank you to Michelle, for being by my side through good times and bad, and giving me the greatest gift of all—our amazing daughter. Thank you to my parents, Chester and Dora Fronczak. Mom and Dad, you saved my life, literally, more times than I can count, and I am forever grateful—and forever your son. I love you. Thank you to my brother, Dave, for waking me up on all those Christmas mornings.

A very special thank-you to CeCe Moore and her amazing team of genealogists—Allison Demski, Carol Rolnick, and Michelle Trostler. You guys spent hundreds of hours building my family tree out of nothing, for no reward other than to help a man who was lost. Thank you so much for your passion, patience, and tenacity—and for giving me my name. Thank you also to my cousin Aimee Gourley, for her tireless devotion to solving this puzzle—and bringing a family together. Thank you to Matt Deighton, Crista Cowan, and everyone at AncestryDNA—you are all amazing and I have learned so much from you. Thank you to Bennett Greenspan and the staff at Family Tree DNA, for all your crucial support—this couldn't have happened without your help. Thank you to everyone at 23andMe and GEDmatch, for being a part of this adventure.

Thank you to the crew at the National Center for Missing and Exploited Children, for taking on my case. Thank you to former FBI Special Agent Bernie Carey and his wife, Mary, for being so lovely and helpful—Bernie, you were there fifty years ago and there again fifty years later when I needed you. And an enormous thank-you to Nino Perrotta, the very best investigator around. Nino, you found the unfindable—twice!—and you helped me uncover the truth.

Thank you to Jonathan Merkh, Jennifer Smith, Bruce Gore, Brandi Lewis—and especially Beth Adams—at Howard Books, for believing in my story and making this book a reality. A big thank-you to the one and only George Knapp, reporter extraordinaire. Without you—and CBS, KLAS-TV, and Coast to Coast AM—none of this would have happened. You took a chance and brought my story to the world. Thank you to Barbara Walters, Andrea Amiel, Lauren Putrino, and the whole gang at ABC, for all your invaluable help along the way. Thanks to Stefano Esposito at the *Chicago Sun-Times* and Josh Levin at *Slate*, for all your help and coverage. Thanks to Frank Weimann, a great literary agent—Tim Robbins sends his regards. And thanks to my friend Alex ("Look at me, Ray!"), for wanting my story to be heard. You took my voice and gave it life. It's been an amazing ride, and we're just getting started!

Thank you to all my newfound family members, who have enriched my life more than you'll ever know—to Lenny Rocco, the best doo-wop singer there is, and his lovely wife, Barbara; to the beautiful Rocco sisters, Joy and Sandy, and their families; to the family of the late Alan Fisch—Randi, Jason, Jenna, and Jessica—for welcoming me so warmly and for being so brave, and to Alan himself—buddy, I wish I'd gotten to know you; to Melissa Duncan and her father, Frank; to Tobe and her daughters; and to Fran Kirby and Ruth Mannis.

Thank you to Kimberly Ingrassia, for contacting me and helping me so much, and thank you to Janet Eckert Ingrassia, for loving me and taking care of me all those years ago, along with your incredible parents, Claire and Fred. Thank you to Sam Miller, for sharing your story and inspiring me with your courage. Thank you to Maritta Brady—you've got a great future in forensics ahead of you. Thank you to Kim, Joe, Thomas, Shelly, Craig, Lindee, Christa, and everyone else who played a part in my story—I will never forget any of you. A special thank-you to Shane, for helping me literally dig up my past. Shane, hug your daughter every day.

Thank you to my foundation—Jimbo, JB, NMR. Thank you to Joe Leyba—baby lambs, brother . . . you got this! Thank you to Montreal— Eddie and Tony, I'm ready for the reunion tour. Thank you to Harley-Davidson, for making the ride better than the destination. Thank you to Rickenbacker bass guitars, for keeping me sane and sounding so good. Thank you to Kristina and Andy—who doesn't love a good mystery, or three? Thank you to Dr. John Nassar, DDS; to Noel, Roger, and the gang at Cactus—and the best jukebox in the city; to 97Rock, Buffalo's classic rock station—the best station to research a mystery by; to Paulie D—we always meet at the crossroads. . . . Not so bad!

A sincere and heartfelt thank-you to all the friends, family, and strangers who followed my case on my Facebook page and elsewhere, and continually sent me kind words of support, useful tips, and strong opinions that all helped bolster my spirits along the way. Please— please—keep following my case at www.foundlingpaul.com, and keep sending in any tips, leads, or information you might have as I continue my search for answers.

Finally, my deepest thank-you to everyone out there who struggles with questions about their families and identities. I am so inspired by your persistence and courage, and I hope and pray you find all the answers you need to live your best, fullest, and happiest lives.

For more about Paul and his case
or to get involved in his search,
please visit:

FoundlingPaul.com